A HISTORY OF GREEK ECONOMIC
THOUGHT

A HISTORY OF GREEK ECONOMIC THOUGHT

BY

ALBERT AUGUSTUS TREVER

PORCUPINE PRESS
Philadelphia

First edition 1916
(Chicago: University of Chicago Press, 1916)

Reprinted 1978 by
PORCUPINE PRESS, INC.
Philadelphia, Pennsylvania 19107

Library of Congress Cataloging in Publication Data

Trever, Albert Augustus, 1874-1940.
    A history of Greek economic thought.

    Reprint of the 1916 ed. published by University of
Chicago Press, Chicago, originally presented as the author's
thesis, University of Chicago.
    Bibliography: p.
    Includes index.
    1.   Economics — Greece — History.   I.   Title.
HB77.T75   1978   330 .09495   78-15142
ISBN 0-87991-861-6

PREFACE

The need of a reinterpretation of Greek economic theory in the light of our modern humanitarian economy is presented in the introduction to this work. If this volume may, in some degree, meet such a need, by awakening the classicist to the existence of important phases of Greek thought with which he is too unfamiliar, and by reminding the economist of the many vital points of contact between Greek and modern economy, our labor will have been amply repaid. There are doubtless errors both in citations and in judgment which will not escape the critic's eye. We trust, however, that the work is, on the whole, a fair representation of the thought of the Greeks in this important field. In the course of our study, we have naturally been obliged to make constant reference to the actual economic environment of the Greeks, as a proper background for their theories. It is therefore our purpose to publish, at some future date, a general history of economic conditions in Greece, which may serve as a companion to this volume.

We gladly take this opportunity to express our gratitude to Professor Paul Shorey, of the University of Chicago, for his suggestion of the subject of this work, as also for his many helpful criticisms and suggestions during the course of its preparation.

LAWRENCE COLLEGE, APPLETON, WIS.
November 1, 1915

CONTENTS

CHAPTER I

INTRODUCTION

For a complete list of scholars who have devoted more or less attention to the economic ideas of Greek thinkers, the reader is referred to the bibliography at the conclusion of this work. On the surface, the list appears to be reasonably extensive. It will be observed, however, that the majority of the works are not of recent date; that many of them deal largely with the practical phase of economics; that most of the larger works on economic history treat Greek economic and social theory in a merely incidental manner, and that nearly all are written from the general standpoint of the economist rather than with the more detailed analysis of the classicist. The work of Souchon, the most extensive, careful, and satisfactory discussion of the subject, is no exception to this latter rule, and since his standpoint is too exclusively that of the older English economists, his criticism of the Greek theories is not always sufficiently sympathetic. The monumental volumes of Poehlmann have treated Greek social theories thoroughly, but the chief interest of the author is rather in the actual social conditions, and his work is marred by a constant overemphasis of the analogy between ancient and modern capitalism and socialistic agitation. Moreover, there is no book in the English language, on Greek economic thought, that treats the subject in anything more than the cursory manner of Haney and Ingram.[1] There is, thus, still a place for a work of this type in the English language, written from the standpoint of the classicist, but with a view also to the needs of twentieth-century students of economics.

The present work aims to fulfil such a need. Its scope differs quite essentially from all other accounts of Greek theory previously published, in that our purpose is not merely to consider the extent to which the Greek thinkers grasped the principles of

[1] F. Wilhelm (*Rhein. Mus.*, XVII, No. 2 [1915], 163, n. 2) says: "Eine Geschichte der theoretischen Behandlung der Oekonomik bei den Griechen ist noch zu schreiben." The present work was undertaken in the year 1911.

the orthodox economy of Ricardo and Mill.   We shall also endeavor to ascertain how far they, by the humanitarian and ethical tone of their thinking, anticipated the modern, post-Ruskin economy, which makes man, not property, the supreme goal, and recognizes the multiplicity of human interests and strivings that belie the old theory of the "economic man."   Our verdict as to the importance of the Greek contribution to economic thought is thus likely to be somewhat more favorable than that which is usually rendered.

We purpose also to emphasize more than is often done the important fact that Greek theory is essentially a reflection of Greek economic conditions, and that a true interpretation of the thought depends upon a clear understanding of the economic history of Greece.   However, as we shall see, this by no means implies that the anti-capitalistic theories of the Socratics are evidence of an undeveloped state of commerce and industry in fifth- and fourth-century Athens.

The method of presentation is primarily chronological.   Thus the ideas of each thinker can be discussed in a more thorough and unitary manner, and more in relation to the contemporary economic conditions that gave rise to them.   Moreover, despite some practical advantages of the topical method, it savors too much of an artificial attempt to force the Greek thinkers on the procrustean rack of the concepts of modern economy.

The general characteristics of Greek economic thought have often been enumerated.   They may be restated with advantage, at this point, together with some additions and needed criticisms.

1. *Simplicity.*—The theory of economics as a separate science never developed in Greece.   The consideration of economic problems was incidental to the pursuit of politics and ethics.   In so far as Greek thinkers treated such subjects, their theories reflect the comparative simplicity of their economic environment.   Without prejudging the issue as to the actual extent of capitalism in ancient Athens, we need only to think away the vast international scope of our modern commercial problems, our giant manufacturing plants with their steam and electric power, our enormous wealth and its extreme concentration, the untold complexity of modern business and finance, the vast territorial expanse of modern nations,

almost all our luxuries and commonplace comforts, to begin to appreciate something of this ancient simplicity.[1] However, as a direct result of this limitation, the Greeks were led to deal with their problems more in terms of men than in terms of things, and thus their economic vision was sometimes clearer and truer than our own. Aristotle struck the keynote in Greek economic thought in stating that the primary interest of economy is human beings rather than inanimate property.[2]

2. *Confusion of private and public economy.*—As a result of this simplicity, the terms οἰκονομία and οἰκονομική were, both in derivation and largely in usage, referred to household management rather than to public economy.[3] Domestic and public economy were regularly defined as differing merely in extent.[4] Aristotle, however, distinctly criticizes the confusion of the two.[5] Moreover, there is no warrant for the frequent assertion that Greek thinkers never rose above the conception of domestic economy. Xenophon's treatise on the *Revenues of Athens*, and Aristotle's entire philosophy of the state are a sufficient answer to such generalizations. The statement of Professor Barker that "political economy," to Aristotle, would be a "contradiction in terms," is extreme.[6] There is also a certain important truth in the Greek

[1] Cf. Zimmern, *Greek Commonwealth²*, pp. 211 ff.; but the statement on p. 222 is extreme: "where competition and unemployment are unknown terms, where hardly anyone is working precariously for money wages or salary."

[2] Cf. Roscher, *Ansichten der Volkswirtschaft³* (1878), I, chap. i, p. 7; Ar. *Pol.* 1259b18–21.

[3] Cf. Plato *Rep.* 498A; Xen. *Econ.*, a treatise on household management; Ar. *Pol.* i. p. 3, on the divisions of οἰκονομία; chap. 8, on whether finance (χρηματιστική) is a part of οἰκονομική; pseudo-Ar. *Economica;* cf. *infra*, p. 63, nn. 5 and 6; p. 82, n. 1; p. 128, for fuller discussion.

[4] Xen. *Mem.* iii. 4. 6 ff., especially 12; *Econ.* xx; Plato *Pol.* 259 B-C; cf., on this passage, Espinas, *Revue des Etudes Grecques*, XXVII (1914), 105; cf. Ruskin: "Economy no more means saving money than it means spending money. It means the administration of a house" (*A Joy Forever*, I, 8, Allen ed., London, 1912, Vol. XVI, 19). We shall frequently quote from this monumental edition of Ruskin.

[5] *Pol.* i. 1. 2: ὅσοι μὲν οὖν οἴονται πολιτικὸν καὶ βασιλικὸν καὶ οἰκονομικὸν καὶ δεσποτικὸν εἶναι τὸν αὐτόν, οὐ καλῶς λέγουσιν.

[6] *Political Thought of Plato and Aristotle*, p. 357; cf. Zmavc, *Zeitschr. f. d. gesammt Staatswissenschaft*, 1902, pp. 59 f., and his references to Boeckh, Meyer, and Beloch; Kautz, *Die Gesch. d. Entwickelung der National Ökonomik*, p. 133, n. 5; for note on the authorship of the *Revenues*, cf. *infra*, p. 63, n. 2.

confusion, which has been too generally missed by modern critics and statesmen—that the public is a great property-holder, and that politics should be a business which requires the application of the same economic and ethical laws as are admitted to govern in private affairs.

3. *Confusion of economics with ethics and politics*—The assertion that Greek economic theory was confounded with ethics and politics has become a commonplace. The economic ideas of Greek thinkers were not arrived at as a result of a purposeful study of the problems of material wealth. All economic relations were considered primarily from the standpoint of ethics and state welfare. "The citizen was not regarded as a producer, but only as a possessor of wealth."[1] Such statements are too commonly accepted as a final criticism of Greek thinkers. Though the confusion was a source of error, and caused Greek economic thought to be one-sided and incomplete, yet some important considerations should be noted.

a) The Socratic philosophers are our chief source for the economic ideas of the Greeks. Too sweeping conclusions should not, therefore, be drawn from them as to the general attitude of the Greeks. Xenophon is much freer from the ethical emphasis than the other Socratics. Thucydides is entirely free from it, and very probably his standpoint came much nearer being that of the average Athenian citizen.

b) The confusion was not merely with individual ethics, for Greek moral philosophy always had the welfare of the state for its goal. Indeed, the basal reason for this close union of economics, ethics, and politics is the true idea that the state should rise above internal strife, and unite all in a care for the common interest.[2]

c) The standpoint of the Greek philosophers is certainly no more to be criticized than is that of the so-called orthodox political economy.[3] They represent two extremes. If the Greek theory

---

[1] Ingram, *History of Political Economy*, p. 12; cf. Souchon, *Les Théories économiques dans la Grèce antique*, p. 34.

[2] Cf. Souchon, *op. cit.*, pp. 31 ff.

[3] Cf. V. Brants, *Xenophon Economiste*, reprint from *Revue Catholique de Louvain*, 1881, pp. 4 ff.

did not give to wealth its full right, and was open to the charge
of sentimentalism, the Ricardian doctrine, with its "economic
man," which eliminated all other ideals and impluses, was an unreal
and pernicious abstraction. Of the two errors, the Greek is the
less objectionable, and is more in accord with the trend of economic
thought today. The best economists are now insisting more and
more on the Greek idea that economic problems must be considered
from the standpoint of the whole man as a citizen in society.
Modern political economy "has placed man as man and not
wealth in the foreground, and subordinated everything to his true
welfare." "Love, generosity, nobility of character, self-sacrifice,
and all that is best and truest in our nature have their place in
economic life."[1] "The science which deals with wealth, so far
from being a 'gospel of Mammon,' necessarily begins and ends
in the study of man."[2] "Es soll kein Widerspruch zwischen
Ethik und Volkswirtschaft bestehen, es soll das Sittengesetz für
die Wirtschaft gelten und in ihr ausgeführt werden."[3] Such
strong statements taken at random from modern economists should
serve to temper our criticism of the Greek confusion. Plato's
definition of economics, as suggested by one of the most recent
historians of economic thought,[4] could easily be accepted by many
a modern scholar: "Economics is the science which deals with the
satisfaction of human wants through exchange, seeking so to regulate the industries of the state as to make its citizens good and
happy, and so to promote the highest well-being of the whole."
The contention of the Socratics, that all economic operations must
finally root in the moral, that all economic problems are moral
problems, and that the province of economics is human welfare,

[1] Ely, *Studies in Historical and Political Science*, 2d series, pp. 48 ff., especially
p. 64, where he states that it is a return to the Greek view.

[2] Ely, *Outlines of Economics*, 1908, pp. 4 ff.; cf. Seligman, *Principles of Economy*,
(1905), pp. 4 ff., especially p. 14, where he even quotes the sentences of Ruskin with
approval: "There is no wealth but life"; "Nor can anything be wealth except to a
noble person" (*Unto This Last*, IV, 77 [Vol. XVII, 105]). All citations will be from
the Allen library edition unless otherwise stated.

[3] Schoenberg, *Handbuch der polit. Econ.* (1890), I, 56.

[4] Haney, *History of Economic Thought*, p. 52; cf. Ely, *op. cit.*, p. 48, n. 1, cited
in n. 1, above, for a similar definition based on Plato.

is thus a dominant twentieth-century idea. And just as the ethical interest of the Greek philosophers caused them to emphasize the problems of distribution and consumption, so these are the phases of economics that receive chief consideration today. To be sure, modern thought appreciates more fully the complementary truth that all our social and moral problems root essentially in economic conditions, though this too was by no means overlooked by Plato and Aristotle.

4. *Ascetic tendency.*—It cannot be denied, however, that, as a result of the overemphasis on the ethical, Greek economic thought was hampered by a certain asceticism. But this was also an outgrowth of pessimistic tendencies in Greek philosophy itself. Moreover, the ascetic ideas of the philosophers cannot be accepted as the common attitude of Athenian citizens, any more than Thoreau can be recognized as a criterion of the economic thought of his day in New England.[1] Asceticism was certainly foreign to the mind of Pericles and Thucydides. In the course of our discussion, also, we shall find that it represents, after all, only one phase of the thought of the philosophers themselves.

5. *Socialistic tendency.*—Since Greek economy was chiefly interested in the problems of distribution, it tended toward socialism, both in theory and in practice. This was also a natural outgrowth of the fact that individual interests were subordinated to public welfare. Though the latter half of the fifth century witnessed a great individualistic movement in Greece, and though individualism and independence are often named as prominent Greek characteristics, yet these terms did not constitute a basal political principle, even in the free Athenian democracy, in the same sense as they do with us today. The life of the Greek citizen was lived far more for the state, and was more absolutely at the disposal of the state, than is true in any modern democracy. In Greece, politics was thus the social science of first importance, and the supreme purpose of all human activity was to make good citizens. State interference or regulation was thus accepted as a matter of course, and the setting of prices, rigid regulation of

[1] Kautz (*op. cit.*, p. 57) goes to the extreme of saying that antiquity represents "die Negation der ökonomischen Interessen und der wirtschaftlichen Arbeit."

grain commerce, exploitation of the rich in the interest of the poor, and public ownership of great material interests such as mines were not revolutionary ideas, but common facts in Greek life.[1] The tendency of the theorists was therefore naturally toward centralization of power in the hands of the state, and an exaggerated idea of the omnipotence of law.[2] Yet despite the error inherent in it, this socialistic tendency of Greek economic thought had its basal truth, which is becoming an axiom of modern economics and statesmanship—the belief that private property is not a natural right, but a gift of society, and hence that its activities should be controlled by society, and made to minister to public welfare. Indeed, we have by no means escaped the error of the Greek thinkers, for one of the most common mistakes of statesmen and political theorists today is an overestimate of the effectiveness of law.

[1] Even abolition of debts and redivision of lands were not unknown in Greek history. Grote (*History of Greece*, III, 105 f. and notes) denies this, but the heliastic oath, which he cites (Dem. *Adv. Timoc.* 746, and Dio Chrysost. Or. xxxi. 332), proves that such measures were agitated, or there would be no reason for protective measures. Cf. *infra*, Plato (*Laws*, 736E), who takes this for granted. Cf. Solon's Fragments; Isoc. (*Panath.* 259) says that it would be hard to find a Greek state, except Sparta, that has not fallen into "the accustomed accidents," viz., στάσιν, σφαγάς, φυγὰς ἀνόμους, ἁρπαγὰς χρημάτων, χρεῶν ἀποκοπάς, γῆς ἀναδασμόν, etc.

[2] Cf. *infra*. for citations and qualifications.

CHAPTER II

ECONOMIC IDEAS BEFORE PLATO, AND REASONS FOR THE UNDEVELOPED CHARACTER OF GREEK ECONOMICS

As stated above, the economic ideas of the Greeks were unsystematized and inextensive.[1] The extant literature previous to Plato presents only incidental hints on matters economic. Hesiod, in interesting antithesis to classical thinkers, emphasizes the dignity and importance of manual labor.[2] The contrast, however, is not so great as it appears, for the labor which he dignifies is agricultural. He constantly urges its importance as the chief source of wealth.[3] On the other hand, he opposes the commercial spirit that was beginning to be rife in his age, and decries the evil of unjust gains.[4] His mention of the fact of competition between artisans of the same trade is of interest for the development of industry in Greece.[5] His *Erga* was, in a sense, the forerunner of the later *Economica* in Greek literature.

Solon proved by his reforms that he had some sane economic ideas as to the importance of labor, industry, commerce, and money in the development of the state. He also showed some insight into the solution of the problem of poverty. His ideas, however, are not definitely formulated in his extant fragments, and belong rather to economic history.[6] The *Elegies* of Theognis

[1] Cf. *infra* for qualifications. Zimmern (*op. cit.*, p. 227) rightly insists: "In spite of what is often said, Greece did produce economists."

[2] *Erga* 308, 314, 397 f.; 311 (ἔργον δ' οὐδὲν ὄνειδος, ἀεργίη δέ τ' ὄνειδος), 310, 303–6, 413. Any material in Homer applies rather to a history of economic conditions. Cf., however, *Il.* xiii. 730–32; iii. 65; xxiii. 667 on specialization of gifts.

[3] Cf. *Erga* and *Theogony* 969–75; cf. n. 2.

[4] Cf. n. 2 above; a common theme of seventh- and eighth-century poets; cf. e.g., Sappho (Bergk-Hiller, *Lyr. G. Vet.* [1897], I, 204, fr. 79 [45]); ὁ πλοῦτος ἄνευ <τὰς> ἀρετὰς οὐκ ἀσίνης πάροικος. Cf. also III, 168, fr. 49 (50), Alcaeus.

[5] *Erga* 25 f.

[6] Cf. his poems, especially fr. xiii. 43 ff.; Ar. *Ath. Pol.* x. 1; Plut. *Solon* 15, 22–24; Kautz, *op. cit.*, pp. 114 f. and note, on Solon and the other lawgivers; Gilliard, *Quelque Réformes de Solon.* Cornford (*Thucydides Mythhistoricus*, p. 66) thinks he was "on the verge" of discovering the law that exports must balance imports.

are full of moral utterances on wealth, emphasizing its temporary nature as compared with virtue.[1] Pythagoras and his followers have often been given a prominent place in the history of communism, but this is probably due to a false interpretation.[2] It is likely, however, that he opposed the evils of luxury, and moralized on the relation between wealth and virtue.[3] Democritus wrote a work on agriculture.[4] Like the other philosophers, he taught that happiness was to be sought in the gold of character, rather than in material wealth.[5] To his mind, poverty and wealth alike were but names for need and satiety (κόρου).[6] Wealth without understanding was not a safe possession, depending for its value on right use.[7] The amassing of wealth by just means, however, was good,[8] though unjust gains were always a source of evil.[9] Excessive desire for wealth was worse than the most extreme poverty.[10] It is possible also that Democritus held to a mild form of the social contract theory of the origin of society.[11] Heraclitus complained bitterly of the unwisdom of the masses and their merely material view of life.[12] He made the common antithesis between material and spiritual wealth,[13] and observed the fact that gold is a universal medium of exchange.[14] Hippodamas of Miletus

[1] *Elegies* 1117 f., 227 ff., 1157 f., 181 f., 267 ff., 173 ff., 351 ff., 393 ff., 523 ff., 621 f., 199 ff., 753, 145 f., 559 f., etc.

[2] On this error, cf. *infra*, on communism before Plato.

[3] Cf. Kautz, *op. cit.*, p. 114; Jamblichus, *De Pyth. vit.*, chap. xii, p. 58; chap. xvi, p. 69.

[4] Diels, *Frag. d. Vorsokratiker* (1912), II, 20, 69.

[5] *Ibid.*, p. 95, fr. 171; p. 73, fr. 40.   [6] *Ibid.*, p. 119, fr. 283.

[7] *Ibid.*, p. 77, fr. 77; cf. Stob. *Flor.* 94. 24; χρημάτων χρῆσις ξὺν νόῳ μὲν χρήσιμον εἰς τὸ ἐλευθέριον εἶναι καὶ δημοφελέα· ξὺν ἀνοίῃ δὲ χορηγίη ξυνή. Cf. Xenophon and Plato, *infra*, on value and wealth.

[8] *Ibid.*, p. 78, fr. 78.   [9] *Ibid.*, p. 105, frs. 200, 218, 221.

[10] *Ibid.*, fr. 219; p. 106, fr. 224. The ethical fragments of Democritus, cited above, may be spurious. Cf. Mullach, *Frag. Phil. Gr.*, I, 138; Zeller (*Gesch. d. Gr. Phil.* I, 2, 925, n. 1) leaves the question open. Diels (*op. cit.*, II, 1912) cites the above passages under the "echte fragmente," though some are starred.

[11] Cf. Barker, *op. cit.*, p. 37.

[12] Diels, *op. cit.*, I, 83, fr. 29; δι δὲ πολλοὶ κεκόρηται ὁκώσπερ κτήνεα.

[13] *Ibid.*, p. 82, fr. 22; cf. Clem. Alex. *Strom.* iv. 2. p. 565, and his comment.

[14] Diels, *op. cit.*, I, 95, fr. 90: πυρὸς ἀνταμείβεται πάντα καὶ πῦρ ἀπάντων, ὥσπερ χρυσοῦ χρήματα καὶ χρημάτων χρυσός.

and Phaleas of Chalcedon proposed new plans for the distribution of wealth, but we have the barest outline of their theories from Aristotle.[1] Their systems will be discussed in a following chapter.

The Sophists, true to their character as philosophers of extreme individualism, developed a new theory of the origin of society. The already current term φύσις, "nature," which had been accepted as a sufficient reason for the state's existence, was now opposed to "law," νόμος, as natural to artificial. The Sophists argued that, in a primitive state of nature, perfect individualism was the rule. Men did injustice without restraint. The weaker, however, being in the majority, and finding it to their disadvantage to compete with the strong, agreed neither to do nor to suffer injustice, and constrained the stronger minority to co-operate in their decision. Thus arose the social contract whereby nature gave up its real instinct for an artificial convention (συνθήκη), and thus society came into being.[2] The theory, at first, though untrue, was not intended to be destructive of moral foundations, but was opposed rather to the traditional idea of the laws of a state as the "decrees of a divinely inspired lawgiver."[3] In the hands of men like Thrasymachus[4] and Callicles,[5] however, it became a means of denying that the life according to nature was bound by any laws which the strong need observe, and that might was the only final law.

In line with their radical individualism, the Sophists were also pioneers in the more cosmopolitan spirit that characterized the Cynics and Stoics. They taught the doctrine of the fundamental worth and relationship of men,[6] and thus, with the Cynics, started the attack upon the theory that upheld slavery as a natural insti-

[1] *Pol.* ii; cf. *infra* for details.

[2] Cf. Glaucon's tentative argument presenting the Sophist theory, *Rep.* 358E ff., very similar to that of Hobbes. Cf. Barker's (*op. cit.*, pp. 27 ff.) excellent presentation of the rise of this theory and its causes.

[3] Cf. A. Dobbs, *Philosophy and Popular Morals in Ancient Greece* (1907), p. 48. For examples, cf. Hippias, cited below, n. 6, or Lycophron, opposed by Aristotle, cited below in Aristotle's criticism of socialism (*Pol.* 1280*b*10–12).

[4] *Rep.* i, and the story of Gyges, *Rep.* ii.

[5] *Gorg.* 482E ff., though Callicles was hardly a Sophist.

[6] E.g., Hippias in *Protag.* 337C, where he says that men are related (συγγενεῖς, οἰκείους) by nature, not by law, and that the law is a tyrant of men that does much violence contrary to nature (παρὰ τὴν φύσιν).

tution.[1] Little further is known of their other social or economic ideas. Protagoras wrote a work on "wages," but it was probably an argument relative to the acceptance of pay by Sophists.[2] In any event, this fact that the Sophists were so ready to be enriched through their lectures is clear evidence that their teaching on wealth was not the negative doctrine of the other Greek philosophers.[3] Prodicus seems to have scorned menial labor as morally degrading, though he agreed with Hesiod in his doctrine of the dignity of all work that is noble.[4] He emphasized the necessity of labor in the production of material good,[5] and, like Democritus, was the forerunner of the Socratics in his insistence upon right use as a criterion of wealth.[6] Hippias prided himself on his accomplishment in many arts,[7] and thus probably did not share the prejudice of the philosophers against manual labor.

Euripides, though markedly individualistic, like the Sophists, shows traces of the older use of nature to explain the necessity of the state. He draws a parallel between the social order and the order of nature, by which law and government are justified, and the right of the middle class of farmers to rule is upheld.[8]

[1] Cf. Alcidamas frag., cited *infra* on Aristotle's theory of slavery, and Ar. *Pol.* i. 3. 1253b20–23; Lycophron (pseudo-Plut. *Pro. Nob.* 18. 2) denies the reality of the distinction between noble and ill-born. Cf. also on Euripides, *infra*. On the development of the opposition to slavery in Greece, cf. Newman, *Pol. of Arist.*, I, 139 ff.

[2] Diog. L. ix. 55: δίκη ὑπὲρ μισθοῦ. Cf. Diels, *op. cit.*, II, 220, 231; Croiset, *Hist. de la Litt. Gr.*, IV, 54. Souchon (*op. cit.*, p. 23, n. 1) thinks that it may have taught the dignity of all labor. Cf. also Plato (*Sophist* 232 D): τὰ πρωταγόρεια . . . . περί τε πάλης καὶ τῶν ἄλλων τεχνῶν. Gomperz (*Die Apologie der Heilkunst*, p. 33) infers that Protagoras had published a *Gesammtapologie der Künste*. Cf. *Pol.* 299C, and Diog. L. ix. 8. 55.

[3] Cf. Plato *Protag.* 328B, where Protagoras states his rule as to charges for his lectures. Cf. Zeller, *op. cit.*, I, 2, 1080 ff., on the earnings of the Sophists. Cf. Plato *Euthyd.* 304C: ὅτι οὐδὲ τοῦ χρηματίζεσθαί φατον διακωλύειν οὐδέν.

[4] Plato *Charm.* 163 B-D on Hesiod.

[5] Xen. *Mem.* ii. 1. 21–34, the story of Heracles (28).

[6] Pseudo-Platon. *Eryxias* 397 D-E, discussed *infra*.

[7] *Hippias Minor* 368 D, where he is presented as the jack of all trades. Cf. *infra* for the antithetic attitude of Plato.

[8] *Orestes* 917–22; *Supplices* 399–456, 238–45; *Phoenissae* 535–51 (Dindorf), cited by Dümmler, *Proleg. zu Platons Staat* (1891), to show that there are traces of a political treatise of the school of Antiphon in Euripides. Cf. Barker, *op. cit.*, p. 25 and note.

He emphasizes the importance of agriculture, and the dignity of the peasant farmer (αὐτουργός), who works his own land, as the stay of the country.[1]   This latter accords well with his cosmopolitan spirit, which he shares with the Sophists. He opposes the artificial distinctions of birth,[2] slavery,[3] and the traditional Greek idea of the inferiority of woman.[4] His attitude toward wealth is that of the moral philosopher rather than that of the Sophist.[5]

Thucydides reveals considerable insight into economic problems, though he does not deal with them directly. Roscher declares that the Greek historian contributed as much as any other writer to give him the elements of his science, since he alone, of all Greek writers, did not confuse his economic ideas with ethics.[6] He recognizes the place of labor in production, and the importance of material wealth as the basis for all higher development.[7] He also has some appreciation of the true nature of capital. In his description of the undeveloped condition of early Greece, which lived from hand to mouth, he writes like a modern economist describing primitive conditions in Europe in contrast to the capitalism of his own day.[8]   Cornford's attempt[9] to discredit Thucydides

---

[1] *Orestes* 917 ff.; cf. also the noble character of the peasant (αὐτουργός) in the *Electra*, who is a noble soul (252 f.), and who speaks the prologue, though he is only a secondary person in the play. Cf. also 367–82.

[2] Fr. 345 (Nauck), the unjust man is ignoble (δυσγενής), though better born than Zeus; frs. 54 (Alex.), 514 (Melanippe), 8 (Electra); cf. n. 1 above, and *infra*. He puts worthy sentiments into the mouths of slaves and dresses his nobles in rags.

[3] *Ion* 854; ἐν γάρ τι τοὺς δούλοισιν αἰσχύνην φέρει || τοὔνομα; frs. 828 (Phrixus), 515 (Melanippe) (Nauck); *Helena* 730; cf. Decharme, Euripide et l'esprit de son théâtre, pp. 162 ff.

[4] His finest portrayals are noble women. He was no woman-hater, but freely presented both sides of female character. Cf. *Medea* 230 ff. and other such passages complaining of woman's lot; fr. 655 (*Protes.*), advocating community of wives. Cf., however, Decharme, *op. cit.*, 133 ff.

[5] Cf. Nauck, frs. 642 (Polyidus), 55, 56 (Alex.), 95 (Alcmene), 143 (Andromeda), 326 and 328 (Danae); cf. Decharme, *op. cit.*, pp. 163 ff. and notes; Dobbs, *op. cit.*, p. 78, n. 5.

[6] *Op. cit.*, p. 7: "Ich auch in volkswirtschaftlicher Beziehung von keinen Neuern mehr als von ihm gelernt habe." Cf. Kautz, *op. cit.*, pp. 123 ff.

[7] Thuc. ii. 40. 1; i. 70. 8; ii. 40. 2; etc.   [8] Thuc. i. 2.

[9] *Thucydides Mythhistoricus* (1907); cf. Shorey's critical review, *Dial*, July–December, 1907, pp. 202 ff.; also W. Lamb, *Clio Enthroned* (1914), especially pp. 34–67. Lamb's citations of Thucydides (pp. 35 f.), present sufficient evidence of the Greek historian's economic insight.

as a historian, and to show that he missed the true cause, economic, of the Peloponnesian War, is not convincing. Cornford both exaggerates the influence of commercial interests in fifth-century Athens and belittles the economic insight of Thucydides. The Greek writer is, however, like Herodotus, a historical source for the actual economic conditions in Greece, rather than an economic theorist.

Aside from the fragmentary hints presented above, Greek economic thought begins with the Socratics, Plato, Xenophon, and Aristotle, and is continued, in a very incidental way, in the orators, and in the Stoics and their contemporaries. As we shall see, however, even in the Socratics, no real science of wealth is developed, in the modern sense. The reason for this lack, which is most commonly emphasized since it is closest at hand, is that the phenomena of actual production were but slightly developed. This explanation is well summarized by Haney[1] as follows: (a) that economic relations between individuals and states were far simpler than now; (b) that international commerce was not encouraged by ancient states, whose ideal was rather national exclusion; (c) that public finance was then very limited and unimportant; (d) that division of labor was not extensive; (e) that the relative lack of security of life and property discouraged exchange and saving; (f) that in all these respects, the situation is analogous to that of mediaeval Europe.

There is certainly much force in this general reason. The development of economic thought must, of course, depend upon the actual conditions under which the thinkers live. We have already admitted also the vast difference between the present economic complexity and the simplicity in ancient Greece. The foregoing summary of Haney, however, is misleading. Though the ideal of Sparta was national exclusion, it was surely not that of Athens and some other Greek states. All extant records agree that Athens, at least, the home of the economic theorists, encouraged international commerce by every means in her power. The division of labor, while insignificant compared with the minute division of modern mechanical industry, was by no means inextensive, as is evidenced by the fact that this is a point on which

[1] *Op. cit.*, pp. 18 f.

Greek thinkers show especial insight. The notion that Greek industry was chiefly limited to household economy, and that the era of capitalism had not yet dawned, has long ago been refuted by Meyer and others. The alleged insecurity of life and property, while relatively true, is exaggerated for Athens, at least. Above all, the common attempt to draw an analogy between classical Greece and mediaeval Europe economically is due to an utter misconception. The period of Greek economic history, which corresponds to that of the Middle Ages, is rather the era of economic awakening, between the middle of the ninth and the end of the sixth century B.C.[1]

Other reasons for the limited development of Greek economic thought are:

a) The dominance of the state over the individual citizen, which fact caused political rather than economic speculation to absorb the attention of Greek thinkers. It is stated that the importance of the individual must be recognized before a science of economics can develop.[2] This reason is also usually overemphasized.

b) The general prejudice in Greece against industry, labor for another, and finance for its own sake. That such a prejudice existed to some degree, arising from the old aristocratic feeling, moral objections, the reflex influence of slavery, the spirit of independence, and the belief that leisure was necessary for the proper performance of the duties of citizenship, is generally admitted. The commonly assumed universality of this feeling is, however, open to grave question. The prejudice against skilled labor was probably limited to the moral philosophers, and perhaps to the more aristocratic portion of the citizens, and we shall see in another

---

[1] "Die wirtschaftliche Entwickelung des Alterthums," *Kleine Schriften*, 1910; cf. also Beloch, *Zeitschr. f. Socialwiss.*, II, 21 ff.; "Griechische Geschichte," *ibid.*; Poehlmann, *Geschichte des antiken Socialismus und Kommunismus*, I (2d ed., 1912, *Geschichte der sozialen Frage und des Socialismus in der antiken Welt*). Citations from Poehlmann throughout the book are to this work unless otherwise specified. He exaggerates the development of capitalism. Meyer and Beloch are also somewhat misleading in their use of the modern terms for Greek conditions. Francotte (*L'Industrie dans la Grèce ancienne* [1900]) is more conservative. For the older extreme conservative view, cf. the works of Rodbertus and Bücher. Cf. *infra* for further notice of the subject.

[2] Haney, *op. cit.*, p. 17.

chapter that the hostile attitude of the philosophers themselves has been considerably exaggerated. The evil effects of slavery also could not have been so marked in Greece, before the age of machinery. Moreover, as Meyer has pointed out, a prejudice against manual labor is evident among the more favored classes in most European countries today, yet it does not appear to retard the advance of industry in the least.[1]

c) The approval of conquest as a legitimate source of wealth. This is somewhat true as applied to the state, but it certainly is irrelevant for the individual citizen of fifth-century Athens. To appeal to Aristotle's list of legitimate employments as evidence of this is to misinterpret his meaning, for he is thinking of a primitive life, not of contemporary Greece.[2]

d) Economic facts are a commonplace of daily life, and familiarity breeds contempt.[3] This statement contradicts the first reason given by Haney. Moreover, it is somewhat unfortunate as applied to Greece, since the very opposite reason is given for the prominence of political speculation—the commonness of practical politics.

e) Perhaps the strongest reason for the comparative unimportance of Greek economic thought is usually not emphasized. It is the patent fact that almost our only extant sources are the Socratic philosophers, who represent avowedly a direct moral reaction against the commercial spirit and money-greed of their age.[4] Thus the limited development of Greek economics, so far from being an evidence of primitive economic conditions in Greece, is a direct argument for the opposite. To be sure, a man with the scientific mind of Aristotle would scarcely have failed to gain a clearer apprehension of certain fundamentals of economics than he did, had his economic environment been more complex. Yet the fact remains that he and Plato are moral prophets, protesting against that very capitalism whose existence many modern historians have sought to deny to their age.

[1] For a full discussion of the Greek attitude toward labor, with citations from ancient and modern authors, cf. *infra*, p. 29, n. 4; pp. 32 ff., and notes; pp. 47 ff. and notes; pp. 69 f. and notes; pp. 93 ff. and notes.

[2] *Pol.* i. 8. 1256b2.   [3] Haney, *op. cit.*, p. 17.

[4] Emphasized by Poehlmann, *op. cit.*, I, 593 f. Our citations will always be from the second edition, 1912.

CHAPTER III

PLATO

As seen above, Plato was the first great economic thinker of Greece.[1] Plato, however, was primarily interested in neither economics nor politics, but in moral idealism. He is pre-eminent, even among the Socratics for this. All his economic thought is a direct outgrowth of it, and is shot through with its influence. Yet, despite this fact, he exhibits considerable insight into some of the basal principles of economics,[2] and his entire *Republic* is founded upon an essentially economic theory of society. He traces its origin to mutual need,[3] and makes little of the innate social impulse, so prominent in Aristotle's analysis.[4] He is the predecessor of Aristotle, however, in opposing the social contract doctrine of the Sophists with its interpretation of law as mere convention, by a natural theory of social origins. To his thought, the very foundations of society are established in eternal justice. They are not the result of mere convention, nor altogether the work of inspired lawgivers, but a complex product of natural and artificial elements.[5]

VALUE

Strictly speaking, Plato's contribution to a theory of economic value and a definition of wealth is practically nil. In his discussion of just price, he merely hints at the fact of exchange value. He implies that, since goods exchange according to definite pro-

---

[1] To judge by Xen. *Mem.*, this might have been said of Socrates had he been a writer.

[2] Robin (*Platon et la science sociale*, p. 239) makes him the forerunner of the triple division of economics—production, exchange, distribution—but this is hardly warranted.

[3] *Rep.* 369 B-C.

[4] *Pol.* i. chap. 2. But in the *Laws*, Plato's theory of origins is more social, tracing society back to clan and family.

[5] Cf. *Laws* 889 D-E, 709 B-D, and Robin, *op. cit.*, pp. 224 f.; also the entire argument of the *Republic* on justice.

portions, they should have a common quality capable of measurement, and that just price corresponds to this.[1] He offers no suggestion as to the nature of this quality, except that, in stating that "the artisan knows what the value of his product is," he seems to be thinking of labor, or cost of production, as the chief element in value.[2]

In other passages, he insists on the doctrine taught previously by Democritus,[3] and later by Xenophon and other philosophers, that so-called goods depend for their value upon the ability of the possessor to use them rightly.[4] This idea is represented in modern thought especially by Ruskin.[5] The theory is, of course, true of absolute value, and, in a sense, even of economic value, in that "all exchangeableness of a commodity depends upon the sum of capacity for its use."[6] It cannot be made a criterion of economic value, though the allied idea, implied by Plato and urged by Ruskin, that the innate quality of the thing, its capacity for good or harm, is a real element in economic value, is being recognized today. This is evident in the increasing hostility toward such so-called commodities as opium and intoxicating liquors. Since we have begun to define political economy in terms of human life rather than in terms of property, Ruskin's definition of wealth is more acceptable: "the things which the nature of humanity has rendered in all ages, and must render in all ages to come . . . . the objects of legitimate desire."[7]

---

[1] Laws 921B. The word is ἀξία.

[2] Ibid.: γιγνώσκει γάρ ὅγε δημιουργὸς τὴν ἀξίαν.

[3] Cf. p. 15, n. 7 above.

[4] Euthydemus 280B-E, 281B, D, 288E–289A; Meno 88D-E.

[5] Unto This Last, IV, 62: "Useful articles that we can use"; 64: "Wealth is the possession of the valuable by the valiant" (Vol. XVII, 86 ff.); Fors Clavigera, Letter 70 (Vol. XXVIII, 712 ff.); Munera Pulveris, I, 14 (Vol. XVII, 154); II, 35 (Vol. XVII, 166 f.). Plato's economic ideas greatly influenced Ruskin. Cf. infra, p. 149, n. 2. Cf. also Vol. XXXVIII, 112; XXXIX, 411, of Ruskin. He says, in the preface to Unto This Last (Vols. XVII, XVIII), that his "real purpose is to give . . . . a logical definition of wealth," which has "often been given incidentally in good Greek by Plato and Xenophon." Cf. ibid., n. 1, for other such references.

[6] Ibid.

[7] Cf. above note and Mun. Pul., II, 30, notes; Fors Clav., Letter 70, 3 (Vol. XXVII, 713), the "good things."

WEALTH

Plato has much to say of wealth, though he deals with it strictly from the standpoint of the moralist. We look in vain for a clear definition, or for a consistent distinction of economic wealth from other goods. His terms are πλοῦτος, used of both material and spiritual wealth; χρήματα, often interpreted literally of "useful things," as the basis of the subjective doctrine of value discussed above; κτήματα, "possessions," and such words as χρυσός and ἀργύριον. His use of these terms, especially the first, is ambiguous. At times he means material goods only; again, like Ruskin, he includes every human good, intellectual and moral as well;[1] again he means "excessive wealth."[2] As a result of his conception of value, he includes in material wealth all those objects that depend for their worth upon wise use and character in the possessor.[3] Material wealth is regularly placed last by Plato, as inferior to all other goods of soul or body, a mere means, and not an end in itself,[4] for virtue does not come from property, but property and all other goods from virtue.[5] Material goods should be the last thing in one's thought,[6] and the fact that people universally put them first is the cause of many ills to state and individual alike.[7] Wealth is not blind, if only it follows wisdom.[8] The things usually called goods are not rightly so named, unless the possessor be just and worthy.[9] To the base, on the other hand, they are the greatest evil.[10] In all of this, Plato is the forerunner of Ruskin, with his

[1] *Fors Clav.*, Lett. 70, 8 f. (Vol. XXVIII, 718 ff.), where he refers to Plato's *Laws* 727A.

[2] Cf. *infra* for citations.   [3] Cf. p. 23 and notes.

[4] *Laws* 697B, 631C, 728A, 870B; *Apol.* 29D-E.

[5] *Apol.* 30B; also *Laws* 743E; *Gorg.* 451E; cf. Ruskin, *Fors Clav.*, Lett. 70, 6 and 11 (Vol. XXVIII, 717), where he cites *Laws* 726–728A, on the value of the soul. He also cites *Laws* 742–743 and *Rep.* 416E (cf. *Mun. Pul.* [Vol. XVII, 89, 148]).

[6] *Laws* 743E.

[7] 831 C-D. Ruskin (*Crown of Wild Olive*, 83 [Vol. XVIII, 456 f.) cites *Critias* 120E ff., in urging the same idea. He also cites Plato's myth of the metals, *Rep.* 416E, in similar vein (*Mun. Pul.*, III, 89 [Vol. XVII, 211]).

[8] 631C cited by Ruskin, *Mun. Pul.*, III, 88 (Vol. XVII, 210).

[9] 661A, 661B; *Rep.* 331A-B.

[10] *Laws* 661B; *Hipp. Maj.* 290D; *Menex.* 246E.

characteristic assertions: "Only so much as one can use is wealth, beyond that is illth"; and "Wealth depends also on vital power in the possessor."[1]

Plato especially inveighs against excessive wealth and luxury.[2] Men are urged not to lay up riches for their children, since great wealth is of no use to them or the state.[3] The prime object of good legislation should not be, as is commonly supposed, to make the state as rich as possible,[4] since excessive wealth and luxury decrease productive efficiency,[5] are incompatible with the highest character or happiness, being based on both unjust acquisition (κτῆσις) and unjust expenditure (ἀναλώματα),[6] produce degeneration in individual and nation,[7] and are the direct cause of war[8] and civic strife.[9] Were it feasible, he would prefer to go back to the simpler life of earlier times, before luxury and the inordinate desire for riches had so dominated all society.[10] Of course he realizes that such a return is impossible, but he has little hope of any other escape from the evils. He is thus led to express the belief that the fewer wants the better, a doctrine common also to Ruskin, Carlyle, and Thoreau.[11]

---

[1] *Mun. Pul.*, II, 35 ff.; he refers to both Xenophon and Plato as being right on this point. Cf. *Fors. Clav.*, I, 8 (Vol. XXVII, 122); *Unto This Last*, 64 (Vol. XVII, 89).

[2] *Rep.* 550D, 373D: ἐὰν καὶ ἐκεῖνοι ἀφῶσιν αὐτοὺς ἐπὶ χρημάτων κτῆσιν ἄπειρον ὑπερβάντες τὸν τῶν ἀναγκαίων ὅρον. On ἄπειρος cf. *infra* under Aristotle. Cf. Dobbs, *op. cit.*, pp. 202 f. and note, on the evil results of excessive wealth and poverty in the Greece of that age. Like Ruskin, *Mun. Pul.*, VI, 153 and note (Vol. XVII, 277), who cites *Laws* 736E; *Aratra Pentelici*, IV, 138 (Vol. XX, 295 f.) on money as the root of all evil, citing *Laws* 705B.

[3] *Laws* 729 A.   [4] 742D.   [5] *Rep.* 421D.

[6] *Laws* 742E, especially πλουσίους δ' αὖ σφόδρα καὶ ἀγαθοὺς ἀδύνατον. For the modern application of this doctrine, cf. *infra;* cf. also 743A, C; *Rep.* 550E, 551A.

[7] *Rep.* 422; cf. 372E ff. on the φλεγμαίνουσα state.

[8] 373E; *Phaedo* 66C. Compare the modern doctrine that lasting peace is impossible under the present economic system.

[9] *Laws* 744D: διάστασις; also a basal idea of the *Republic*.

[10] This is the spirit of the *Republic* throughout, but cf. especially 369C–374D, and p. 25, n. 7.

[11] *Laws* 736E: καὶ πενίαν ἡγουμένους εἶναι μὴ τὸ τὴν οὐσίαν ἐλάττω ποιεῖν, ἀλλὰ τὸ τὴν ἀπληστίαν πλείω. Cf. *infra* on Xenophon for similar ideas. Carlyle, *Sartor Resartus*, chapter on "Everlasting Yea": "The fraction of life can be increased in

However, Plato has no prejudice against moderate wealth. His sermons are directed against excessive commercialism, which puts money before the human interest,[1] thereby causing injustice, degenerate luxury, vicious extremes of wealth and poverty, political graft, individual inefficiency, and wars both within and without the state. Though his philosophy leads to asceticism, and his attitude toward wealth seems, on the surface, to breathe this spirit, yet Plato is not an ascetic in his doctrine of wealth, as is often wrongly asserted. He describes the true attitude as that which partakes of both pleasures and pains, not shunning, but mastering them.[2] He recognizes an assured competency to be practically a prerequisite for the development of the good life,[3] while, on the other hand, he considers poverty to be an evil only second to excessive wealth.[4]

To be sure, Plato's demand for a limitation of private and national wealth, and his general negative attitude are, if interpreted rigidly, unfruitful and economically impossible.[5] It is not business that should be curbed, but bad business.[6] Individual or nation cannot become too prosperous, provided there is a proper distribution and a wise consumption of wealth, and Plato's idea that great prosperity is incompatible with this goal can hardly be accepted by modern economists.

Nevertheless, there is much of abiding truth in his doctrine of wealth. Aside from the profound moral value of his main contention, we may state summarily several points in which he remark-

value not so much by increasing your numerator as by lessening your denominator." Ruskin, *Time and Tide*, II, 5 ff. (Vol. XVII, 319 ff.); cf. 320, n. 1, for other references. Thoreau: "A man is wealthy in proportion to the number of things he can let alone"—an overemphasized truth.

[1] So Socrates (*Apol.* 41E, 29 D-E) and Jesus (Matt. 6:33).   [2] *Laws* 634A.

[3] *Rep.* 329E–330A, 330D–331B; cf. also the prayer of *Phaedrus* 279C: τὸ δὲ χρυσοῦ πλῆθος εἴη μοι ὅσον μήτε ἄγειν δύναιτ' ἄλλος ἢ ὁ σώφρων; *Laws* 679B; *Gorg.* 477E: τίς οὖν τέχνη πενίας ἀπαλλάττει; οὐ χρηματιστική; cf. also 452C.

[4] Cf. preceding notes; also *Rep.* 421D-E; *Laws* 744D.

[5] Bonar (*Philosophy and Political Economy*, pp. 13 f.) criticizes *Rep.* 400–402 for not seeing that unlimited wealth is necessary for the realization of the highest art and beauty.

[6] Plato also emphasizes this, *Laws* 743E, 870B: οὐ χρὴ πλουτεῖν ζητεῖν τὸν εὐδαίμονα ἐσόμενον, ἀλλὰ δικαίως πλουτεῖν καὶ σωφρόνως; 660E; though he implies that unlimited wealth is necessarily evil.

ably anticipated the thought of the more modern humanitarian economists: (1) in the fact that excessive private wealth is practically impossible without corresponding extremes of poverty, and that such a condition is a most fruitful cause of dissension in any state; (2) in the fact that extremes of wealth or poverty cause industrial inefficiency; (3) in the prevalent belief that no man can gain great wealth by just acquisition, since, even though he may have done no conscious injustice, his excessive accumulation has been due to unjust social conditions; (4) in the growing belief that expenditures of great private fortunes are not likely to be helpful either to individual or to community, but are too liable to be marked by foolish luxury and waste that saps the vitality of the nation; to Plato, such are mere drone consumers of the store ($\tau\hat{\omega}\nu$ $\dot{\epsilon}\tau o\acute{\iota}\mu\omega\nu$ $\dot{\alpha}\nu\alpha\lambda\omega\tau\acute{\eta}s$, ... $\kappa\eta\phi\acute{\eta}\nu$);[1] in this, he was a forerunner of Ruskin, who opposed the old popular fallacy that the expenditures of the wealthy, of whatever nature, benefit the poor;[2] (5) in the dominant note in economic thought today, so emphasized by Plato and Ruskin, that the prime goal of the science is human life at its best —as Ruskin states it, "the producing as many as possible full-breathed, bright-eyed, and happy-hearted human creatures";[3] (6) in the fact that the national demand for unlimited wealth is now recognized, as Plato taught, always to have been the most fruitful cause of international differences; (7) in the fact, which is receiving ever-greater recognition by modern economists and statesmen, that the innate quality of the object for good or harm must be considered in a true definition of economic wealth.[4]

PRODUCTION

Plato seems to have had little positive interest in the problems of production. He was too much engrossed with suggesting means for limiting excessive acquisition. He was, however, quite apt

---

[1] *Rep.* 552B-D; cf. Robin, *op. cit.*, p. 243, n. 1, on $\kappa\eta\phi\acute{\eta}\nu$.

[2] In *Mun. Pul.*, III, 91 (Vol. XVII, 213), he makes Circe's swine a type of false consumption; cf. *Fors Clav.*, Letter 38 (Vol. XXVIII, 30 ff.); *Mun. Pul.*, Pref., 16 (Vol. XVII, 139 f.); *Queen of the Air*, III, 124 ff. (Vol. XIX, 404 ff.); *Pol. Econ. of Art*, I, 48 ff. (Vol. XVI, 47 ff.); *Unto This Last*, IV, 76 (Vol. XVII, 102); Mill also attacked this idea.

[3] *Unto This Last*, II, 40 (Vol. XVII, 56); cf. also *Mun. Pul.*, II, 54 (Vol. XVII, 178 f.).

[4] Discussed above.

in his use of illustrations from industrial life.[1] He was also apparently the first to give a real classification of trades,[2] as follows: furnishers of raw materials (πρωτογενὲς εἶδος), makers of tools (ὄργανα), makers of vessels for conserving products (ἀγγεῖα), makers of vehicles (ὄχημα), manufacturers of clothing and means of defense (προβλήματα), workers in fine arts (παίγνιον), producers of food (θρέμμα)—a fairly inclusive catalogue for that age; if commerce and the learned professions were included. But some of the classes overlap, since they follow no necessary principle of division. He divided productive arts into co-operative (συναιτίους), which provide tools for manufacture, and principal (ἀιτίας), which produce the objects themselves.[3] They were further divided into productive arts (ποιητικαί), which bring something new into existence, and acquisitive (κτητικαί), which merely gain what already exists. In the latter class, he placed all commerce, science, and hunting.[4] Plato would thus appear to exclude commerce and the learned professions from the true sphere of production. This, however, is only apparent, in so far as legitimate exchange is concerned. He clearly understood that the merchant and retailer save the time of the other workers,[5] and that they perform a real service to the community, in that they make necessary exchange convenient and possible.[6] He thus recognized them as producers of a time and place value, and he cannot be accused of the physiocratic error, which denied productivity to all workers except those who produce directly from natural resources.[7] His distinction

[1] Cf. *Pol.* 281D–283A, for an excellent description of the weaving industry; also *Crat.* 388C ff.; *Phileb.* 56B, on carpentry.

[2] *Pol.* 287D–289B; cf. Espinas, *op. cit.*, pp. 35 f.; "L'Art économie dans Platon," *Revue des Etudes Grecques*, XXVII (1914), 106 ff.

[3] *Pol.* 281D-E; cf. also *Phaedo* 99A-B; *Phileb.* 27A; *Timaeus* 46C-D.

[4] *Sophist.* 219A-D. Bonar's (*op. cit.*, p. 20) criticism of this on the ground that learning may produce something new, while the arts may merely change the shape of things, takes Plato too seriously. We have here only a characteristic Platonic generalization. Cf. Shorey, *Unity of Plato's Thought* (1903), p. 64, n. 500, on the foregoing passages from *Sophist.* and *Pol.*; cf. Robin, *op. cit.*, pp. 231 f.

[5] *Rep.* 371C.

[6] *Laws* 918B-C, especially πῶς γὰρ οὐκ εὐεργέτης πᾶς ὃς ἂν οὐσίαν χρημάτων ὠντινωνοῦν, ἀσύμμετρον οὖσαν καὶ ἀνώμαλον, ὁμαλήντε καὶ σύμμετρον ἀπεργάζεται.

[7] Cf. DuBois, *Precis de l'histoire des doctrines économiques dans leurs rapports avec les faits et avec les institutions*, pp. 45-47, comparing Plato and Aristotle on this

of productive and acquisitive arts can, furthermore, hardly be interpreted as intending to limit production to the material merely, though learning is relegated to the acquisitive class. Such an interpretation would be out of harmony with the whole trend of his thought.[1] His further classification of productive agencies as creative (ἕνεκα τοῦ ποιεῖν τι) or preventive (τοῦ μὴ πάσχειν)[2] substantiates this, for many of the preventive agencies are intellectual and scientific.

The general attitude of Plato toward economic production may be inferred from his insistence upon the thorough application of the division of labor for the perfection of industry.[3] He evidently recognized it as the necessary basis of all higher life. We have seen above, also that one of his chief objections to excessive wealth or poverty was the fact that they caused inefficiency in production.

Agriculture.—Of the three factors that enter into production— land, labor, and capital—the most important in the mind of the Greek thinkers was land. The relative prominence of agriculture was partly the cause of this, but in the case of the philosophers, their ethical passion, their idea of the necessity of leisure for personal development, and their conservative attitude toward industry and commerce were the chief motives that impelled them to urge their contemporaries back to the simple life of the farm.[4]

point. *Laws* 743D and Plato's attitude on agriculture (cf. *infra*) might seem to point the other way. Cf. *infra*, p. 41, nn. 7–10. Espinas (*Revue des études Grecques*, XXVII [1914], 247, n. 1) is extreme in calling him a physiocrat. The term would more nearly apply to Aristotle.

[1] Ar. (*Pol.* vi [iv]. 1291a12–19) so interprets him, because he finds the origin of the state in physical needs (*Rep.* 369C ff.), but this is a carping criticism. Blanqui is hardly fair to Plato on this point (*Histoire de l'économie politique en Europe*, p. 88). Cf. above, p. 22, n. 4, on Plato's other theory of origins.

[2] *Pol.* 279C.

[3] Cf. *infra* and Poehlmann, *op. cit.*, I, 574.

[4] As we shall see, the third reason has been exaggerated for the philosophers. On the favorable attitude to labor at Athens, cf. V. Brants, *Revue de l'instruction publique in Belg.*, XXVI (1883), 108 f., 100 f.; he distinguishes between the *doctrine philosophique* and the *doctrine politique*. So also Guiraud, *La main-d'œuvre industrielle dans l'ancienne Grèce* (1900), pp. 36–50; Zimmern, *op. cit.*, pp. 382 ff., 256–72. For the older view of general prejudice against free labor in Greece, cf. Drumann, *Arbeiter und Communisten in Griechenland u. Rom* (1860), pp. 24 ff. Francotte (*L'Industrie*) takes the more conservative position. Cf. *infra* for further notice of this problem.

The aristocratic feeling, still strong in European countries, that landed property is the most respectable, probably also had some influence, though land was not so distinctively in the hands of the upper classes in Attica.

Though the praise of agriculture was a characteristic feature of Greek literature in all periods, it was not at first a conscious economic theory.[1] Later, toward the end of the fifth century, it became a definite ethico-economic doctrine of the philosophers, as a criticism of their times, and as an appeal to what was deemed to be the more healthful life of the earlier days.

Plato does not devote so much attention to this theme as do Xenophon and Aristotle. His standpoint, however, is practically the same, though his tendency toward the physiocratic error is not so marked. In his second state, he orders that agriculture shall be the only means of money-making,[2] and he even strikes the modern note of conservation, in his directions for the care of land, waters, springs, and forests.[3] On this point, he and the other Greek thinkers accord well with the economy of the past decade with its urgent preachment, "Back to the land," though the modern watchword has, of course, a more economic emphasis.

Capital.—Though the function of capital, aside from natural resources, was a familiar fact in the Athenian life of the fifth and fourth centuries B.C.,[4] there is scarcely any consideration of it by the theorists before Aristotle. Plato has no definition of capital, nor indeed scarcely any recognition of the fact of its existence.[5] His emphasis on the virtue of economy, however, and his criticism of those who spend the "stored wealth," imply the idea that wealth should be used not merely for enjoyment, but also for productive

---

[1] Hesiod *Erga; Theog.* 969–975, though even here it is opposed to commerce.

[2] *Laws* 743D, but he would even limit this, so that it may not become a sordid occupation.

[3] *Laws* 760E–761C, 763D. Ruskin cites this in *Fors Clav.;* cf. Vol. XXIX, 546.

[4] Cf. pp. 19 f., and notes; cf. also p. 106, n. 1. The extensive commerce of Athens necessitated the presence of a comparatively large amount of money capital, and a large amount was also invested in slaves. For further notice, cf. *infra,* p. 68, nn. 8 ff., on the terms.

[5] But cf. *Laws* 742C (κεφάλαιον), and *infra,* under Xenophon, on the terms for capital.

purposes.[1] His strictures upon interest show that he has but slight appreciation of the productive function of money-capital.[2] *Labor and industry.*—On the other hand, Plato has considerable insight into the rôle of labor in production. To be sure, he shares with the other philosophers a certain prejudice against manual labor as degrading to freemen.[3] The mechanical arts call forth reproach.[4] Free citizens should not be burdened with such ignoble occupations,[5] and any person who disobeys this rule shall lose his civic rights until he gives up his trade.[6] Agriculture alone shall be open to them, and only so much of this as will not cause them to neglect their higher welfare.[7] However, this prejudice has been read into some passages in Plato by a forced interpretation. The assertion of Socrates,[8] that craftsmen have not temperance (σωφροσύνη), since they do other people's business, is made merely to draw Critias into the argument. The statement that all arts having for their function provision for the body are slavish,[9] does not necessarily imply prejudice against physical labor. Such arts are slavish, to Plato, because they have no definite principle of service as gymnastics has. He is merely illustrating the point that it is an inferior type of statesmanship that works without a definite principle for the highest political welfare. The idea, expressed in the *Politics*,[10] that the masses (πλῆθος) cannot acquire political science is a criticism against unprepared statesmanship rather than against labor. Indeed, Plato asserts the same of the wealthy.[11]

---

[1] Cf. *Rep.* 552B, and p. 27. Kautz (*op. cit.*, p. 119) overemphasizes this; cf. Souchon, *op. cit.*, p. 91, n. 2, who observes, however, that Plato, by his insistence upon collectivism in landed property implies that "la terre est toujours un capital, et que la fortune mobilière ne l'est jamais."

[2] Cf. *infra* on money.

[3] On the general attitude toward labor in Athens, cf. p. 30, n. 4. On Plato's regard for the laborer, cf. *infra*, under distribution.

[4] *Rep.* 590C, but only for him whose higher nature (τὸ τοῦ βελτίστου εἶδος) is naturally weak, though the implication is that this is characteristic of the artisans. Cf. Poehlmann, *op. cit.*, II, 49 f.

[5] *Laws* 842D, 806D-E, 741E, 846D, 919D.

[6] 847A.   [8] *Charm.* 163A-C.   [10] 292E, 289E-290A.

[7] 743D.   [9] *Gorg.* 517D-518E.   [11] *Ibid.* 300E.

Moreover, the following facts should be observed: that the prejudice of Plato against the manual arts is chiefly limited to the *Laws;* that even there his prejudice is primarily against retail trade rather than against industry;[1] that in so far as a real hostility exists, its true source is not in any opposition to labor or industry *per se,* but rather in the political belief that only as citizens have leisure for politics can prepared statesmen take the place of superficial politicians,[2] and in the moral feeling that constant devotion merely to the physical necessities of life causes men to neglect the primary purpose of their existence.[3]

Modern scholars have usually been extreme in their interpretation of Plato on this point.[4] Such unwarranted generalizations as the following are common: "Il ne découvre dans les professions qui tendent au lucre qu'égoisme, bassesse d'esprit, dégradation des sentiments." "Platon et Aristote voient dans le commerce et dans l'industrie deux plaies de la société; ils voudraient les extirper à'fond, si cela était possible."[5] One of the worst misinterpretations has been perpetrated by Roscher, in inferring from the *Republic* (372 ff.) that Plato "das Leben der Gewerbetreibenden als ein Leben thierischen Behaglichkeit schildert, sie wohl mit Schweinen vergleicht."[6] Such absurdities are unfortunately not rare, though they might be avoided by a careful reading, even in a translation.[7]

---

[1] Cf. *Rep.* 371C for a contrast in his attitude toward the two; cf. Bonar, *op. cit.,* pp. 21 f.

[2] *Laws* 846D, 847A.   Ruskin (*Fors Clav.,* Letter 82, 34 [Vol. XXIX, 253 f.]) contrasts the fevered leisure that results from extreme money-making with the true leisure, citing *Laws* 831.

[3] *Laws* 743D.   The aristocratic Greek feeling of independence against selling one's powers to another, and the fact of the frank acceptance of slavery, by most contemporary thinkers, as the natural order, also exerted some unconscious influence.

[4] Cf. *infra* for citations from Zeller, and Poehlmann's able, but somewhat extreme, defense of Plato (*op. cit.,* II, 36 ff.). He cites Adam Smith, *Wealth of Nations,* V, I, Pt. 2, art. 2, in similar vein to Plato, on the ill-effects of mechanical labor, despite his undoubted interest in the industrial arts.

[5] Francotte, *L'Industrie,* I, 246, in reference to the *Laws.*

[6] *Op. cit.,* p. 26, n. 2.

[7] Eisenhart (*Geschichte der Nationalökonomie,* p. 5) also says that Plato calls "Volkswirtschaft gerade zu den Staat der Schweine." Dietzel ("Beiträge zur Geschichte des Socialismus und des Kommunismus," *Zeitschrift für Literatur und Geschichte der Staatswissenschaften,* p. 397, n. 1) criticizes both the foregoing.

It should not be overlooked either that Plato's utterances on labor are by no means all negative. Skilled labor is recognized in several of the minor dialogues as fulfilling an actual need in civilization. Laborers are represented as having their part in knowledge and virtue,[1] and are admitted to be the necessary foundation of all human well-being.[2] A positive interest is also manifested by Plato in labor and the proper development of the arts in both the *Republic* and the *Laws*. He constantly harps on the necessity of each doing his fitting work, and doing it well, and in his opinion happiness consists in this rather than in idleness.[3] Indeed, that each one perform well the task for which nature has fitted him is the definition of justice itself.[4] The indolent rich man is a parasite and a drone, a disease of the state. This is Plato's favorite figure in both the *Republic* and the *Laws*, a figure that is suggestive of Hesiod, the pioneer champion of labor.[5] He is even ready to admit that it is, after all, not the kind of labor but the character of the workman that ennobles or degrades any work.[6] In fine, his attitude toward the mechanical arts is similar to that of Ruskin, who also thinks that manual labor is degrading.[7]

[1] *Sympos.* 209A; *Phileb.* 56C.   [2] *Protag.* 321E.

[3] *Rep.* 420E, 421C; *Laws* 779A, 807A-E, 808C. The passages in the *Laws* apply particularly to the work of the soldier and the citizen. Cf. Ruskin, *Unto This Last*, I, 22 (Vol. XVII, 40) for a similar idea that the function of the laborer is not primarily to draw his pay, but to do his work well.

[4] *Rep.* 433A.

[5] *Rep.* 552A, C, 564E; cf. *Laws* 901A, where he refers to the passage in Hesiod's *Erga* 304: κηφήνεσσι κοθούροις. Cf. p. 27, n. 1, above. Poehlmann (*op. cit.*, II, 87 f.) points to Plato's demand that woman be freed, so that the total number of free workers may be increased, but Plato is thinking only of the ruling class.

[6] *Laws* 918B–919C, referring to retail trade; but if he could admit it for this, he surely could for the industries. Cf. Aristotle's passage on liberal and illiberal work (*Pol.* 1337b5–22).

[7] *Mun. Pul.*, V, 105 and note (Vol. XVII, 234 f.), where he refers to Plato's diminutive, ἀνθρωπίσκοι, as applied to laborers (*Rep.* 495C; *Laws* 741E); *Time and Tide*, 103 (Vol. XVII, 402), 127 (p. 423 and note); *Crown of Wild Olive*, 2 (Vol. XVIII, 388), on the furnace; *Lectures on Art*, IV, 123 (Vol. XX, 113); on the evil effects of arts needing fire, as iron-working, where Xen. *Econ.* iv. 2, 3 is cited. He makes frequent reference to the Greek attitude, e.g., Vol. XVIII, 241, 461, and above. But he was not absolutely opposed to machinery; cf. *Cestus Aglaia*, 33 for what is called the finest eulogy of a machine in English literature. He even anticipated the great future mechanical development (*Mun. Pul.*, 17).

But as with Plato, the chief secret of his prejudice lies in the fact that laborers usually do their work mechanically, without thought. He believes that "workmen ought often to be thinking, and thinkers ought often to be working." He is willing to classify all work as liberal on this basis, the only distinction being the amount of skill required.[1] However, in agreement with Plato's idea, he would set the roughest and least intellectual to the roughest work, and this he thinks to be "the best of charities" to them.[2] With Plato, he is also convinced that, under actual conditions of labor, the degradation is very difficult to avoid, and therefore he would emphasize chiefly agricultural labor, where education of head and hand are more fully realized.[3]

It is, however, in Plato's constant insistence upon the principle of the division of labor, as a prerequisite for any succces in the mechanical arts or elsewhere, that he reveals insight into, and interest in, productive labor. This is the basal idea in the *Republic*. It is also one of the chief regulations in the *Laws*, where its direct application to the artisan is a clear evidence that he appreciates the economic significance of the principle.[4] To him, it is the foundation of all human development. Society finds its source in mutual need ($\dot{\eta}$ $\dot{\eta}\mu\epsilon\tau\epsilon\rho\alpha$ $\chi\rho\epsilon\acute{\iota}\alpha$). Man is not self-sufficient ($\alpha\dot{\upsilon}\tau\acute{\alpha}\rho\kappa\eta s$). Reciprocity is necessary even in the most primitive state.[5] Out of this necessary dependence arises the division of labor, a beneficent law, "since the product is larger, better, and more easily produced, whenever one man gives up all other business, and does one thing fitting to his nature, and at the opportune time."[6]

---

[1] *Stones of Venice* (Vol. X, 201); cf. also IV, 6 (Vol. XI, 202 f.), where he cites Plato *Alc.* I. 129.

[2] *Fors. Clav.*, VII, 9 (Vol. XIX, 230).

[3] Cf. Vol. XXVII, Intro., p. lxv.

[4] *Rep.* 370A-C and many other passages. Cf. *infra; Laws* 846E–847A. Cf. *infra* on the unfair interpretation of *Rep.* 421A by Zeller and others. Plato implies by the passage merely that specialization is more important for the statesman than for the cobbler (421C).

[5] *Rep.* 369C. Adam Smith makes this the basal fact of exchange (*Wealth of Nations*, I, ii).

[6] *Rep.* 370C: πλείω τε ἕκαστα γίγνεται καὶ κάλλιον καὶ ῥᾷον, ὅταν εἷς ἓν κατὰ φύσιν, καὶ ἐν καιρῷ σχολὴν τῶν ἄλλων ἄγων, πράττῃ. He first states the principle less plausibly as a literary device, *Rep.* 369C; cf. 433A.

The basis of this law Plato finds in the fact of the diversity of natures, which fits men for different tasks.[1] In this he differs from Adam Smith, who believes that the differences of natural talents in men are much less than is generally supposed. Smith makes the propensity to barter the source of specialization, which, in turn, is based on the interdependence of men. He thus considers the diversities in human nature to be the effect rather than the cause of the division of labor.[2] Plato, however, is probably nearer the truth, since the very reason for mutual interdependence is diversity of nature.[3]

The advantages of specialization, according to Plato,[4] are four, as stated above. It enables one to accomplish more work with greater ease, more skilfully, and at the proper season. The second and fourth of these are not mentioned by Adam Smith, but he notes the resulting increase in opulence for all the people, and the development of inventive genius. He also observes that the division of labor causes the growth of capital, and that this in turn increases specialization.[5] Of course Plato could not appreciate the important fact of the influence of the division of labor on the development of inventive genius, since he lived before the age of machinery.

Plato is also a forerunner of Adam Smith in his recognition of the fact that the division of labor depends for its advance upon a great increase in the size and complexity of the state.[6] It means a multiplication of trades, a development of industry,[7] the entrance of the retail trader (κάπηλος),[8] and the invention of money as a means of exchange.[9] The necessity of the division of labor between states is also recognized. It is impossible to establish a city where it will not be in need of imports (ἐπεισαγωγίμων). International trade therefore arises, and with it are born the merchant (ἔμπορος)

---

[1] Rep. 370C, B.   [2] Op. cit., I, chap. ii.

[3] So Herbert Spencer, Principles of Sociology (1900), III, 342-49. Cf. also Ruskin, Fors Clav., IV, 15 (Vol. XXVIII, 160).

[4] Rep. 370B-C, 374B-E.

[5] Op. cit., I, chap. i. Plato implies the increase in wealth. Haney (op. cit., p. 41) observes that Plato thought especially of the advantages of division of labor to the state, rather than to the individual. Cf. further Wealth of Nations, II, Intro.

[6] Rep. 370C-371B; cf. DuBois, op. cit., p. 37.

[7] Rep. 370C-D.   [8] 371C.   [9] 371B; Laws 918B.

and the sailor class, together with all those who are engaged in the labor of the carrying trade.[1] Thus Plato, the idealist, and reputed enemy of trade and industry, develops them directly out of the basal principle of his *Republic*. He appreciates the necessity of a full-fledged industry and commerce to the existence even of a primitive state, and his hostility to them is actually directed only against what he terms their unnatural use.[2] Moreover, in his opinion, one function of the division of labor should be to limit them to the performance of their proper tasks, and keep them from degenerating into mere money-making devices. It should also result in limiting such vocations to the less capable classes since the rulers should be artisans of freedom.[3]

It would take us too far afield to discuss the diverse ways in which Plato uses his principle. We may observe in passing, however, that he applies it to war, in his interesting criticism of the citizen-soldier;[4] to the finer arts, even when they are quite similar to each other;[5] to politics, as noted above; to justice and the moral life in general;[6] and to the intellectual life, in his unsparing criticism of the superficial versatility and dilletantism of the contemporary Athenian democracy, which trusts the government to any incompetent, professes to be able to imitate everything, and makes the many-sided Sophist ($\pi o\lambda\lambda\alpha\pi\lambda o\hat{v}s$) the man of the hour.[7] Though he begins with the development of the principle as an

---

[1] *Rep.* 370E–371A. In the *Laws*, he does not extend the principle to international trade. Cf. Bonar, *op. cit.*, p. 17.

[2] Poehlmann (*op. cit.*, II, 185 f.) notes a contradiction between Plato's insistence upon the division of labor and his desire for the simple life. But the philosopher is aware of this, and knows that the simpler ideal is impossible. Cf. V. Brants, *Revue de l'instr. pub. en Belg.*, XXVI (1883), 102–4, on the fact of the extensive division of labor in Athenian industry.

[3] $\delta\eta\mu\iota o\upsilon\rho\gamma o\grave{v}s$ $\dot{\epsilon}\lambda\epsilon\upsilon\theta\epsilon\rho\iota\alpha s$; *Rep.* 395C, 434A-D; cf. also 420B-421B. In the *Laws*, the artisans and traders are non-citizens (846D, 847A, 918B-C), not because of prejudice primarily, but for the sake of better government.

[4] *Rep.* 374B-E.

[5] 395A-B; cf. Adam's note to 395A, explaining *Sympos.* 223D, where Plato asserts the opposite. He thinks Plato is speaking ideally in the *Republic* passage, but here of the actual fact. But cf. Shorey, *Unity*, etc., p. 78, n. 597.

[6] *Rep.* 433A-B, D, 434A-D, 432A, 443-444A, 396D-E; *Charm.* 161E. In his broad application of the law, he has advanced beyond Adam Smith. Cf. Souchon, *op. cit.*, p. 81 and n. 2.

[7] *Rep.* 397E-398A.

economic fact, his primary interest in it is as a moral and intellectual maxim. The fact that the cobbler sticks to his last is only a symbol (εἴδωλον) of justice.[1] Nevertheless Plato does appreciate to a remarkable degree the economic bearings of the law, and his discussion of it is notably scientific and complete.[2] He sometimes pushes its application to an extreme, though such instances are perhaps meant in a playful Socratic vein.[3] At least, like Ruskin, he understands that extreme specialization must produce narrow and one-sided men, and that progress revolts against its too rigid application.[4] He is aware too that the division of labor breaks down in the case of the poor unemployed of the state, since they have no special work.[5]

SLAVERY

Plato is not blind to the ethical aspects of the problem of slavery. In his first healthy state (ὑγιείνη), slavery and war are conspicuously absent, and it is the natural inference that the author believed these to be necessary evils of the more complex state.[6] He appreciates the dangers of absolute power, even in private life, and believes that few men can stand the strain.[7] He conceives human nature as a unity that defies absolute division into separate classes.[8]

[1] 443C–D; cf. Nettleship *Lectures on the Republic of Plato*, p. 71.

[2] Oncken observes (*Geschichte der Nationalökonomie*, pp. 34–36) that while Smith drew from the law the idea of freedom of trade and industry, Plato inferred the strictest subordination of these to the will of the state, and that he also based the caste system on the principle. For the alleged caste system, cf. Souchon, *op. cit.*, p. 82, and *infra*, under distribution. Aristotle's state implies even a more rigid separation of the capable few. On Plato's insight into economic principles, cf. Robin, *op. cit.*, pp. 229 ff. He criticizes Guiraud for belittling the value of Plato's social ideas, and urges that he should be judged, not by the worth of his proposed remedies, but by his scientific insight (p. 252).

[3] *Rep.* 395A–B; 374E, 395B; εἰς σμικρότερα κατακερματίσθαι.

[4] *Apol.* 21C–22E; cf. *Rep.* 495D–E, though it applies rather to the evil effects of the banausic life. Cf. Bonar, *op. cit.*, p. 16. Ruskin (*Stones of Venice*, VI, 16 [Vol. X, 196]), says: It is "not the labor that is divided but the men—divided into segments of men." It stunts their faculties.

[5] *Rep.* 552A.   [6] 396C–373E; cf. Bonar, *op. cit.*, p. 27.   [7] 579D.

[8] Cf. Zimmern, *op. cit.*, p. 389, note; *Laws* 777B: δῆλον ὡς ἐπειδὴ δύσκολόν ἐστι τὸ θρέμμα ἄνθρωπος καὶ πρὸς τὴν ἀναγκαίαν διόρισιν, τὸ δοῦλόν τε ἔργῳ διορίζεσθαι καὶ ἐλεύθερον καὶ δεσπότην οὐδαμῶς εὔχρηστον ἐθέλει εἶναι τε καὶ γίγνεσθαι. On his alleged caste system, cf. above, n. 2, and *infra*.

Though he does not renounce slavery in the *Republic*, he would limit it to the barbarians and to those who seem unfit for the higher life.[1] It plays a remarkably small part in his first state, and it would seem that his idealism is here struggling against what he feels to be an economic necessity. In the *Laws*, he frankly accepts the necessity, and puts even agriculture, as well as the other industries, into the hands of slaves.[2] However, they are not to be treated as animals, but as rational men, in whom a proper usage may develop a certain degree of morality and ambition for good work.[3] To be sure, his purpose is economic rather than ethical—to make the slaves satisfied with their lot, and thus better producers.[4] He makes no mention of freedom as a reward for good behavior, though he elsewhere provides for the existence of freedmen in the state, and stipulates that they shall not become richer than their former masters.[5]

MONEY

As Plato was the first of extant Greek thinkers to grasp the principle of the division of labor, so he was the first to give any hint as to the origin of money. He states that it came into use by reason of the growth of necessary exchange, which in turn resulted from increased division of labor.[6]

The function of money he defines somewhat indefinitely by the term "token of exchange,"[7] an expression suggestive of Ruskin's

---

[1] *Rep.* 469C; cf. *Pol.* 309A.

[2] *Laws* 806D. For Ruskin on slavery, cf. *infra* on Aristotle.

[3] *Laws* 776D–777E. Espinas (*Revue des Etudes Grecques*, XXVII [1914], 256) observes that Plato adopts the mean between the two extremes in his attitude to slaves.

[4] Cf. Xen. *Ath. Pol.* i. 10–12 on the easy life of slaves in Athens, and Zimmern, *op. cit.*, pp. 382 f., who points out that this resulted from economic necessity. Cf. 777C-D; cf. *Rep.* 578D–579A on the dangers and troubles arising from extensive slaveholding.

[5] *Laws* 915A ff., another striking evidence of the actual status of freedmen and slaves in Athens.

[6] *Rep.* 371B. The word is νόμισμα, something established by usage, hence "current coin," not necessarily suggestive of intrinsic worth, as are χρήματα and the metals. Cf. Ar. *Clouds* 248 for a play on the word, θεοὶ ἡμῖν νόμισμ' οὐκ ἔστι. Cf. the simile, *Frogs* 720, and *Phaedo* 69A, for an analogy between it and wisdom.

[7] *Rep.* 371B: ξύμβολον τῆς ἀλλαγῆς.

definition "a ticket or token of right to goods."[1] It seems to imply that money is not itself a commodity to be trafficked in. In the *Laws*, he specifies more clearly the functions of this symbol. It acts as a medium of exchange and as a measure of value.[2] The latter office is performed by reason of the fact that money is a common denominator of value, changing products from incommensurable (ἀσύμμετρον) and uneven (ἀνώμαλον) to commensurable and even.[3]

Since Plato did not consider money to be a commodity to be bought and sold, and since he did not appreciate its productive function as representative capital, his theory of interest was superficial. His attitude toward it was somewhat similar to that of many people today toward speculation in futures in the stock market, as a practice contrary to public interest and policy. The application of the term τόκος to interest by Plato[4] and Aristotle, as though interest were the direct child of money, is probably only a punning etymology, and not intended seriously. It can therefore hardly be used, as it often is, to prove the superficiality of the theory of the Socratics. Plato, however, would have no money-making by usury,[5] nor indeed any loaning or credit at all, except as an act of friendship.[6] Such contracts should be made at the loaner's own risk,[7] and held legal only as a punishment for breaking other contracts.[8] He calls the usurer a bee that inserts his sting, money, into his victims, thereby beggaring them and enriching himself.[9]

Such strictures against interest were common in mediaeval Europe, reappeared in Ruskin,[10] and are implied in the present

---

[1] *Fors Clav.*, IV, 11, note (Vol. XXVIII, 134 f.); cf. also Vol. XVII, 50, 194 f.

[2] 742A-B: νόμισμα δ' ἕνεκα ἀλλαγῆς; 918B: ἐξευπορεῖν καὶ ὁμαλότητα ταῖς οὐσίαις, referring directly to traders.

[3] *Laws* 918B.   [5] *Laws* 743D.

[4] *Rep.* 553E; for Aristotle, cf. *infra*.   [6] 849E.

[7] 742C, 915D-E; *Rep.* 556A-B; *Laws* 850A.

[8] 921C, an obol per month.   [9] *Rep.* 555E.

[10] *Fors. Clav.*, notes to Letter 43, 14 (Vol. XXVIII, 121 f.), notes to Letter 81, 16 (Vol. XXIX, 212), where he refers to Plato and Aristotle; *Mun. Pul.*, IV, 98, note (Vol. XVII, 220), where he absolutely condemns it; On the Old Road, Vol. XXXIV, 425, on usury, ends with a citation from the *Laws* 913C; ἃ μὴ κατέθου, μὴ ἀνέλῃ.

opposition, in some quarters, to so-called "unearned income."[1]
The motive in mediaeval times, however, was distinctively religious, and was also partly due to the absence of a developed capitalism. With Ruskin and modern theorists, on the other hand, the
objection is, at bottom, socialistic. The motive of the Socratics
was essentially moral and political.

Plato's other error concerning money, as above observed, was
that it need possess no intrinsic value for domestic use. He looked
upon gold and silver as causes of degeneration in state and individual,[2] and would therefore have put a ban on them for use within
the state.[3] To his mind, a mere state fiat was sufficient to give
currency and value.[4] This doctrine has also often recurred in the
history of economic thought, as in Ruskin and the Greenback
party of a generation ago.[5] The error, however, was not so grave
in Plato's case, for he, at least, recognized the need of the precious
metals for international purposes.[6] Moreover, in his proposed
state of such limited extent, the problem would have been far
simpler, and he would have distinguished between actual conditions and possibilities in Greece and his admittedly more or less
utopian ideal.

EXCHANGE

Exchange in Greek economy held a very minor place, compared
with its dominant importance in modern theory. It was discussed chiefly in a negative manner, as the object of the moral and
aristocratic prejudice of Greek thinkers. We find, however, some
appreciation of its true place in the economic life of a state. Plato
divides trade, ἀλλαγή or ἀγοραστική, into αὐτοπωλική, which sells
its own products, αὐτουργῶν, and μεταβλητική, which exchanges
the products of others. He further divides the latter into καπηλική,
the exchange within the state, which he calls one-half of all the

---

[1] E.g. J. Scott Nearing's recent book on *Income*.

[2] *Laws* 679B, 831C; *Rep.* 545B ff., 548B. Cf. Ruskin on the evils arising from
money, Vol. XX, 295 f.

[3] *Laws* 743D, 742A-B, 801B.   [4] 742A.

[5] Ruskin, *Mun. Pul.*, I, 25. He thinks it is a relic of a barbarism that will dis-
appear as civilization develops.

[6] *Laws* 742A-B.

exchange, and ἐμπορική, foreign commerce.¹ He finds its origin in the division of labor, and in the mutual interdependence of men and states.² He understands the necessity of the reciprocal attitude in international, as well as in private, exchange, and thus has a clearer insight than the mercantilists and some modern statesmen. A state must raise a surplus of its own products, so as to supply the other state from which it expects to have its own needs satisfied.³

Since a tariff on imports played little part in Greek life, except in so far as it was imposed for sumptuary or war purposes,⁴ the perplexing modern problem of the protective tariff scarcely came within the horizon of Greek thinkers. Plato would prohibit the import of certain luxuries, as a moral safeguard. He divides merchandise into primary and secondary products, and would not permit the import of the latter.⁵ Elsewhere, however, he legislates against imposts upon either imports or exports, though unconscious of the significance of his suggestion.⁶

He appreciated something of the function of exchange in society. It performed a very important service, as a mediator between producer and consumer.⁷ Like money, it served to equalize values, and thus acted as an aid to the satisfaction of needs.⁸ When limited to this primary function, it was of advantage to both parties to the exchange,⁹ and merchants and retailers had then a real part in the production of values.¹⁰

The sweeping assertion is too often made that the Greek people were hostile to trade, and therefore that their theorists were especially opposed to it. We have already seen how false this idea is

¹ *Sophist.* 223C-D; cf. *Pol.*, 289E for the triple division of commercials, κάπηλοι, ἔμποροι, and ἀργυραμοίβοι; cf. *Phaedo*, 69A for a figurative use of ἀλλαγή.

² *Rep.* 370A-E, home; 370E-371E, foreign; cf. Adam Smith's idea above.

³ 370E-371A; Cornford (*op. cit.*, p. 66) wrongly asserts that Plato did not know the law that exports must balance imports. Cf. *op. cit.*, p. 37.

⁴ Boeckh, *Die Staataushaltung der Athener*, I, pp. 382 ff.; Zimmern, *op. cit.*, 1st ed., p. 317. But cf. Brants, *Xenophon Economiste*, p. 18, n. 2 and references, on the protectionist tendency of the commercial policy of Athens.

⁵ *Laws* 847C; Souchon (*op. cit.*, p. 102) sees in this a mercantile trend, but the purposes are entirely different.

⁶ 847B. ⁷ *Rep.* 371C-D. ⁸ *Laws* 918B-C. ⁹ *Rep.* 369C.

¹⁰ On the relation of exchange to production, cf. above, p. 28.

for the Greeks themselves,[1] but it also needs a great deal of quali-
fication in the case of their writers. Their hostility is directed
especially against the more petty business of retail trade (καπηλική)
rather than against the extensive operations of the merchant
(ἔμπορος). But their opposition even to this is not entirely undiscriminating. We have seen that Plato clearly understands the
necessity of exchange to the life of the state.[2] He admits that
even retail trade is not necessarily evil.[3] The chief reason why it
appears so is because it gives free opportunity for the vulgar greed
of unlimited gain, which is innate in man.[4] If the noblest citizens,
who are governed by rational interests, should become retailers
and innkeepers, the business would soon be held in honor.[5]

Plato, however, would limit exchange to its primary function
as defined above.[6] Like Ruskin, he believes that, whenever it is
pursued merely for private gain, it becomes a source of degeneration
to individual and state. It is then akin to the fraudulent or
counterfeit pursuits (κιβδήλοις).[7] The retailers in well-ordered
states are generally the weakest men, who are unable to undertake
other work.[8] The rulers in the *Republic* must keep themselves
entirely free from the trammels of trade, lest they become wolves
instead of shepherds,[9] though Plato is grappling here with a very
real problem that still faces us—how to prevent graft among
public servants.[10] In the *Laws*, retail trade is entirely prohibited
to citizens,[11] and permitted only to metics and strangers,[12] and,
indeed, only to those whose corruption will be of least injury to the
state.[13] These aliens are not to be permitted to gain overmuch
wealth,[14] and they must depart from the state, after twenty years'

---

[1] Pp. 19 ff.   [3] *Laws* 918B.   [5] 918E.

[2] P. 41 and notes.   [4] 918D.   [6] P. 41 and notes.

[7] *Laws* 918A, 920C. He seems to feel that trade as regularly pursued is a form of
cheatery, in which one gains what the other loses. Cf. Ruskin, *Unto This Last*, I,
22 (Vol. XVII, 40 f.); IV, 66 ff. (Vol. XVII, 90 ff.); *Mun. Pul.*, IV, 95 ff. (Vol. XVII,
217 ff.), where he refers to *Rep.* 426E, on the difficulty of curing this disease of traders;
cf. Vol. XVII, *Intro.*, p. xlvi, citing Xen. *Mem.*, iii. 7. 5, 6, on those who are "always
thinking how they may buy cheapest and sell dearest."

[8] *Rep.* 371C.   [9] 416A–417A.

[10] Cf. 415E, χρηματιστικάς in contrast to στρατιωτικάς.

[11] 741E, 743D, 919D.   [12] 920A.   [13] 919D.

[14] 915A-B, though it applies especially to freedmen.

residence, with all their belongings.[1]   Retail trade, even in their
hands, must be strictly limited to the demands of the state,[2] and
confined to the market-place for the sake of publicity.[3]   All
exchange must be honest, dealing with unadulterated products
(ἀκίβδηλον).[4]   There shall be no dickering over sales, but only one
price shall be set upon goods each day.   If this is not accepted, the
goods must be removed from sale until the following day.[5]   If
possible, the executors of the laws should try to fix a just schedule
of prices, to allow of moderate gain, and should see that this is
observed by the retailers.[6]   As a climax to all these precautions,
Plato would have the rulers take pains to devise means whereby
the retailers shall not degenerate into unbridled shamelessness
and meanness of soul.[7]   Under such limitations, he has faint hopes
that retail trade may be freed of its stigma, so as to do least harm
to those who pursue it, and to benefit the whole state.[8]

It need not be observed that this attitude of Plato toward trade
and commerce is alien to the spirit of economic progress, and that
no advanced civilization could be developed on such a basis.   His
profuse legislation, too, as above outlined, strikes a modern as
naïve and visionary.[9]   No man, however, is more aware of this
than Plato himself.   He should be judged, not in a spirit of rigid
literalism, but with a sympathetic criticism which tries to under-
stand the psychological reasons for his attitude.   His suggestions
are not offered as a proposed scheme for actual legislation,[10] but

---

[1] 850B-C, and n.1, above.   [2] 919C.

[3] 849D-E, 850A, 915D; cf. *infra* on this and the other regulations in their application to modern economics.

[4] 916D-E; cf. 917.   [5] 917B-D.

[6] 920B-C.   Plato's market regulations would exclude all selfish competition and
all gain, beyond mere return for labor expended, from exchange, and would base it
upon a mutual spirit of reciprocity.   Thus here, as often, he is the model for Aristotle,
who usually fails to recognize his debt.   Espinas (*Revue des Etudes Grecques*, XXVII
[1914], 246) is hardly in accord with the modern spirit in declaring that competition
is the social bond, and that Plato misconceives the nature of this bond.

[7] 920A-B, 919D.   [8] *Laws* 920C.

[9] Zimmern (*op. cit.*, p. 280, n. 1) calls it "grandfatherly."

[10] But cf. Robin, *op. cit.*, p. 212, n. 1, who argues that many of his suggestions are
based on actual legislation in Athens or elsewhere in Greece.   Cf. also Hermann,
Ges. Abh. (1849), pp. 141, 153, 159, whom he cites; J. Schulte, *Quomodo Plato in*

rather in the spirit of the moralist, who, observing that almost inevitable evils accompany retail trade and commercialism, with human nature as it is, and that commerce, the servant of man, has become his master, sees almost the only hope of escape in its limitation to what is barely necessary. The age-long problem of a greedy commercialism, which is blind to the appeal of all other goods when profits are at stake, Plato certainly saw clearly, and outlined with the hand of a master. The problem faces us still, in a form even more acute, but the protests of Plato, Ruskin, and Carlyle are bearing positive fruit today, in a political economy that takes as its supreme goal human life at its best.

But aside from these generalities, a sympathetic study of Plato's thought on exchange reveals an insight into certain specific points, of interest to modern economics, which are commonly overlooked. His protest against the former axiom of economics, that the prime purpose of trade is profit, and that the mere fact that goods change hands, necessarily increases the wealth of a country, is substantially correct.[1] Commerce for commerce' sake is a clear case of mistaking the means for the end, and is contrary to sound economics as well as ethics. The objections of Plato and Ruskin[2] against the principle too generally accepted by business and economy of the past, at least tacitly, that "it is the buyer's function to cheapen and the seller's to cheat," are being recognized today as worthy of consideration.

The anxiety of Plato over the effect of trades or professions upon character is well worthy of modern imitation, and this is, to a considerable extent, an economic as well as a moral question. Zimmern[3] has well observed: "Our neglect to study the effect of certain modern professions upon character, when we are always

legibus publica Atheniensium instituta respexerit (1907, dissertation), and the bibliography cited there. But he deals very little with Plato's economic and social laws.

[1] Plato saw that it might add a time and place value (p. 41, and notes).

[2] Cf. above, p. 42, n. 7; also Fors Clav., Letters 45, 82; Crown of Wild Olive, II, 75 f. (Vol. XVIII, 450 f.). He argues that there should be no profit in exchange, beyond merely the payment for the labor involved in it. He insists that "for every plus in exchange there is a precisely equal minus." Cf. infra on Aristotle for a similar idea, pp. 107 ff.

[3] Op. cit., p. 278, n. 2; cf. above, pp. 42 f.

insisting, and rightly, upon the importance of a character-forming education, is one of the strangest lapses, due to the sway of nineteenth-century economics."

As we have seen, one of the chief purposes of Plato in his limitation of commerce was to eliminate graft from the government. Though his remedy was not acceptable, yet his remarkable appreciation of a very grave problem that still faces us should be recognized. Furthermore, no better solution for it has ever been offered than the separation of politics from big business. This was the underlying principle of his suggestion, and it is in accord with the trend of modern statesmanship.

Another impelling motive of Plato in his stringent legislation was to render impossible the development of extremes of wealth or poverty in the state. Again, we should credit him with having clearly appreciated the problem, though we may criticize his attempted solution. The great commercial prosperity of today has made the situation vastly more acute, and still economics has no satisfactory solution to offer. After all, in the light of modern tendencies toward the regulation of industry and commerce, some of Plato's ideas do not seem so "grandfatherly," but rather prophetic, and in accord with sound economy. His legislation against the sale of adulterated products,[1] and in favor of publicity in business,[2] and state supervision of prices[3] has a startlingly modern ring.

POPULATION

The problem of population and food supply, which disturbed Malthus and some of the other English economists, was also a cause of concern to Greek thinkers. This might well be expected, since it is a recognized fact that the source of the grain supply was always a matter of grave concern to Athens and many other Greek cities.[4]

---

[1] Cf. p. 43.   [2] *Ibid.*

[3] *Ibid.* Cf. Ruskin's more socialistic idea that all retailers be made salaried officers (*Time and Tide*, XXI, 134 [Vol. XVII, 427]).

[4] Cf. e. g., Dem. *De corona* 87; *Cont. Lept.* xx. 31; *Cont. Andr.* xxii. 15; *Cont. Lacrit.* xxxv. 50; Lysias xxii; Hdt. vii. 102; Thuc. iii. 86, and many other passages. For modern discussions, cf. Droysen, *Athen und der Westen* (1882), pp. 41 ff.; Grundy, *Thucydides and the History of His Age* (1911), pp. 58–95; Zimmern, *op. cit.*, 1st ed., pp. 349 ff.; Gernet, "L'Approvisionment d'Athènes en blé," *Mélanges d'histoire, ancienne*, 1909; Beloch, *G. G.*, I, 406 f.; *Bevölkerung im Alterthum* (1898), p. 30, etc.

Plato states the problem clearly and hints at a solution, when he says that the natural increase of population in his state shall not exceed the economic basis for it.[1] In the *Laws*, he suggests specific means for preserving the proper number by restraining over-productive people, and by encouraging the opposite.[2] If such general provisions should not prove sufficient, he would then resort to colonization.[3] On the other hand, should population be greatly depleted by war or disease, he would even open the doors of citizenship to the undesirable classes.[4] His interest in the problem of population, however, is primarily moral and social rather than economic. Moreover, in antithesis to Malthus, he limits his consideration to a very small, artificially constructed state. With the narrow political vision of a Greek, he thinks that the production of a *multitude* of "happy-hearted" men in a state is impossible.[5]

DISTRIBUTION

As stated in the Introduction, the economic interest of Greek thinkers was particularly alive in the fields of distribution and consumption. It is here that they are especially interesting and suggestive.[6] However, they dealt very little with the important principles of distribution as laid down by modern economists. Theories of the several elements that enter into distribution—wages, profits, and rent—are for the most part conspicuously absent.[7]

The problem of distribution is also hardly considered from the modern standpoint. We look in vain for a treatment of the

[1] *Rep.* 372C: οὐχ ὑπὲρ τὴν οὐσίαν ποιούμενοι τοὺς παῖδας.

[2] *Laws* 74cD; but his specific methods for carrying out his difficult suggestion, if he had any to offer, were probably impracticable, judging by his discussion of women and children in the *Republic*. Ruskin's suggestions for meeting the problem are colonization, reclamation of waste lands, and discouragement of marriage (*Unto This Last*, IV, 80 [Vol. XVII, 108]).

[3] *Laws* 740E; Ar. (*Pol.* 1265*b*6–12) unfairly criticizes him for limiting the amount of property, and making it indivisible, while failing to provide against a too high birth-rate.

[4] 741A.   [5] Cf. Ruskin, cited above, p. 27.

[6] For the Greek term, cf. *infra* on Aristotle.

[7] Cf., however, Xen. *Mem.* ii. 7. 12–14, discussed *infra*, which may be a suggestion of a theory of profits.

modern dominant question of the relation between capital and labor. Moreover, the Greek theories of distribution are, on the whole, not the outgrowth of the sentiment of human sympathy for the poor and the common laborer, which is so prevalent today. The purpose seems to be to guard against dishonesty rather than oppression from either contracting party.[1] This lack in Greek theory is not strange, in an age when slaves took the place of machinery, so that capital and labor were largely united in them, while the majority of free laborers worked directly for the public, or on the land.[2] The goal of the theorists, therefore, is the conservation of the state rather than the relief of any class of the citizenship.

Plato discusses the importance of a proper distribution of wealth in the *Republic*, but the point that looms large to him is the fact that excessive wealth or poverty is likely to endanger the stability of the state.[3] As seen above, also, some of his regulations in the *Laws* seem to strike a modern note. He would have a state commission fix prices,[4] would permit the state to limit the freedom of inheritance,[5] and perhaps even intervene in securing a just wage.[6] Yet in all of this, the dominant motive is to avoid civic discord.

Before proceeding to the larger subject in distribution, Plato's theory of private property, we will discuss briefly his attitude toward the laboring classes.[7] It is commonly asserted that the

[1] *Laws* 921A-D, discussed on p. 39, n. 8; cf. also 847B.

[2] The passages above cited, n. 1 above, need not imply labor for capitalists. It does not appear that there was ever a considerable body of free citizen laborers at Athens, who worked for capitalists, though the number of free workers, aside from labor on the farms, was fairly large. Cf. *C.I.A.* for records of such labor on the buildings of the acropolis; Boeckh, *op. cit.*, I, 58: "Der geringere war durch seine Umstände so gut als der arme Schutzverwandte oder Sklave zur Handarbeit genöthigt." On the favorable attitude toward free labor at Athens, cf. above, p. 29, n. 4. Poehlmann (*op. cit., in loc.*) takes the opposite view as to the number of free laborers for capitalists.

[3] *Rep.* 552B–D, a characteristic passage; *Gorg.* 507E; *Laws* 757 B.

[4] 920C.   [5] 740B ff., 923; but his purpose is to keep the allotments intact.

[6] 847B: μισθῶν δὲ αὐτοῖς περὶ καὶ τῶν ἀναιρέσεων τῶν ἔργων, καὶ ἐάν τις αὐτοὺς ἕτερος ἢ κεῖνοί τινα ἄλλον ἀδικῶσι, μέχρι δραχμῶν πεντήκοντα ἀστυνόμοι διαδικαζόντων, etc.; perhaps a strained interpretation.

[7] On his attitude to industry, cf. pp. 32 ff.

Greek philosophers had little or no regard for the masses. As usually expressed, however, the statement is very unfair, and especially to Plato. Such extreme assertions as the following are frequent: "They [the masses] are of no account altogether."[1] Plato in the *Republic* "voue à l'ignominie, au mépris, à la misère, à la servitude éternelle la classe des ouvriers."[2] "Für die des Erwerb obliegenden Personen bedarf es keiner Erziehung."[3] "Plato, in treating of the ideal state, deems it not worth while to concern himself with the trading and artisan classes."[4] "Und im übrigen will er sie [the masses], wie es scheint, durchaus sich selbst überlassen."[5]

To be sure, as above admitted, the interest of Greek thinkers was not marked by the modern sentiment of sympathy for the laborer. Their writings are characterized by a certain aristocratic feeling, and they do not emphasize the worth or importance of the masses. Yet they are far from being indifferent or hostile to them.

Aristotle himself was the first to make this false criticism of Plato.[6] But the author of the *Republic* foresaw that he might be misinterpreted, and excused himself for his indefiniteness in the details of the ideal state.[7] Moreover, Aristotle's criticism is not borne out by a study of the *Republic*. Plato implies with sufficient clearness that his communistic regulations are limited to the two upper classes.[8] It is not true either, as Aristotle asserts,[9] that there is a rigid caste system in the *Republic*. The very opposite principle is laid down.[10] The myth of the three metals presents

[1] Bonar, *op. cit.*, p. 29.

[2] Bussy, *Histoire et Réfutation du Socialisme* (1859), p. 119.

[3] Oncken, *op. cit.*, p. 34.   [4] Haney, *op, cit.*, p. 16.

[5] Zeller, *Phil. Gr.*, II, 1 (1889), 907; cf. also above, pp. 32 f. Historians of economic thought generally state the case extremely; e. g., Kautz, *op. cit.*, p. 59; Blanqui, *op. cit.*, p. 45; Souchon also, to some extent. Poehlmann (*op. cit.*, II, 36-108) errs in the opposite way.

[6] *Pol.* ii. 5. 1264a11-17, 36-38; 1264b11-13.

[7] 423D: ὡς δόξειεν ἄν τις; also 425D, both cited by Poehlmann.

[8] 415E-417B, 420A-421C admit of no other interpretation. Cf. 421C, how he turns to the next related point (τοῦ τούτου ἀδελφόν) the question of the effect of wealth or poverty on the artisans (τοὺς ἄλλους δημιουργούς). Cf. also *infra* for other citations.

[9] *Pol.* 1264a36-38, repeated by many moderns.   [10] *Rep.* 415B-C.

an aristocracy based strictly on intellectual and moral excellence. No arbitrary obstacle hinders either the degradation or the rise of any individual from his class. It depends entirely upon the possession of the gold of character and mentality, for which all may strive. Moreover, the life of the so-called first caste is literally dedicated to the best service of the rest. If this be aristocracy, we cannot have too much of it.[1]

Neither is Aristotle's criticism warranted, that Plato makes the happiness of the whole state something different from the sum of its parts.[2] He merely states the principle, universally true, that no class has a right to expect to be happy at the expense of the whole state, and that, in the long run, the prosperity of each is bound up in the prosperity of all. Indeed, he puts the very objections of Aristotle and Grote into the mouth of Adeimantus, and answers them satisfactorily, in his illustration of the painted statue.[3] There could hardly be a better example of Plato's lofty ideal, that each part is to contribute its share toward the utility, beauty, and happiness of the whole, and that through this co-operation each realizes the highest quantum of happiness for himself. This doctrine of mutual interdependence is the basal principle of Christianity, taught by Jesus and Paul in a strikingly similar figure of the body and its members,[4] though naturally Plato's idea of brotherhood is narrower in scope.

The common assertion that Plato has no regard for the artisan class, then, is unwarranted.[5] The entire *Republic* is built upon the opposite principle, to prevent exploitation of the lower by the upper classes; and his comparison of good and evil rulers to

---

[1] Cf. the undiscriminating statement of Souchon, *op. cit.*, p. 41: "Et il n'y a guère eu, au cours de l'histoire de la science politique, de conception plus aristocratique que le mythe fameux des trois races d'or, d'argent et d'airain."

[2] *Pol.* 1264b15–25, repeated by Grote and others.   [3] *Rep.* iv. beg.-421C.

[4] I Cor. 12:14 ff.; for other evidence of Plato's interest in all classes, cf. 519E ff., and the entire argument against Thrasymachus, Book I.

[5] *Rep.* 421A, cited by Zeller, *op. cit.*, II, 1, 907, as evidence of this, states merely that it is more important that there be efficient rulers than efficient cobblers. Cf. Poehlmann, *op. cit.*, II, 36–108, a masterly defense of the *Republic* on this point, criticizing both Zeller and Gomperz. He errs on the other side, however, as e.g., p. 96, where he infers from *Rep.* 462C that Plato intended his communism to apply to the whole people.

shepherd dogs and wolves[1] is a precursor of the famous passages of Milton and Ruskin on the same theme. All classes of citizens in the state are brothers.[2] The rulers are saviors (σωτῆρας), allies, shepherds (ποίμενες), nurses (τροφέας), paymasters, and friends.[3] This happy unity (ὁμόνοια), or harmony (ξυμφωνία), of all classes is to Plato the highest goal toward which the true statesman should strive,[4] and the point of next highest importance to the communism of the guards is the proper regulation of wealth and poverty for the artisans.[5] The mere fact that he does not believe the artisans to be capable of political independence by no means indicates that he is indifferent to their social or economic welfare. It is to conserve this that he would put the government into the hands of the most capable,[6] and, in any event, the artisans are not to be held in subjection so much by external force as by their own free self-restraint.[7] This, in itself, is sufficient evidence that Plato intended to include the third class in his lower scheme of education, a fact borne out also by other passages.[8]

It must be admitted that a somewhat different spirit pervades the *Laws*, where he seems to have despaired of the lofty ideal of the *Republic*. He relegates the working classes to non-citizenship. But here, also, he is still anxious that they shall have the sort of education that befits their station,[9] and that justice be done them.[10] He also provides against the existence of beggary in the state.[11] Whatever may be said of his aristocratic spirit, therefore, he cannot be justly accused of the gross indifference of the early nineteenth-century economy and of modern capitalism toward either masses or public, in their concern for material wealth.[12]

---

[1] 416A-B, 417B.

[2] 415A, introducing the alleged aristocratic myth.

[3] 463B, 417B, 416A, 547C.   [4] 431E–432A, 443E, 423D.

[5] 421C-E, cited on p. 48, n. 8. Cf. Poehlmann, *op. cit.*, II, 91.

[6] 590C.   [7] 431D-E, 434C.

[8] 378B, E, 377B, insisting upon proper stories for all children; 915E–520A, implying that the artisans shall share in all benefits of the state up to their capacity.

[9] 643B-C.   [10] 847B, 921C-D.   [11] 936B-C.

[12] Mill is an exception, but despite his thoroughgoing definitions of economics.

COMMUNISTIC AND SOCIALISTIC IDEAS

The Greek theory of distribution was employed chiefly in the criticism of the institution of private property, and in the suggestion of more or less communistic systems to succeed it. This tendency, however, was not like the modern either in motive or in general type. Modern socialism aims to be scientific, and professes to build a scientific system on a basis of economic laws. Greek socialism had no such aim. It did not lay claim to any relation to economic law, but frankly presented itself for what it was, a politico-moral sentiment. Other points of distinction will be observed as we proceed, but this primary one must not be overlooked, if either the spirit or the meaning of the Greek social theory is to be understood.

Two considerations made the communistic sentiment a normal one to the Greek democrat. (*a*) The institution of private property had not become so thoroughly imbedded in the very foundations of society as it has today. The custom of family tenure was not entirely forgotten, and in some backlying districts may well have been still in vogue.[1] In some states, also, a part of the land was probably still held in common by the citizenship. The frequent establishment of cleruchies in conquered territories, in which the land was regularly assigned by lot, and the ever-recurring revolutions, which usually resulted in confiscation of the land in favor of the victorious party, must have assisted materially in unsettling the confidence of the Greeks in private property as a basal institution of society. The actual existence of a polity like that of Sparta, where private ownership does not seem to have been so absolute,[2] doubtless also exerted its influence on the imagination of Greek thinkers. (*b*) As is generally recognized, the Greek, far more than the modern, took for granted the subordination of the individual citizen to the state. We have also seen that he tended to magnify the power of legislation as sufficient to encompass any reform, even in the face of economic laws. To him, therefore, the

---

[1] Cf. Ar. *Pol.* ii. 1266*b*17–24.

[2] On the Spartan system, cf. Guiraud, *La Prop. fonc.*, pp. 41 f.; Poehlmann, *op. cit.*, I, 75–98, both of whom oppose the more extreme theory of communism in Sparta.

demand that the state be made the dispenser of private property did not seem unnatural.[1] We should be on our guard, however, against exaggerating the extent of this sentiment among the Greek writers, or against reading into them the modern socialistic doctrines.

A consideration of the predecessors of Plato in social speculation may be conveniently introduced at this point, before we proceed to the discussion of the *Republic*. Some have thought to find traces of communism in Homer. The evidence of any real communism, however, is very slight, and the frankly individualistic spirit of the poems is against it. Moreover, this is a problem that concerns the economic conditions rather than the theory.[2] Little is definitely known of Pythagoras and his school, but it is improbable that he either taught or practiced a real communism.[3]

As for Hippodamas of Miletus, it is difficult to gain a clear idea of his ideal state from Aristotle's meager description,[4] but it seems not to have been markedly socialistic. He divides his body of ten

[1] On this general subject, cf. Guiraud, *La Prop. fonc.*, 573 f.; cf. S. Cognetti de Martiis, *Socialismo Antico* (1889), pp. 515–17, on socialistic tendencies in Greek constitutions and politics.

[2] E.g., Esmein, *Nouvelle Revue historique*, 1890, pp. 821 ff. For a refutation, cf. Poehlmann, *op. cit.*, 1st ed., pp. 20 ff.; Guiraud, *op. cit.*, p. 37; Souchon, *op. cit.*, pp. 135 f.

[3] For a refutation of the common error, cf. Zeller, *op. cit.*, I, 1, 317, n. 1, and 318, n. 2; Guiraud, *op. cit.*, pp. 574 f. and 7–11; Souchon, *op. cit.*, pp. 136–39 and notes. The earliest witnesses for Pythagorean communism, Epicurus, in Diog. L. x. 2, and Timaeus of Tauromenium, *ibid.*, viii. 10 are remote from his time and untrustworthy. The later writers (Diog. L. viii. 10; Aul. Gell. i. 9. 12; Hippolytus *Refut.* i. 2. 12; Porphyry *Vit. Pyth.* 20; Jamblichus *De Pyth. vit.* 30, 72, 168, 257, etc.; Photius, under κοινά) quoted, and made the tradition general. The older writers know nothing of the tradition. Moreover, some passages give evidence of private property among the Pythagoreans (Diog. L. viii. 1. 15, 39). The origin of the tradition has been plausibly assigned to a misunderstanding of the proverb κοινὰ τὰ τῶν φίλων, and to the doctrine of moral helpfulness among the Pythagoreans. S. Cognetti de Martiis (*op. cit.*, pp. 459ff.) calls it *socialismo cenobito*.

[4] *Pol.* ii. 8. Hippodamas the Pythagorean, cited by Stob. *Flor.* xliii (xli). 92 f., should not be confused with him. The former wrote in the Dorian dialect, and differs materially in his ideas. His three classes are rulers, soldiers, and all laborers, including merchants and farmers. He says nothing of the division of the land or who shall own it, but provides that the third class furnish a living to the rest. But cf. Robin, *op. cit.*, p. 228, n. 1, who identifies them.

thousand citizens into artisans, farmers, and soldiers.[1] He makes
a corresponding triple division of the land—sacred, to provide for
the expense of worship; public, for the support of the soldiers;
private, to be owned and worked by the husbandmen.[2] Thus
only the farmers are to own land, and the question as to who shall
work the land for the military class is left in obscurity.[3] It seems
likely that Hippodamas intended that the farmers should work
all the land, and own one-third of it for their own support. His
system contains some communistic elements, as the fact that two-
thirds of the land is public, but it is certainly not socialistic
in spirit and purpose. The prime interest of Hippodamas was
very probably not in a system to supplant private property, but
rather in a plan of assured support for the priestly and military
classes.[4]

Phaleas of Chalcedon, according to Aristotle's description,
approaches much nearer to the modern socialistic idea.[5] Aristotle
makes him a type of those thinkers who lay chief stress on the
right system of property as the necessary basis of civic peace.[6]
His central tenet is equality of possessions and of education for all
the citizens,[7] but he seems to have specified only landed property.[8]
This demand, though only landed property is included, seems to
strike a truly modern socialistic note. But nowhere better than
here may we see the gulf that separates ancient and modern socialism. The avowed interest of Phaleas is not in the masses. The
artisans are all to be public slaves.[9] His interest is rather in the
classes, and not even in these primarily, but rather in the state

---

[1] *Pol.* 1267b31–33. Cf. Cornford's visionary article (*Class. Quart.*, VI [1912],
246 ff.), in which he seeks to prove that the tripartite psychology of Plato's *Republic*
is an inference from this triple division of society. Cf. a similar idea of Pohlenz,
Aus Plato's Werdezeit (1913), pp. 229 ff.

[2] ii. 8. 1267b33–36.　　　[3] 1268a34 ff.

[4] So Souchon, *op. cit.*, p. 141, who makes him an individualist.

[5] *Pol.* ii. 7.　　　[6] 1266a37 f.

[7] 1266a40: φησὶ γὰρ δεῖν ἴσας εἶναι τὰς κτήσεις τῶν πολιτῶν; 1266b31-33, to be
realized in an old state, partly by allowing only the rich to give dowries and only the
poor to receive them; 1266b2-4.

[8] Ar. (1267b10) criticizes him for this.

[9] 1267b15; cf. Poehlmann, *op. cit.*, II, 7 f.

itself. His entire system has for its fundamental motive the avoiding of civic discord in the state.[1]

The ideal state of Plato's *Republic* has often been presented by socialists and other modern writers as the great prototype of all socialistic doctrine. We must consider to what extent such a view is justified. In his famous myth of the three metals, Plato divides his citizens into three classes—rulers, auxiliaries, and farmers and artisans.[2] His avowed purpose here, as indeed throughout his *Republic*, is to secure the highest degree of happiness for all the citizens.[3] In order to gain this end, he provides for a most thoroughgoing system of communism, including all property, both for production and for consumption, except such as is necessary for the immediate need.[4] He extends it even to the common possession of wives and children,[5] that all private interests may be reduced to a minimum.[6] He provides further for a common work[7] and education[8] for men and women.

Such, in brief, is the system proposed in the *Republic*.[9] Superficially considered, it would seem to be the parent of modern socialism and communism. There is, however, actually but slight similarity between them. The so-called communism of Plato extends only to the first two classes, which can include but a small minority of the citizenship.[10] Thus the masses, with whom modern

---

[1] 1266a37 f.; 1267a1 f. Aristotle's account of these writers, as of Plato, is incomplete and unsatisfactory.

[2] *Rep.* 415A; cf. above, pp. 48 ff. on this and the following note.   [3] 420B-C.

[4] 416D-E, 458C; cf. also *Critias* 112B-C, where common houses, common meals, and the prohibition of gold and silver are presented as an ideal.

[5] 457D.   [6] 462B-C.

[7] 451D–455D. Poehlmann points to this doctrine of the *Ebenbürtigkeit* of women as an advanced ground even for Christianity.

[8] 451E.

[9] Guiraud (*La Prop. fonc.*, p. 578) distinguishes these elements in Plato's system, *Republic* and *Laws:* exclusive right of property vested in the state; use of land granted to a part of the citizens; distribution of the product among all the citizens; obligation to work, tempered by equality of service; inequality of classes, and equality of men in each class; heredity of profession, corrected by selection of talents.

[10] Cf. pp. 48 f. and notes. Even Aristotle admits (1264a33) that Plato makes his husbandmen absolute owners of their lots, on condition of paying rental. The rulers alone (μόνοις) are to keep themselves from silver or gold (417A). Cf. Book IV, beg.: οἷον ἄλλοι

socialism is especially concerned, are not directly touched by his system. Again, the primary motive of Plato's communism is not the modern motive at all. His thought is not to secure a just share for all in the products of industry. Though he recognizes the importance of providing against the evils of extremes of wealth and poverty,[1] the motive is not the material interest of any class. It is an intense desire for unity and for escape from civic strife in the state,[2] for provision against graft, corruption, and tyranny in the rulers,[3] and for insuring as efficient work as possible.[4] Like Ruskin, Plato is no democrat. Equality is not in his thought.[5] Unlike many a modern socialist, he realizes that absolute arithmetical equality is impossible, and that if gained it would be the greatest injustice. He knows that the true equality must be proportional, demanding not that each receive exactly the same,

ἀγρούς τε κεκτημένοι καὶ οἰκίας οἰκοδομούμενοι, etc.; 420A, 416D-E, 458C, 464B-D, where the community is applied to the guards only, and 464A-D, where the same is true of family communism. Doubtless he would have extended it farther, had he thought it feasible (462B-C), but Poehlmann (*op. cit.*, I, 569 f.; II, 96 f.) overemphasizes this demand of Plato. Adler (*Geschichte des Socialismus und Kommunismus von Plato bis zur Gegenwart*, p. 44), DuBois (*op. cit.*, p. 40), Oncken (*op. cit.*, p. 34), Souchon (*op. cit.*, 148); Malon (*op. cit.*, pp. 90 f.), Shorey (*Class. Phil.*, October, 1914, art. on "Plato's *Laws*") all agree with the foregoing conclusion. Francotte (*L'Industrie*, II, 258 ff.) leaves the question open, but (261 f.) observes that the third class is at least restrained from extremes of wealth and poverty.

[1] 421D, 421E-422E.

[2] *Ibid.*, the fundamental idea of the *Republic*. L. Stein (*Sociale Frage*, p. 164) rightly says: "Denn der Kommunismus Platons ist seinem Schoepfer nicht Zweck, sondern blosses paedagogisches Mittel."

[3] 415E-416A, 417B, 420D, 421A, 421C. He would also avoid vulgarization of the rulers through trade (416E-417A).

[4] 421D.

[5] Ruskin thinks that inequality of possessions, in itself, does not necessarily mean either evil or good for a nation (*Unto This Last*, II, 31 [Vol. XVII, 46 f.]); he argues that each is born with an absolutely limited capacity, and calls the idea of natural equality of men "radical blockheadism" (*Fors Clav.*, VIII, Letter 95, 6 [Vol. XXIX, 496]); cf. *Unto This Last*, III, 54 (Vol. XVII, 74); *Modern Painters*, III, Pt. IV, chap. x, 22 (Vol. III, 189); *Seven Lamps of Architecture*, IV, 28 (Vol. VIII, 167); *Fors Clav.*, II, Letter 14, 4 and note (Vol. XXVII, 248); *Stones of Venice*, III, 4 (Vol. XI, 260), all of which emphasize its impossibility. He strongly opposes socialism, cf. above, and *Mun. Pul.*, 21 (Vol. XVII, 144), though his economic ideas contained essentially the germ of modern socialistic doctrine.

but that each receive his due.[1] His third class, comprising a large majority of the citizens, is practically without political activity, a fact in marked contrast to the modern social-democratic spirit. His emphasis is not economic and material, as is that of modern socialism, but political and moral.[2]

In fine, the *Republic* contains some socialistic elements. Plato's restriction of the freedom of the individual so as to subserve the interest of the whole,[3] his tendency to magnify the power of law in the face of economic principles and of human nature,[4] his interest in the welfare of the common people, his declaration against inequality of fortune, his denial of the right of private property for the upper classes, and his proposed community of wives and children, a measure too radical for the better type of modern socialism,[5] all seem socialistic in trend.

The tendency to magnify the power of law, and the submission of individual to state interest, however, were characteristics of Greek civilization, and not distinctly Platonic or socialistic. His interest in the welfare of the masses, as we have seen, was not primarily economic, but had for its ulterior motive the preservation of the peace of the state. His denial of private property and family interests to the guards, and his opposition to extreme wealth or poverty were, as seen above, devoid of socialistic motive. Moreover, in his hostility to retail trade, he was not moved by

[1] Cf. his ironical criticism of democratic equality in Athens, 558C: ἰσότητά τινα ὁμοίως ἴσοις τε καὶ ἀνίσοις διανέμουσα; *Laws* 757B-D, 744B-C; cf. *infra* for Aristotle's idea. Cf. p. 61, n. 1 for further notice of these passages.

[2] Poehlmann (*op. cit.*, I, 553, n. 3) is extreme in asserting that Plato's account of the growth of the proletariat, and the rise of class struggles (Book VIII) contains "alle wesentlichen Züge des Bildes, welches die moderne Plutokratie gewährt," and (560), "Das vierte Jahrhundert v. Chr. hat uns den Kampf vorgekämpft in welchem wir selbst mittenhineinstehen."

[3] Pohlenz (*op. cit.*, p. 240) makes his socialism a reaction against the individualism of Pericles, but makes the extreme assertion: "Die Grundlage auf der Plato seinen Idealstaat aufbaut, ist der strengste Socialismus."

[4] Cf. p. 43, n. 10. He evidently recognizes his ideas on the family and on the philosopher-king as utopian; cf. also 425D-E; but Poehlmann (*op. cit.*, II, 144–52) opposes this view. Cf. Shorey, *Class. Phil.*, October, 1914, pp. 357 f., on the idea of law in the *Laws* and *Politics*.

[5] When advocated, it has not been with the lofty motive of Plato.

the modern socialistic demand for immediate contact between producer and consumer. The conditions that called forth such a demand were not then in existence,[1] as is also true of the modern agitation for a proper distribution of the profits of industry. Above all, Plato made no pretense to any economic basis for his communism, but presented it as a moral and political ideal. The *Republic* cannot therefore be classified as truly socialistic either in motive or in general plan.[2]

In any event, there is nothing in common between the high moral idealism of Plato's so-called communism and the crass materialistic communism that is the subject of Aristophanes' satire in the *Ecclesiazusae*. Dietzel[3] has well pointed out that the latter is extremely individualistic, atheistic, and immoral, demanding all from the state with no return; that the *Republic*, on the other hand, demands the loftiest morality and renunciation, and is a direct protest against such tendencies in Athens as are attacked by the comic poet. As he shows, the two are as far apart as are the watchwords, "All for self," and "All for all."

[1] Poehlmann (*op. cit.*, I, 579, 598) admits this. Guiraud (*La Prop. fonc.*, p. 594) points out that the analogy with modern socialism is difficult, owing to the modern abolition of slavery, great extent of states, and large increase in personal property.

[2] So Souchon, *op. cit.*, pp. 145 ff.; Guiraud (*La Prop. fonc.*, p. 638) well says: "Si ces derniers [modern socialists] reussissaient à appliquer leurs projects, les sociétés qui sortiraient de leurs mains n'auraient pas la moindre ressemblance avec la société hellenique." Cf. also *ibid.*, p. 594, where he distinguishes between Plato and modern socialists. Francotte (*L'Industrie*, II, 250, n. 1) makes the *Republic* essentially socialistic, though he admits that it has not the modern aim (p. 255). Poehlmann (*op. cit.*, II, 123–43) makes it a "Koinzidenz der beiden Prinzipieen" (p. 143). Wolf (*Gesch. d. Ant. Kommun. u. Individ.*, p. 96) distinguishes Plato's two aims as a strong community spirit, and a strong central authority, devoid of selfish interest. Cf. S. Cognetti de Martiis, *op. cit.*, pp. 524–89, on the *Socialismo filosofico* of the *Republic*.

[3] *Vierteljahrschrift f. Staats u. Volkswirtschaft*, I, 375 ff. Of course Aristophanes may have caricatured Plato as he did Socrates in the *Clouds*. However, since both were opposed to extreme individualism, and since the comedy was written before the *Republic*, it is improbable. But cf. Drumann, *Arbeiter u. Communisten in Griechenland u. Rom* (1860), pp. 133 f., who thinks the poet was satirizing the oral discussions of Plato. Pohlenz (*op. cit.*, pp. 223–28) argues for an earlier edition of the *Republic*, and states that, though the comedy is not a direct satire on the *Republic*, yet its numerous specific ideas and expressions that are similar to Plato's warrant the conclusion that the poet followed Plato. Cf. also S. Cognetti de Martiis, *op. cit.*, pp. 541–61, on the relation of the two.

Plato's idea that society is the exact counterpart of the individual in the large, however, is quite analogous to the modern comparison of society to an organism.[1] Both are wrong in attempting to press the analogy too far, yet they contain a truth of profound importance, which is at the foundation of the marked change in the spirit of economics in recent years. It is the notion of solidarity, which demands that the individual shall no longer seek the content of his being in himself alone, but also in the conditions that shall produce the highest life for the commonwealth.

In the *Laws*, Plato reluctantly abandons some of the utopian suggestions of the *Republic* for a more practical legislation,[2] though his ideal is really unchanged. Communism of property and of the family are both discarded even for the rulers, as feasible only for a supernatural order of beings.[3] As a noble ideal, however, it still hovers before him.[4] Private property is permitted to the citizens,[5] but under protest, and if practicable, Plato would like to prohibit it, as the primary root of all social disturbance and corruption.[6] He would advocate, therefore, a return to the old régime of family tenure, somewhat on the model of the Spartan system.[7] He would also hamper this by limitations so as to make it no real ownership at all. The land is to be practically state property, over which the citizens exercise merely the right of use.[8] It is to be divided into lots of equal value, corresponding exactly to the number of citizens.[9] Natural disadvantages shall be compensated for by an increase in the size of the lot, and part of each allotment shall be near, and part at a distance from the city, that all may be on an equal footing,

[1] 434D-E, and the entire plan of the *Republic*. Cf. Poehlmann, *op. cit.*, I, 527 ff.; also II, 210 f., on Plato's idea of a pre-established harmony between individual and common good.

[2] Poehlmann (*op. cit.*, II, 205 ff.) suggests that this change resulted from Plato's experiences with Dionysius of Syracuse, but it may be easily accounted for by the natural conservatism of age. Cf. Shorey, *Class. Phil.*, IX (1914), 353.

[3] 739D, 740A.   [4] 739C-E, 807B.   [5] 737E, 741C

[6] 831C-D, though it refers to the love of wealth, 807B, 713E.

[7] Cf. Guiraud (*La Prop. fonc.*, pp. 582 f.; cf. *infra* for details.

[8] 740-741A, 923A-B, a remarkable passage, which declares that they are not full owners either of themselves or their property, but that they belong to the whole race, past, present, and future (ξύμπαντος δέ τοῦ γένους ὑμῶν τοῦ τε ἔμπροσθεν και τοῦ ἔπειτα ἐσομένου), and especially to the state.

[9] 737E, 745C-E.

and alike ready to defend against invasion.[1] In order that no citizen may lose his lot, and no man may possess more than one, very stringent regulations are advised.[2] No lot may be purchased or sold,[3] confiscated,[4] or divided by will to more than one heir,[5] and no citizen, in any manner whatsoever, may become owner of more than one lot.[6] The living of the other members of the family is arranged for by a provision for a general distribution of the product of the soil, in imitation of the Cretan law.[7] The annual product of grain and cattle shall be divided into three equal parts, one for citizens, one for their servants, and one for the artisans, metics, and strangers. The first two parts shall not be subject to sale, but each head of a family shall receive from them enough to nourish his family and slaves.

It is evident from all these regulations that Plato's citizens do not actually own their lots, but merely enjoy the usufruct of them from the state on certain conditions. He takes away with one hand what he gives with the other. Under such a system all his precautionary measures could not have prevented the growth of an even more oppressive poverty, unless the growth of population could be checked.

The regulations limiting the acquisition or possession of personal property are even more stringent, though here an absolute equality is not attempted. He seeks, however, to prevent the rise of inequality of fortunes, at the very threshold, by making undue acquisition difficult or even impossible for the citizens. All money-making occupations are practically closed to them[8]—trade,[9] the mechanical arts,[10] and even agriculture, so far as their own personal work is concerned. The latter is given over to slaves,[11] the arts and trade to aliens, with strict limitations to be enforced by the officers of the market.[12] As seen above, two-thirds of the farm products are not to be subject to commercial dealings.[13] The loan of money at interest is forbidden, and he who disobeys will

---

[1] 745C-E. [2] 740B. [3] 741B-C. [4] 745A, 855A-B, 754E-755A, 744E.

[5] 740B, 923C. If the family is large, the women are to be married off, and the men adopted by the childless (740C). Personal property may be willed to the other children (923D); cf. also above, pp. 45 f. and notes.

[6] 740C, 741B-D. [8] 741E. [10] 846D, 847A, 919D.

[7] 847E-848C. [9] 847D, 919D. [11] 806E.

[12] 920A; cf. above, on exchange. [13] 849C.

risk the loss of both principal and interest.[1] A bulky coinage of
baser metal is provided for the daily use of private citizens, such
as will not pass current in another country.[2] No dowries are to be
given or received,[3] and there shall be no hoarding, but the entire
produce of the lots must be annually distributed for consumption
among the whole population of the state.[4] To make assurance
doubly sure, Plato prohibits his citizens from owning personal
property above four times the value of the lot,[5] or four minas.[6]
Any amount in excess of this must be handed over to the state on
pain of severe fine for disobedience.[7] This is to be accomplished
by the regulation that all property except the lot must be publicly
registered, and failure to fulfil this obligation entails the loss of
all but the original lot, and public disgrace.[8]

In all this drastic limitation of property rights, Plato's chief
motive is to render excessive wealth or poverty impossible,[9] and
to harmonize the citizenship by reducing all inequalities to a minimum.[10] This he purposes to accomplish, not merely by the foregoing restrictions, but also by means of a common education,[11]
and by the institution of the *sussitia*.[12] He makes the road to comparative equality easier than in his first state by relegating all
the third class, the artisans, merchants, and farmers, outside the
pale of citizenship.[13] The actual difference, however, is not so
great as it might appear. In the *Republic* there is equality in the
upper class, while in the *Laws* there is comparative equality among
the citizens who comprise only the upper class. In neither case
is there a real equality in the whole state. Plato is well aware
that only approximate equality can be attained, and that differences

---

[1] Cf. p. 39 and notes.   [2] Cf. p. 40 and notes.   [3] 742C.   [4] Cf. p. 59 and notes.

[5] 744E. The entire wealth will thus vary from the bare lot to five times its
value. Cf. Jowett, *Dialogs of Plato*, 3d ed., V, 127, though the division into four
classes might mean that the highest was only four times the lot value. Espinas
(*Revue des Etudes Grecques*, XXVII [1914], 237) accepts the former interpretation.

[6] 754D-E. The value of the lot was thus only a mina.   [7] 744E, 745A.

[8] 745A, 754D-E (which requires it only for the excess), 755A. Espinas (*op. cit.*,
pp. 118 ff.) emphasizes the ascetic tendency of his regulations.

[9] 729A ff., 919B, 936B-C, against beggars.

[10] 744B-E, and above notes.   [11] Book VII.

[12] 780B; women and children separate, 806E; on its Cretan origin, 625E ff.

[13] 846D, 847A, D, 919D, 806E.

not only in property, but also in birth, virtue, strength, and beauty, are bound to exist.[1] He would therefore have taxes and distributions unequal in the same ratio, so as to avoid dissatisfaction and dispute.[2] The difficulties incident to such a scheme of legislation he would obviate by starting a new state in virgin soil.[3]

Souchon[4] recognizes the Plato of the *Laws* as a true socialist, and points to his attempt to prevent all inequality, and to his extreme state intervention as characteristic elements of socialism. Plato certainly does approach nearer to a real socialism in the *Laws* than in the *Republic*. In addition to the points noted by Souchon, there may be observed the application of the system of equality to the whole citizenship, though at the cost of shutting out all the workers; the strong sense of the social function of property;[5] the practical denial of real private ownership of land; the demand for publicity in business, which is one of the chief suggestions for the regulation of corporations today;[6] the active interest in the conservation of natural resources, which, while not socialistic, lies in the direction of greater social control;[7] and the fact that distribution of the products of industry is made practically a function of the state.[8] The demand for equality and unity is also somewhat analogous to the modern socialistic hostility to competition, which Ruskin calls the "law of death."[9] It may be

[1] 744B; cf. pp. 55 f. on equality; cf. 757B-D, contrasting the mere arithmetical equality (τὴν ἀριθμῷ ἴσην), which is easily realized, and the true equality, which is very difficult. This latter apportions to each in accord with his nature (πρὸς τὴν φύσιν αὐτῶν). The two are almost opposites (ἐναντιαῖν). Espinas (*op. cit.*, p. 236) thinks that the division into property classes in the *Laws* is an attempt to realize this principle.

[2] 744B. [3] 736C-D, 704.

[4] *Op. cit.*, p. 143; cf. also pp. 163–65, where he compares it to modern collectivism; cf. p. 162; also Poehlmann, *op. cit.*, II, 295.

[5] 923A; cf. 877D, and much of the legislation on property, above.

[6] Cf. pp. 59 f. and notes. The modern analogy is not close, yet in each case the aim is to prevent undue gains whereby the public is oppressed.

[7] Cf. p. 30, n. 3.

[8] Cf. p. 59 and notes. The socialistic tendency to overemphasize the power of law is also strong here as in the *Republic*. But cf. p. 36, n. 4, and *Laws* 807B, 746A-B, 747B.

[9] *Time and Tide*, IX, 5–9. *Modern Painters*, V, Pt. 8, chap. i, 6 (Vol. VII, 207). Espinas (*Revue des Etudes Grecques*, XXVII [1914], 246) calls this Platonic denial of "conflict of interest" in trade "le thème éternel de la chimère socialiste."

added further that Plato's description of the economic strife in his day is slightly suggestive of the criticism of capitalism by modern socialism.[1] However, the basal motive of Plato is, again, not that of modern socialism. His aim is still primarily moral and political rather than material,[2] and he exhibits less interest in the welfare of the laborers than he does in the *Republic*.[3] Moreover, his demand for equality is prompted by exactly the same motive as was active in the *Republic*, not to ameliorate the condition of the laborer, whom he has relegated to slavery, but to avoid the hated civic discord (διάστασις) and to preserve the unity of the state.[4] The equality too, is in no sense analogous to that sought by modern socialism, for, as seen above, it is merely equality within a class, comprising the aristocratic minority of the state, and does not touch the working masses at all.[5] In fine then, though there are perhaps enough truly socialistic elements in the *Laws* to warrant the classification of Souchon, yet if Plato's ideal were realized, it would be mainly a restoration of the old economic régime in Greece, based on agriculture and the family tenure of property. Such an ideal, modern socialists would doubtless fail to recognize as having much in common with their own.[6]

[1] *Laws* 626E: τὸ πολεμίους εἶναι πάντας πᾶσιν; cited by Poehlmann, *op. cit.*, I, 557; but he exaggerates the analogy.

[2] Cf. 742D-E, 743D-E, 729A, and the remarks on retail trade, 918B–919E, 870B; cf. also, above, on wealth.

[3] As seen above, they are all slaves or strangers. A direct comparison is hardly possible, since in the *Republic*, the masses are the majority of the citizens, while in the *Laws*, there are none.

[4] 744D; cf. Shorey, *Class. Phil.*, IX (1914), 363: "Plato's object, however, is not socialistic equalization of the 'good things' of life, but the enforced disinterestedness of the rulers, and the complete self-realization of every type of man, in limitation to his own proper sphere and task."

[5] Cf. pp. 55 and 60, on equality; also note 4, above.

[6] Francotte (*L'Industrie*, II, 250) suggests that *l'étatisme*, "nationalism," would be a more applicable term for the *Laws*. He distinguishes this from socialism, as being not so thoroughgoing a limitation of the individual as is the "socialism" of the *Republic*. Cf. Shorey, *Class. Phil.*, IX (1914), 358, on the famous "communistic" passage in *Laws* 739C: ὄντως ἐστὶ κοινὰ τὰ φίλων, etc. He calls it a "rhetorical exaltation of that ideal unity of civic feeling, which Demosthenes upbraids Aeschines for not sharing." For further communistic ideas of Plato, cf. his incomplete romantic story of Atlantis in the *Critias*. The ideal is similar to that of the larger works. Cf. Poehlmann, *op. cit.*, II, 348 ff.

CHAPTER IV

XENOPHON

Xenophon was a man of affairs, whose interests touched the practical life of the world on many sides, as is evidenced by the broad scope of his extant works. He was also, however, a pupil of Socrates. In his economic thought, therefore, he vacillates between the positive interest of the practical economist and the negative criticism of the Socratics.[1] On the whole, his practical bent dominates, and is especially exhibited in his essay on the *Revenues of Athens*,[2] as also in the fact that he was the first writer to produce a work devoted entirely to economics.[3] The spirit of the moral philosopher, on the other hand, is prominent wherever the influence of Socrates is felt, as in the first chapters of the *Economicus* and in the *Memorabilia*. When the Socratic ideal dominates, he, in common with other Greek thinkers, confuses economics with ethics, and private with public economy.[4] He makes the science of economy deal with the management of private estates,[5] and believes with Plato and Ruskin that the same qualities are necessary for the successful handling of the affairs of either house or state.[6]

[1] We shall not try to distinguish between the actual ideas of Xenophon and those which he reports objectively as Socratic.

[2] On the Xenophontine authorship of the *Revenues*, cf. Croiset, *op. cit.*, IV, 393 and notes; Christ, *Griechische Literatur-Geschichte*, 4th ed., pp. 367 f. and notes. Other authorities are cited there.

[3] The οἰκονομικός, at least, the first extant, devoted to private economy, and especially agriculture, but revealing a practical interest in the details of the production of wealth. Cf. *infra* for further discussion of *Economica* in Greek literature.

[4] For some qualifications, cf. above, Introduction.

[5] *Econ.* i. 2: οἰκονόμου ἀγαθοῦ εἶναι οἰκεῖν τὸν ἑαυτοῦ οἶκον; cf. 3: τὸν ἄλλου δὲ οἶκον. οἶκον is used of one's entire property (5).

[6] *Mem.* iii. 4. 6; cf. further above, p. 9, n. 4. Cf. Ruskin, *Pol. Econ. of Art*, I, 12: "Precisely the same laws of economy, which apply to the cultivation of a farm or an estate, apply to the cultivation of a province or an island." Cf. the story in Hdt. v. 29 on this idea. Espinas (*Revue des Etudes Grecques*, XXVII [1914], 111) contrasts Xenophon, to whom the royal administration is a greatly expanded private economy, with Plato's absorption of all private economy by the state.

VALUE

Xenophon insists strongly on utility or serviceableness as a necessary quality of property (χρήματα, κτήματα). By this, however, he means primarily, not potential· utility in the object, but ability of the owner to use rightly.[1] Even exchangeability does not insure value in anything, unless the seller can use to advantage that which he receives in return.[2] This idea of value is true enough from the ethical standpoint, and should not be left out of account, as is being recognized by modern economists. But to attempt to build a theory of economic value on such a basis, as Ruskin does,[3] would result in hopeless confusion. Value is not merely an individual and moral, but also a social and economic, fact.

A hint of exchange value is given in the implied classification of goods as usable or salable.[4] But there is no discrimination between useful things in the economic and uneconomic sense. In the *Revenues*, on the other hand, when free from Socratic influence, Xenophon makes a positive contribution to the theory of value. He observes that the exchange value of goods varies with· supply and demand, and that this law is, in a sense, self-regulative by the

---

[1] *Econ.* i. 7–15; cf. 10: ταὐτὰ ἄρα ὄντα τῷ μὲν ἐπισταμένῳ χρῆσθαι αὐτῶν ἑκάστοις χρήματά ἐστι, τῷ δὲ μὴ ἐπισταμένῳ οὐ χρήματα. Cf. p. 23 and notes on Plato and Ruskin. H. Sewall ("Theory of Value before Adam Smith," *Publications of the American Economic Association*, II, Part III, p. 1) says that the conception of value (ἀξία) as a quality inherent in the thing was not questioned, but Xenophon seems to question it here. As she observes, n. 1, the term originally meant "weight," at first weight in money, as well as actual worth.

[2] i. 11 f.

[3] *Unto This Last*, beginning; cf. preceding n. 1; Ruskin took *Xen. Econ.* as the foundation on which he built all his own economic studies. Cf. *Unto This Last*, Pref., Vol. XVII, pp. xlix and 18; Vol. XXXI, Introd.; pp. xv ff. It was the first in his *Bib. Pastorum*. Cf. his Preface to his translation of the *Economicus; Arrows of the Chace*, Vol. XXXIV, 547; *Letters*, II (Vol. XXXVII, 350). In *Mun. Pul.*, IV, 105 (Vol. XVII, 230); also on pp. 288 and 88, he refers to Xenophon's "faultless" definition of wealth, citing *Mem.* ii. 3. 7. Cf. also Vol. XXXI, pp. xvii and 27. Fontpertuis ("Filiation des idées économiques dans l'antiquité," *Jour. des écon.*, September, 1871, p. 361) thinks this is at bottom the true theory of value.

[4] *Econ.* i. 2: ἀποδιδομένοις μὲν οἱ αὐλοὶ χρήματα, μὴ ἀποδιδομένοις δὲ ἀλλὰ κεκτημένοις οὔ, τοῖς μὴ ἐπισταμένοις αὐτοῖς χρῆσθαι. Brants (*Xen. Econ.*, p. 8) overemphasizes this.

fact that workmen tend to enter other fields of activity whenever any industry becomes unprofitable through an oversupply of its products.[1]

WEALTH

The double standpoint of Xenophon is well illustrated in his doctrine of wealth. On the one hand, he values it highly, and tries to deduce practical rules for its increase and enjoyment.[2] On the other hand, like Socrates and Plato, he makes derogatory comparisons between economic and spiritual wealth.[3] As in the case of value, he offers no clear definition of economic wealth ($\kappa\tau\hat{\eta}\sigma\iota\varsigma$). It is defined indiscriminately as "whatever is useful to life," and "useful" is "everything that anyone knows how to use."[4] But, as seen above, this is a purely subjective notion, and is only one element in economic wealth.[5] He also defines it ($\chi\rho\dot{\eta}\mu\alpha\tau\alpha$) as "the excess of goods over needs," making it a merely relative term:[6] but here again the thought is ethical rather than economic, an attempt to teach the somewhat ascetic principle that a man's riches are measured by the paucity of his wants.[7] The hostile or indifferent attitude to wealth is also assumed in the comparison of it with so-called mental wealth and wisdom[8] and in the implication that it involves many cares.[9] The idea so prominent in Plato, however, that the acquisition or expenditure of great wealth

---

[1] *Rev.* iv. 6–10, a remarkable passage, though he fails to include silver in the law. Cf. Kautz, *op. cit.*, p. 129; Kaulla, *Die geschichtliche Entwickelung der modernen Werttheorien*, p. 2.

[2] Especially in the story of Isomachus (*Econ.*), and the *Revenues*.

[3] Cf. *infra*; also Espinas, *Histoire des doctrines economiques*, p. 20.

[4] *Econ.* vi. 4; cf. i. 7 ff., cited above, p. 64, n. 1.

[5] P. 64 and notes. Büchsenschütz (*Besitz und Erwerb*, p. 15) criticizes it as too broad, including spiritual goods; too narrow, including only what one can use.

[6] In *Econ.* ii. 2–8, Socrates' comparison of himself with the wealthy Critóboulos; *Hiero* iv. 6–10; *Mem.* iv. 2. 37 f.; i. 6. 1–10, where Socrates defends his own simple life, especially 10: ἐγὼ δ' ἐνόμιζον τὸ μὲν μηδενὸς δεῖσθαι θεῖον εἶναι. If meant in the economic sense, this would approach a definition of capital, as "excess of goods over needs."

[7] Cf. p. 25, n. 11, on the similar modern doctrine.

[8] *Symp.* iii. 8 and iv. 34–44, given as the doctrine of Antisthenes, the Cynic, though with apparent approval; *Mem.* iv. 2. 9.

[9] *Econ.* xi. 9.

is not consistent with justice, is not emphasized by Xenophon. He calls that man happiest who has best succeeded in just acquisition, and who uses his wealth in the best manner.[1]

PRODUCTION

The Greeks had no specific word for production, as we have, since industry, though well developed, was not a dominant feature of Greek life, and economics had not become a separate science. The word ἐργασία, meaning "labor" or "business," served the purpose. The term was used of productive labor,[2] of building or manufacturing,[3] of work in raw materials,[4] most commonly of agriculture,[5] of industries in general,[6] of the trades, commerce, or other business for money-making,[7] and of a guild of laborers.[8] The term ἡ ποιητικὴ τέχνη, "the productive art," which approaches more nearly to a specific, technical expression, was also used.[9] Thus, though there is no clear-cut term for production, the statement of Zimmern[10] that the Greeks had no better word for "business" than ἀσχολία, "lack of leisure," is hardly warranted.

Xenophon was far more interested than Plato or Aristotle in the problem of practical production. His shrewd discussion of agriculture, and his urgent appeal to Athens to increase her revenues by systematic exploitation of the mines, and by the encouragement of industry and commerce, reveal a mind awake to economic advantage. Though at times he seems almost to make war and agriculture the only true means of production, it is evident that he has a live interest in all means of acquisition.[11] Toward the theory of production, however, his contribution is not large. In

---

[1] *Cyrop.* viii. 2. 23.　　　[2] *Mem.* ii. 7. 7; *Rev.* iv. 29.

[3] Thuc. vii. 6. 2, of walls; *Gorg.* 449D, ἱματίων; *Theaet.* 146D, ὑποδημάτων; Xen. *Econ.* vii. 21, ἐσθῆτος.

[4] Hdt. i. 68; *Charm.* 173E; Thuc. iv. 105.　　　[5] Ar. *Frogs* 1034; Isoc. *Areop.* 30.

[6] Isoc. *Areop.*, 146d, cited *infra* on the terms for capital; *Ad Nicocl.* 18C.

[7] *Mem.* iii. 10. 1; Dem. xxxiii. 4.　　　[9] Ar. *N. Eth.* vi. 4. 2 ff.

[8] *C.I.A.* 3924: ἡ ἐργασία τῶν βαφέων.　　　[10] *Op. cit.*, 1st ed., p. 55.

[11] *Econ.*, especially chaps. v–vii; iv. 4; *Mem.* ii. 1. 6; *Econ.* v. 17: εὖ μὲν γὰρ φερομένης τῆς γεωργίας ἔρρωνται καὶ ἄλλαι τέχναι ἅπασαι, ὅπου δ' ἂν ἀναγκασθῇ ἡ γῆ χερσεύειν, ἀποσβέννυνται καὶ αἱ ἄλλαι τέχναι σχεδόν τι καὶ κατὰ γῆν καὶ κατὰ θάλατταν, a very true statement, which does not belittle other industries.

the *Economics*, he recognizes the importance of labor and natural resources in production, and in the *Revenues*, he sees the necessity of capital.[1] But naturally, like Aristotle and the southern planter, he confuses capital with labor, in the person of the slave.[2] The fable of the dog and the sheep reveals a knowledge of the machinery of production, and some insight into the proper relation between the employer and the laborer.[3] Xenophon's distinct contribution to future economic thought, however, consists in his appreciation of the fact that economic production has its definite limits; that the same ratio of profits cannot be increased indefinitely by the constant addition of more labor and capital, but that these must be proportioned to the greatest possible return.[4] To be sure, he does not appreciate the scientific significance of the principle. His purpose is rather to emphasize the danger of overproduction, and he even fails to grasp the necessary application of this danger to the silver mines. However, as the enunciator of the principle, he may be called the forerunner of the doctrine of diminishing returns.

As seen above, special emphasis was laid by Xenophon upon natural resources as an element in production, both in land and in the mines. His great interest in and eulogy of agriculture as the basal industry, upon which all other sources of wealth depend,[5] have caused him to be classed with the physiocrats of modern time but such an interpretation is hardly warranted. Without doubt, agriculture is, in his opinion, the supremely honorable occupation. It shares with war the right to be placed above all other vocations.[6] It permits the maximum of leisure and physical development, and is not unworthy of the personal attention of a prince.[7] It is the

---

[1] *Ibid.* v. 2; iii. 15. 11, 16; *Rev.* i. 2 ff., etc.   [2] *Pol.* i. 8 and 9.

[3] *Mem.* ii. 7. 13 f., from Socrates. Cf. *infra* under distribution, on this.

[4] *Rev.* iv. 5–7; Cossa, *op. cit.*, p. 148; Kautz, *Histoire des doctrines économiques*, p. 127; Fontpertuis, *op. cit.*, p. 367.

[5] *Econ.* v. 17, cited on p. 66, n. 11, perhaps the strongest statement of the economic importance of agriculture in Greek writers. Ruskin follows Xenophon in his high appreciation of agriculture. He thinks it should be largely done by the upper classes (*Mun. Pul.*, 109 [Vol. XVII, 235]); cf. also Vol. VII, 341, 429; Vol. X, 201.

[6] *Econ.* iv. 4; cf. *Rev.* v and *Cyrop.* iii. 2. 17, which favor peace for the sake of economic advance.

[7] *Econ.* iv. 8 to end of chapter, especially 21.

most pleasant, most productive, most dignified, of callings; the best exercise for the athlete, the finest school for education in patriotism and justice, and it offers the greatest opportunity for the exercise of hospitality to men and reverence to gods.[1] Indeed, it is the first of all occupations for an honorable and high-minded man to choose.[2] Here we have the highest eulogy of agriculture in Greek literature. It is in essence a sound statement, and offers a needed message for today.

Though Xenophon recognized the practical importance of capital in industrial enterprises,[3] he developed no theory of it in his writings. He appreciated, however, the value of being able to keep a surplus.[4] The term ἀφορμή, as used by him of the provision of raw material for weaving, probably signified nothing more than it would have done to any Athenian business man of his time.[5] The word originally meant a "starting-point," especially in war.[6] Later, it signified the "means" or "resources" with which one begins a project,[7] especially in business. It was an easy step from this general business use to the meaning, "financial capital" of a banker.[8] Other terms for capital were ἐνεργά, used of interest-bearing capital in antithesis to ἀργά, of goods merely for use;[9] κάρπιμα, "goods that yield a produce," as opposed to ἀπολαυστικά, "goods to be enjoyed,"[10] which is suggestive of Mill's[11]

---

[1] *Econ.*, v. 1; 2–16; vi. 9–10; cf. Fontpertuis, *op. cit.*, pp. 362 f.

[2] *Econ.* vi. 8.   [3] Cf. *Revenues*.

[4] *Econ.* ii. 10, περιουσίαν. Brants thinks (*Xen. Econ.*, p. 13) that the theory is implied in his principle of sparing (*Mem.* ii. 7). Blanqui (*op. cit.*, I, 81) emphasizes *Econ.* i. 7–15 as defining productive and unproductive wealth, but this merely distinguishes wealth from non-wealth, from the standpoint of consumption.

[5] *Mem.* ii. 7. 11 f.   [6] Thuc. i. 90. 2.

[7] Cf. n. 1, although Liddell and Scott cite the passage as having the meaning of "capital"; *Mem.* iii. 12. 4, where it need mean no more than wealth; *Econ.* i. 1. 16; Dem. xxxvi. 54: πίστις ἀφορμὴ πασῶν ἐστὶ μεγίστη πρὸς χρηματισμόν. Here πίστις is almost called capital. Cf. p. 106, n. 3.

[8] Dem. xxxvi. 11: καίτοι εἰ ἦν ἰδία τις ἀφορμὴ τουτῳὶ πρὸς τῇ τραπέζῃ; xiv. 36; Lysias fr. 2. 2, p. 343, ed. Thalheim; *Rev.* iii. 9 and 12 and iv. 34 are also used of large financial undertakings; cf. Harpocration's definition; ὅταν τις ἀργύριον δῷ ἐνθήκην, ἀφορμὴ καλεῖται ἰδίως παρὰ τοῖς Ἀττικοῖς; for the term in Ar. *Pol.* vi. 1320a35–1320b17 cf. *infra*. Cf. Isoc. *Areop.* 146d for a similar passage.

[9] Dem. xxvii. 8 and 13.

[10] Ar. *Rhet.* i. 5. 7.   [11] Laughlin, ed., 1907, pp. 66 and 93.

definition, "that part of his possessions . . . . which he designs to employ in carrying on fresh production," and of his two kinds of capital, "circulating" and "fixed"; ποιητικά, "things for further production," as opposed to πρακτικά, "things merely for use";[1] κεφάλαιος, of capital as opposed to interest or income.[2] The term ἔρανος, also, since it came to mean a "contribution of money," was often used of a loan, and therefore approached the signification of "money capital."[3]

Xenophon is considerably more favorable to labor and the industrial life than are the other Socratics. He quotes Socrates with apparent approval, that to do something well is well-being, while he who does nothing well is neither good for anything nor beloved of God.[4] Work is far better than idleness. It produces more happiness, makes the laborer more temperate and just, and is the *sine qua non* for the independent life.[5] This is a strong plea for industry, and is especially significant, since it refers primarily, to manufacture rather than to agriculture. The reference, however, is to women workers, whose loss of leisure would not be an injury to the state. Each person is encouraged to provide for himself, and to do his work in the best possible manner,[6] and the maxim of Epicharmus, "For labor, the gods sell all goods to us," is heartily approved.[7] All the foregoing passages are Hesiodic in their insistence upon the value of industry.[8] But apart from his evident acceptance of the doctrine of Socrates, as quoted above, Xenophon exhibits a positive interest in labor. His attitude

---

[1] Ar. *Pol.* 1254a1 ff.; cf. *infra* on Aristotle ("Production"); pseudo-Ar. *Econ.* ii. 1346b14.

[2] Plato *Laws* 742C; Dem. xxvii. 75.

[3] Lycurg., p. 150, 22: τοὺς ἐράνους διενεγκεῖν; Dem. xxi. 184 f.; cf. Dem. lix. 8 for the interesting figurative use, τὸν αὐτὸν ἔρανον ἀποδοῦναι, "to pay him in his own coin"; also Lycurg., p. 168, 143.

[4] *Mem.* iii. 9. 14 f.; cf. Brants, *Xen. Econ.*, p. 10, for passages on Xenophon's attitude to labor.

[5] *Mem.* ii. 7. 7 f. Guiraud (*La Main-d'œuvre indust.*, p. 46) thinks that this passage is a good commentary on Pericles' oration (Thuc. ii). Both see in labor, not an inevitable evil, but a good. Guiraud holds that this was the general attitude in Athens. Cf. this chapter, pp. 36–50, on "Opinions des Grecs sur le travail."

[6] *Mem.* ii. 8. 1–5. [7] ii. 1. 20.

[8] Cf. Döring, *Die Lehre des Socrates als soziales Reform-System*, pp. 387 ff.

toward the advancement of industry and commerce is thoroughly modern, except that he does not contemplate the employment of free citizen labor.[1] He emphasizes labor almost as strongly as natural resources as an important factor in production. He believes also that industrial thrift and prosperity are the best means of realizing a more quiet and orderly state.[2]

Even the practical Xenophon, however, is not free from the moral-aristocratic prejudice against mechanical arts ($\beta\alpha\nu\alpha\upsilon\sigma\iota\kappa\alpha\iota$) for the better class of citizens. He admits that they are justly spoken against, and held in ill-repute, since they tend to weaken the laborer both in body and in soul.[3] The artisans have no leisure to give either to their friends or to the state, and in a warlike state the citizens cannot be thus employed.[4] The artisan is also servile because of his ignorance of the higher moral sentiments ($\tau\grave{\alpha}$ $\kappa\alpha\lambda\grave{\alpha}$ $\kappa\alpha\grave{\iota}$ $\dot{\alpha}\gamma\alpha\theta\grave{\alpha}$ $\kappa\alpha\grave{\iota}$ $\delta\acute{\iota}\kappa\alpha\iota\alpha$).[5] All this sounds like Plato, but Xenophon differs, in that he is in no wise opposed to the unlimited development of industry and commerce, provided the drudgery of it may be done by non-citizens.

The principle of the division of labor is clearly stated by him, but here again he differs from Plato in that his prime interest is practical and economic rather than moral. He presents it as the reason why royal dishes are superior in flavor to others, and makes the acute observation that the division of labor is not so fully applied in the small city, because there are not enough consumers to support a man in one trade. In the large city, on the other hand, the consumers are so numerous that even the trades themselves are divided and subdivided. Thus much greater skill is developed, and better results realized, for he who spends his time in work of the narrowest compass ($\beta\rho\alpha\chi\upsilon\tau\acute{\alpha}\tau\psi$) must accomplish this in the best manner.[6] He does not specify the advantages of the division of labor to industry, except that it results in greater

[1] Rev., especially i. 2 ff. and iv; Econ. v. 2; iii. 15; ii. 16; Kautz, op. cit., p. 126. But cf., on the other hand, Xen. Laced. Pol. on the restrictions in Sparta against acquisition of wealth by trade and arts; cf. also (Xen.). Rep. Ath. ii. 11 ff.

[2] Rev. iv. 51.

[3] Econ. iv. 2; vi. 5-7; agriculture and war are not included.

[4] iv. 3.   [5] Mem. iv. 2. 22.

[6] Cyrop. viii. 2. 5 f.; cf. also ii. 1. 21, of military labor.

skill, but he reveals especial insight in stating so clearly the relation of the market to the development of the principle.[1] In this, he is the forerunner of Adam Smith, who observes that a minute division of trades cannot exist except in the larger cities, especially in coast and river towns.[2] The assertion of Haney,[3] that the Greeks referred only to a "simple separation of employments," is certainly unwarranted in the light of this passage, for Xenophon expressly distinguishes here the simple from the more complex subdivision. He says that some are employed on men's shoes, others on women's; some do the sewing (νευρορραφῶν), others do the cutting (σχίζων), and that the same also is true in the manufacture of clothing.[4] This passage is also an evidence that the development of industry in fourth-century Athens must have been extensive. Xenophon also, like Plato, observed the fact that the diversity in the natures of men is the basis for the division of labor,[5] though he did not follow him in his doctrine that men and women should have the same work.[6]

Unlike Plato, the idealist, Xenophon, the practical man of affairs, takes the institution of slavery for granted, seemingly unconscious of any ethical or economic problems involved.[7] However, as a matter of common-sense, he advises that slaves be treated with consideration. He would give them a proper degree of liberty,[8] and arouse them to do their best[9] by a fair system of rewards and punishments. In the case of those slaves who hold positions of trust, he advises that their affections should be won by kindly treatment, and even by making them sharers in the prosperity of the household.[10] Slavery is, of course, a condition most irksome to the free-born. The unfortunate Eutheros would almost prefer starvation.[11]

---

[1] Cf. p. 70. [2] *Op. cit.*, I, iii.

[3] *Op. cit.*, p. 40; cf. also Dühring, *Kritische Geschichte der Nationalökonomie und des Socialismus*, p. 22.

[4] *Cyrop.* viii. 2. 5 f., cited above. [7] *Econ.* iii. 4; v. 16; ix. 11; xiii; *Rev.* iv. 17 ff.

[5] *Mem.* iii. 9. 3. [8] *Econ.* iii. 4.

[6] *Econ.* viii. [9] v. 16; xiii.

[10] *Econ.* ix. 11; cf. p. 38, n. 4, on the actual status of slaves at Athens.

[11] *Mem.* ii. 8. 4.

MONEY

In his treatise on the *Revenues of Athens*, Xenophon shows some appreciation of the theory of money. He appears to take for granted that money must have intrinsic value. At least, he understands that silver is a commodity whose value is affected by its use as such, as well as by its employment for currency.[1] He also apprehends the value of a silver currency for international commerce.[2] His naïvely enthusiastic argument for the indefinite, increase of the stock of silver, however, is suggestive of the mercantile fallacy, which identified money with wealth.[3] But perhaps he is merely using for practical purposes of argument the fact that the Athenians were accustomed to look upon silver as the metal for fixed and constant value.[4] In any event, he sees that the increase of silver must be attended by a corresponding increase in business activity, if its value is not to depreciate,[5] and he cannot be accused of the error of the mercantilists, that a country is impoverished by the export of money.[6] He must also have understood clearly the importance of stability of value in a currency, since he deems it necessary to show that the increased output of silver will not decrease its value, and that silver is the least changeable of the monetary metals.[7] Despite his enthusiasm for his thesis, which causes him to exaggerate the stability of silver, he does not fail to grasp the direct effect of supply and demand upon it,[8] just as upon gold[9] and other commodities.[10] He shows also some under-

[1] *Rev.* iii. 2: ὅπου γὰρ ἂν πωλῶσιν αὐτό, πανταχοῦ πλεῖον τοῦ ἀρχαίου λαμβάνουσιν.

[2] *Ibid.*; cf. Souchon, *op. cit.*, p. 114.

[3] *Rev.* iv, especially 7–12; Haney (*op. cit.*, chap. iv) and Simey ("Economic Theory among the Greeks and Romans," *Economic Review*, October, 1900, p. 472) point to *Rev.* iii. 2 as distinguishing between money and wealth, but this hardly balances the above passage. *Econ.* i. 12–14 means merely that silver is not wealth unless properly used.

[4] So Brants, *Xen. Econ.*, p. 21; cf. Lenormant *é La Monnaie dans l'antiquité*, I, 179; III, 3.

[5] *Rev.* iv. 8.

[6] *Rev.* iii. 4; v. 3; iii. 2; cf. Ingram, *History of Political Economy*, p. 15; Kautz, *op. cit.*, p. 129; Roscher, p. 12.

[7] *Rev.* iv. 5–11.   [8] iii. 2; and iv. The demand will increase with the supply.

[9] iv. 10: χρυσίον ὅταν πολὺ παραφανῇ, αὐτὸ μὲν ἀτιμότερον γίγνεται, τὸ δὲ ἀργύριον τιμιώτερον ποιεῖ.

[10] iv. 5–7.

standing of the quantitative theory of the relation between gold and silver.[1] It need hardly be added that, in strong contrast to Plato, his attitude toward the precious metals, especially silver, is very favorable.[2]

EXCHANGE

Xenophon presents no theory of exchange,[3] though he is frankly interested in the advance of commerce and trade. In his opinion, the greater their development, the better it is for the city of Athens.[4] He is full of practical suggestions to stimulate commercial activity.[5] So assured is he of the prime importance of extensive commerce to a nation, that, in the spirit of modern commercialism, he insists upon the necessity of peace for its sake.[6] To his mind, increased trade means not only material advantage, but social and political as well, in that greater prosperity, more labor, and a better distribution will mean greater satisfaction, and hence less danger of revolution in the state.[7] He entertains none of the prejudice of the other Socratics against the money-makers' art, a fact which may well be a warning against the too ready acceptance of their attitude as the usual verdict of the Athenian citizens.[8] In his practical suggestions for the development of commerce there is a hint of the protective principle. He advises that certain advantages be granted to shipowners so as to induce them to increase their shipping.[9] But the purpose is not to limit the advantage to Athenian merchantmen, nor to restrict import trade. It is rather the opposite. He would enrich the city by tribute on both imports and exports, imposed for sumptuary and revenue purposes,[10] and

[1] iv. 10.

[2] iv, especially 7–9, 11; he has no word against them. *Lac. Pol.* vii shows that he favors their free use.

[3] Brants (*Xen. Econ.*, pp. 17 f.) says that he grasped both bases of exchange, division of labor, and natural diversity of products, but he bases it on *Rep. Ath.* ii. 12. 3.

[4] *Rev.* iii., especially 5; *Hiero* ix. 9; ἐμπόρια ὠφέλει πόλιν.

[5] iii. 3. 4. 12 f.   [6] iii. 4; v–vi.   [7] vi. 1.

[8] *Econ.* ii. 18: χρηματιστής; cf. iii, where Socrates teaches the art. Cf. above, p. 17, on the Sophists' attitude.

[9] *Rev.* iii. 4.   [10] iii. 5.

would also develop a public merchant-marine for rent to merchants, as a further source of income.[1]

POPULATION

In antithesis to Plato and Aristotle, the problem of population has no difficulties for Xenophon. He does not deem it advisable to set a limit on the population of the state. On the contrary, he conceives it as one of the advantages of his plan in the *Revenues*, that thereby the city would become very populous, and thus land about the mines would soon be as valuable as that in the city itself.[2]

DISTRIBUTION

Xenophon is far less concerned about the problem of distribution than Plato. He has no suggestions as to wages, profits, or prices, no ideal state where an equitable distribution shall be realized, no yearnings after equality, or complaints against the evils of extreme wealth or poverty. Like Plato, he would avoid civic discord in the state,[3] but by the increase of production and exchange rather than by their limitation. In Socrates' parable of the dog and the sheep, he presents a suggestion of a theory of profits, but his plea is for the employer instead of the laborer. The right of the former to share in the profits of the business is based on his service as overseer of the work, and as protector of the workmen.[4]

Our author does not definitely reveal his attitude toward the poorer masses, but it seems probable that he had little interest in them, except in so far as their condition might affect the fortunes of the state. He was, of course, opposed to giving them full political rights,[5] and would probably have preferred a system such as that in Plato's *Laws*, where all free citizens have sufficient income so that they can give their time largely to the state, and

---

[1] iii. 14.   [2] iv. 50.   [3] *Rev.* vi. 1.

[4] *Mem.* ii. 7. 12–14. Poehlmann's attempt to turn the argument about, so as to favor the laborer, is strained (*op. cit.*, I, 288), though the passage may be a sidelight on the economic conditions in early fourth-century Athens. Cf. *Mem.* ii. 8. 4–5, where, as Poehlmann (*op. cit.*, I, 286 f.) points out, the free laborer was coming to feel himself to be on the same status with the slave.

[5] Cf. e.g., his opposition to the free democracy of Athens, for evidence of which we do not need to depend upon the *Ath. Pol.*

where all laborers are slaves. He did not think of suggesting that the poorer citizens work in the mines, or even that aliens do so, but suggested rather that each citizen have the income from three state slaves.[1]

While Xenophon is not usually considered among the socialists of Greece, he approaches perhaps even nearer than Plato to one phase of modern socialism. Like Plato, he opposes the extreme individualism of the political and private life of his day.[2] He also reveals the Greek feeling of the social obligation of private property.[3] Again, as do Plato and modern socialists, he magnifies the power of law to transform economic or social conditions.[4] But in advocating the modern doctrine of the socialization of industry, with an economic, and not a moral or political, motive, he has advanced beyond either Plato or Aristotle, and approaches modern socialism.[5] As seen above, however, his economic motive is not interest in the welfare of the masses, for by his scheme they would all be slaves. He desires only to abolish poverty among the citizens.[6] He would have the state become entrepreneur, not merely in one, but in many branches of industry. State merchant shipping,[7] public ownership of slaves,[8] public exploitation of the mines,[9] public buildings near the mines, for rental to strangers,[10] are all in his plan. The rich must finance the scheme, but their profit will be 18, 36, or even 200 per cent.[11] Companies are to be organized so as to obviate individual risk.[12] Thus will poverty be no more, plenty

---

[1] *Rev.* iv. 17; cf. p. 70; but p. 69 might point the other way.

[2] *Mem.* iv. 4. 16; ἄνευ δὲ ὁμονοίας οὔτ' ἂν πόλις εὖ πολιτευθείη οὔτ' οἶκος καλῶς. οἰκηθείη.

[3] *Econ.* xi. 9, 13.

[4] Cf. how naïvely he takes for granted the feasibility of his schemes in the *Revenues*. Cf. the opening sentence of the work, "As are the governors [προστάται], so are the governments [πολιτεῖας] "cited by Poehlmann (*op. cit.*, I, 299) as the illusion of socialism; but it might easily be expressed by a conservative. Plato (*Rep.* 544D) expresses a similar idea.

[5] *Rev.* iii and iv.

[6] iv. 33. The mines were already publicly owned, for the most part, but they were privately worked. Cf. Ardaillon, *Les Mines du Laurion dans l'antiquité* (Paris, 1897).

[7] iii. 14.   [9] iv.   [11] iii. 9 f.

[8] iv. 17.   [10] iv. 49.   [12] iv. 30–32.

for all will reign, and there will be an era of prosperity and security for the state.[1]

His thesis is, in a word, that what private capital can accomplish for the enrichment of itself alone, state capital can accomplish to better advantage for the enrichment of the whole citizenship,[2] a doctrine which strikes a truly modern socialistic note.

[1] iv. 33; 49–52; vi. 1. Cf. the excellent résumé of the whole plan by Poehlmann (*op. cit.*, I, 299 ff.), though he reads into it too much of the modern socialistic spirit; e. g., 306–8, he makes it an example of the so-called psychological necessity by which socialism develops out of capitalism.

[2] Cf. especially iv. 14: τῆς μέντοι πόλεως πάνυ ἄξιον θαυμάσαι τὸ αἰσθανομένην πολλοὺς πλουτιζομένους ἐξ αὐτῆς ἰδιώτας μὴ μιμεῖσθαι τούτους.

CHAPTER V

THE ORATORS—DEMOSTHENES, ISOCRATES

Though the Attic orators constitute a very important source for our knowledge of economic conditions in Athens, they furnish but little definite material for a history of Greek economic thought. From the standpoint of theory, their chief value consists in the fact that they all reveal a positive interest in wealth and all the phenomena of practical economy. In this respect, they present a striking contrast to the negative attitude of the Socratics, and thus serve to correct our conception of the economic ideas of the average Athenian citizen. Specific consideration need be given only to Demosthenes and Isocrates.

The positive interest of Demosthenes in commerce and finance has already been indicated by some passages,[1] and this fact is so evident throughout all his orations that further citations are unnecessary. Instead, we may note briefly some slight hints in him of the negative moral attitude of the philosophers. He emphasizes the dominating influence of money in warping the judgments of men.[2] He praises the simple life of the previous generation, and criticizes in contrast the private luxury of his own day.[3] According to him, it is considered to be rare for a business man to be both diligent (φιλεργόν) and honest (χρηστόν).[4] In his assertion that poverty compels freemen to turn to menial work (δουλικά) and that many freewomen (ἀσταί) have been driven by the stress of the times to such vocations,[5] some aristocratic prejudice against common labor seems to be implied. A similar attitude toward traders and money-dealers is at least suggested by his question as to what is the worst (πονηρότατον) element in the

---

[1] E.g., p. 106, n. 3, citing *Or.* xxxvi. 44 on πίστις.

[2] *Peace* 12, though the emphasis is on bribery.

[3] *Olynth.* iii. 25 f.; *Cont. Aristoc.* xxiii. 207 f.; *Or.* xiii. 29 f. (Dem.), though the emphasis in all is upon patriotism. In these passages, he idealizes the past in the manner of Isocrates; cf. *infra*, p . 143, n. 8.

[4] *Or.* xxxvi. 44, *For Phormio.*   [5] *Or.* lvii. 45.

state.[1] His scornful mention of Stephanus as one who loans money at interest, and takes advantage of another's need,[2] is a slight reminder of the philosophic prejudice against interest, though here he is doubtless emphasizing loans for consumption merely, at an exorbitant rate.[3] But these traces of the Socratic attitude toward wealth are of very little significance, in the face of the evident economic interest that characterizes all the orations of Demosthenes.

Isocrates may, in a sense, be reckoned among the Socratics, and he exhibits more of their spirit in relation to wealth than do any of the other orators. He would have men strive for honest character rather than for wealth, since it is not always gain to acquire and loss to spend. The result depends rather upon the occasion and virtue.[4] Noble character is of more value than great riches,[5] for good reputation is not purchasable (ὠνητή) with money, but is itself the source of material possessions, and it is immortal, while wealth is only temporal.[6] Material and spiritual wealth are thus contrasted in true Socratic manner;[7] right use is emphasized,[8] and the common insatiety and injustice of money-makers is opposed.[9] Folly and license are named as the usual accompaniments of wealth, in contrast to the moderation that characterizes the poor and lowly.[10] But, like Plato, Isocrates considers neither luxury nor penury to be the ideal condition,[11] and clearly appreciates the evil effect of poverty in arousing discontent and civic strife in the state.[12]

[1] *Cont. Aristoc.* 146; *Cont. Aristog.* xxv. 46, his scornful figurative use of the term κάπηλος.

[2] *Cont. Steph.* i. 70: ἀλλὰ τοκίζων καὶ τὰς τῶν ἄλλων συμφορὰς καὶ χρείας εὐτυχήματα σαυτοῦ νομίζων.

[3] *Olynth.* i. 15, referring to those who borrow money at high interest, and thus lose their property, may also be noted. Cf. pp. 105 f. and notes.

[4] *Nicocl.* 3. 50, against injustice in money-making.   [5] *Ibid.* 59.

[6] *Cont. Nicocl.* (2). 32; *Peace* 32; cf. p. 26, n. 1, for Plato's idea.

[7] Cf. also *Paneg.* 76.   [8] *Cont. Nicocl.* (2). 4.

[9] *Peace* 7; moderation in money-making is most difficult for most men; cf. also 34 and 93 f.

[10] *Areop.* 4.   [11] *Cont. Nicocl.* 2; *Panath.* 184.

[12] *Areop.* 51, 53, 83; νῦν δὲ πλείους εἰσὶν οἱ σπανίζοντες τῶν ἐχόντων, a striking commentary on the economic conditions in the Athens of his day. In 44, poverty is called a source of crime. All these passages idealize the past.

But despite this moralizing tendency, he agrees with the other orators in appreciating highly the economic importance of the manual arts.[1] He points also, with apparent pride, to the extensive commerce of Athens as compared with that of other states,[2] and one of his chief arguments for peace is that thereby the city will be filled with merchants and strangers and metics.[3] This entire plea for peace, which he bases so largely on economic advantage, has a decidedly modern ring. He understood well the importance of industrial development in the general prosperity of a democracy. In almost Aristotelian language, he pictures how in the good old days the rich were accustomed to give the poor a start in business (ἀφορμή), either in agriculture, trade, or the arts.[4] This positive economic interest is further evidenced by his emphasis upon the increased skill that results from the application of the division of labor.[5]

Isocrates, like Plato, was especially opposed to civic strife and the extreme individualistic communism that demanded a redivision of lands and abolition of debts.[6] In the ideal past of his dreams, there were no extremes of wealth and poverty, private property was safe, and revolutions did not rend the state. Now, on the other hand, all is changed. Sparta is the only state that has not been torn by the bitter party strife.[7] He contrasts the high regard in which the wealthy were held in his boyhood with the present jealous discontent. To be known as a wealthy man now is almost equivalent to being considered criminal and is a thing for which to apologize.[8] This attitude toward the rich, of which Isocrates complains, is significant in the light of similar tendencies in our own democracy today.

Again, in agreement with Plato and Aristotle, Isocrates opposes the doctrine of mere arithmetical equality, and insists that the true

---

[1] *Paneg.* 29, 33, 40; *Areop.* 74.   But cf. *Panath.* 29 for a hint of prejudice against them.

[2] *Paneg.* 42.   [3] *Peace* 20 f.

[4] *Areop.* 32 f.; cf. *infra*, p. 97, n. 6, for a fuller interpretation of Aristotle's passage; cf. *Letter to Timoth.* 3; *Areop.* 44.

[5] *Bousiris* 16.   [6] *Areop.* 35.

[7] *Panath.* 259; *Paneg.* 79; cf. also citations on poverty, above.

[8] *Or.* 15. 159 f.

equality apportions to each what befits his capacity.[1] But though he is hostile to the crasser type of communism, he makes the chief characteristic of the ideal past a noble community feeling and spirit of co-operation. In that happy time, the common weal was first in the thought of all, each had regard for others' interests, the poor were not jealous of the rich, and the rich assisted the poor.[2] At times, he even approaches the modern humanitarian sentiment for the submerged classes. He defines true national prosperity as a condition in which no citizen is lacking the means of livelihood,[3] and thinks the poor might well be pardoned for their indifference to public welfare, in their anxiety over the daily means of subsistence.[4] He also states the somewhat socialistic principle so emphasized by Plato, that the character of the state will be like that of the ruler.[5]

[1] *Areop.* 21 f.

[2] *Areop.* 35: αἱ δὲ χρήσεις κοιναί; 31 f., 51; for further mention of these idealizations of ancient Athens and Sparta, cf. *infra*, p. 143, n. 8.

[3] *Areop.* 53.

[4] *Ibid.* 83: ὁπόθεν τὴν ἀεὶ παροῦσαν ἡμέραν διάξουσιν.

[5] *Cont. Nicocl.* 31: ὅτι τὸ τῆς πόλεως ὅλης ἦθος ὁμοιοῦται τοῖς ἄρχουσιν.

CHAPTER VI

ARISTOTLE

In the writings of Aristotle, we find a much richer source for a history of Greek economic thought. Though no extant work of his is devoted to economics, he left a multitude of writings on diverse subjects, as a monument to his wonderful versatility and tireless industry.[1] Of these, the *Politics* and the *Ethics* are especially fruitful in economic ideas, though, as in the case of Plato, such material is incidental to the main discussion. His general attitude toward wealth and some of its problems, we shall find to be often substantially in agreement with that of Plato. His economic vision was prejudiced by the same ethico-aristocratic spirit. Yet his practical, scientific mind caused him to deal with many economic questions more extensively, more directly, and more incisively than is true of any other Greek thinker. Caution must be observed, however, against reading into his statements more meaning than he purposed to convey. He was not the creator of the science of political economy,[2] though his apprehension of many of the chief concepts of economics was probably clearer than has often been admitted by modern economists.[3]

At the very threshold of economic speculation, Aristotle advanced beyond Plato and Xenophon, in that he perceived the fallacy in the confusion of household and public economy. He saw

[1] Cf. *infra* for the *Economica*, which is generally recognized to be from a later member of the Peripatetic school, about 250–200 B.C.; cf. Susemihl, *Economica*, Intro. to the ed.; Croiset, *op. cit.*, IV, 710; Zeller, *op. cit.*, II, 2, 944 ff. Moreover, it deals chiefly with the practical phase of economics. On the other hand, we shall cite *Eud. Eth.* and *Mag. mor.* under Aristotle, since, though later than him, they merely imitate his thought, in so far as they touch economics. For the numerous and diverse writings ascribed to Aristotle, cf. Christ, *op. cit.*, IV [1905], 684 ff.

[2] B. St. Hilaire (preface to his French translation of the *Politics*, pp. 4–11) calls him "le créateur de l'économie politique." Zmavc (*Archiv f. d. Gesch. d. Philos.* [1899], pp. 407 ff.) also tends to overestimate him.

[3] Zmavc (*ibid.* and also *Zeitschr. f. d. gesammt. Staatswiss.* [1902], pp. 48 ff.) emphasizes this fact.

that they differed, not only in size or numbers, but in essential type.[1]　In his later discussion of wealth, however, he overlooked his distinction, and fell into the old Greek confusion.

VALUE

The extent of Aristotle's contribution to the theory of value has been very diversely estimated.[2]　In a classic passage of the *Politics*, he distinguishes between the two uses of an object, the direct use for which it was produced, and the indirect as an article for exchange.[3]　This has often been heralded as an anticipation of Adam Smith's distinctions between value in use and value in exchange.[4]　Such an interpretation, however, is hardly warranted.[5] The entire emphasis of Aristotle in the passage is upon use rather than upon value.　The exchange use is declared subordinate, and the context shows that the purport of the statement is to teach the uneconomic doctrine that exchange ($\mu\epsilon\tau\alpha\beta\lambda\eta\tau\iota\kappa\dot{\eta}$) is an artificial use, especially when pursued for gain.

Moreover, the passage fails to develop the definition further by distinguishing between economic utilities that involve a cost of production, and other necessities that are devoid of exchange value because of their universality.[6]　Need is recognized as an element in exchange value,[7] but it is not differentiated from economic demand that has the means to purchase.　All that can safely

---

[1] *Pol.* i. 1. 1252a7–13, cited on p. 9, n. 5, a criticism of Plato's *Politics* 258E–259C; on the truth in this confusion, cf. p. 10.　Even Adam Smith said: "What is wise with a family can hardly be foolish with a great kingdom."

[2] Besides St. Hilaire and Zmavc, cited above, among those favorable are Cossa, *Hist. des doctrines economiques*, p. 149; Blanqui, *op. cit.*, I, 49, 86.　More reserved are Souchon, *op. cit.*, p. 127; DuBois, *op. cit.*, p. 50; Haney, *op. cit.*, pp. 47 f.; unfair interpretation, Dühring, *op. cit.*, pp. 20 f.

[3] i. 9. 1257a6–9: ἑκάστου γὰρ κτήματος διττὴ ἡ χρῆσίς ἐστιν ἀμφότεραι δὲ καθ' αὐτὸ μὲν ἀλλ' οὐχ ὁμοίως καθ' αὐτό, ἀλλ' ἡ μὲν οἰκεία ἡ δ' οὐκ οἰκεία τοῦ πράγματος οἷον ὑποδήματος ἥ τε ὑπόδεσις καὶ ἡ μεταβλητική.

[4] *Wealth of Nations*, I, chap. iv.

[5] Cf. Souchon, *op. cit.*, p. 127; Haney, *op. cit.*, p. 47.

[6] Unless this is implied in κτήματος, 1257a6, as ἔστι γὰρ ἡ μεταβλητικὴ πάντων (14 f.) might seem to indicate.　Zmavc (*Archiv.*, etc., p. 410) points to 1253b33–39, on the automatic tripods of Hephaestus, as implying it, but if so it was unintended by Aristotle.　But cf. *infra*, pp. 84 and 86, n. 4, where it is recognized.

[7] 1257a11; 5–19, but not specifically stated, and the term χρεία does not occur here.

be said of this statement of Aristotle, therefore, is that he accidentally hit upon a basal distinction, which, had it been his purpose, he might have used as starting-point for the development of the modern theory of value.

Certain other passages from his writings reveal a clearer apprehension of the distinction. In the *Rhetoric*, he states the principle that exchange value is measured by rarity, though this may not be a criterion of the actual value of the commodity to life.[1] The latter is measured by its necessity or practical utility.[2]

A paragraph from the *Nicomachaean Ethics*, though it does not treat the problem directly, is also an evidence of Aristotle's insight into the elements of economic value.[3] It has been strangely slighted by most historians of economic thought, though its significance has been recognized by editors of the *Ethics*.[4] It grows out of his discussion of fair exchange, which is a part of the larger subject of justice. He observes that a proportional equality (κατὰ τὴν ἀναλογίαν ἴσον) between diverse products must exist before exchange can take place,[5] since the labor involved in their production is not equal.[6] This equality he obtains through a proportion, in which the objects of exchange stand in inverse ratio to the producers.[7] The equalization of the commodities is thus based, according to Aristotle, upon an estimate of the labor or cost of production in each case.[8] Again, he points out that the

---

[1] i. 7. 14: καὶ τὸ σπανιώτερον τοῦ ἀφθόνου, οἷον χρυσὸς σιδήρου ἀχρηστότερος ὤν· ἄλλον δὲ τρόπον τε ἄφθονον τοῦ σπανίου, ὅτι ἡ χρῆσις ὑπερέχει · τὸ γὰρ πολλάκις τοῦ ὀλιγάκις ὑπερέχει · ὅθεν λέγεται ἄριστον μὲν ὕδωρ. Cf. Pind. *Ol.* i. 1 and Cope-Sandys ed. of Ar. *Rhet.* (I, pp. 130 f., 1877).

[2] *Ibid.* [3] V, v. 8–14. 1133a5–1133b10 ff. [4] E.g., Stewart.

[5] 1133a5–12; 15 f.; 18; cf. *Eud. Eth.* vii. 10. 1243b28–38.

[6] *N. Eth.* 1133a5–12, etc., 12 f.: οὐθὲν γὰρ κωλύει κρεῖττον εἶναι το θατέρου ἔργον ἢ τὸ θατέρου. The emphasis seems to be on quality of labor, as suggested by κρεῖττον. Cf. both ὅσον and οἷον (15) and p. 84 n. 3.

[7] *Ibid.* 7–10; by joining means and extremes together, the proportionate exchange is effected. Cf. also 1133b4 ff.; 1133a32 f. As observed by Ritchie (Palgrave's *Dictionary*, art. "Aristotle") and H. Sewall (*op. cit.*, p. 3, n. 2), the proportion is clearer to moderns if we make our standard one hour of labor of each workman instead of the men themselves.

[8] Stewart (*Notes to N. Eth.*, I, 449) suggests that this gives what the economists call "natural value," but that the market value oscillates from this because of supply and demand.

standard by which all products are measured is need or demand
($\chi\rho\epsilon la$) for reciprocal services,[1] thereby making demand a social
fact dependent upon organized society.   It is, in his thought, the
"common denominator of value" which finally determines the
actual basis on which all goods are exchanged or services rendered.
Elsewhere Aristotle's conception of value is more individualistic,
like that of Xenophon and Plato, but Haney[2] overlooks this passage
in asserting that his notion of value is "purely subjective."   It is
not merely "equal wants" that are considered, as he states, but
equal costs as well.[3]   This demand, or common measure of value,
is expressed in terms of money ($\nu o\mu\iota\sigma\mu a$).[4]

It is clear then, from this passage in the *Ethics*, that Aristotle
understood that economic value is determined by demand, as measured in money, and by labor invested or cost of production.[5]   This
latter element, of course, involves the condition that the product be
limited in supply, though this is not expressly stated.[6]   To be sure,
the interest of the moral philosopher is also paramount here,[7] as in
the *Politics* passage.   The thought is centered on fair exchange, as a
phase of justice, rather than upon the problem of value.   Nevertheless, his discussion reveals a clear insight into demand and cost of
production as the two most important elements in economic value.[8]

[1] 1133a25–27; 1133b6 f.   Cf. p. 34, n. 5, for Plato's use of the term.

[2] *Op. cit.*, pp. 47 f.

[3] Cf. the discussion and notes above; also 1133a15 f., where both elements seem
to be recognized, though the meaning of the passage is disputed. Cf. *infra*, p. 108, n. 3.

[4] 1133a19 ff.; 29; 1133b10 ff., cited *infra*, on money.   It clearly distinguishes the
quality of exchangeableness.   Cf. iv. 1. 1119b26 f., cited *infra*, n. 7.   Cf. pp. 38 f. for
Plato's theory.

[5] So Stewart, *op. cit., in loc.;* Zmavc, *Archiv.*, etc., p. 415, who criticizes Karl
Marx (*Kapital*, 4th ed., I, 26) for denying this.   Barker (*op. cit.*, p. 379) says that
Aristotle did not recognize the "seller's cost of production"; but cf. 384, where he
implies the opposite.

[6] But cf. his definition of wealth, pp. 85 f.

[7] Bonar (*op. cit.*, p. 40) criticizes him for this.   The words $\dot{a}\xi la$ and $\tau l\mu\eta$ are not
used in the passage, but for the former in a very clear economic sense, cf. iv. 1. 1119b26–
27; $\chi\rho\dot{\eta}\mu a\tau a$ $\delta\dot{\epsilon}$ $\lambda\dot{\epsilon}\gamma o\mu\epsilon\nu$ $\pi\dot{a}\nu\tau a$ $\delta\sigma\omega\nu$ $\dot{\eta}$ $\dot{a}\xi la$ $\nu o\mu l\sigma\mu a\tau\iota$ $\mu\epsilon\tau\rho\epsilon\hat{\iota}\tau a\iota$.

[8] For further discussion of this *Ethics* passage, cf. *infra* on money, exchange, and
distribution.   *Mag. mor.* i. 33. 1193b19–1194b2 repeats the idea, citing Plato *Rep.*
on the exchange of the four producers in his primitive state.

WEALTH

Since Aristotle had a better apprehension of the theory of value than other Greek thinkers, we may expect him also to define more clearly the concept of wealth. In the *Politics*, he names the following attributes of genuine (ἀληθινός) wealth (πλοῦτος): necessary to life; useful to persons associated in a household or a state; capable of accumulation (θησαυρισμός); limited in extent (οὐκ ἄπειρος).[1] According to Mill,[2] from the "economic" standpoint, wealth is "all useful and agreeable things" of a "material nature" possessing "exchange value"; and, to have exchange value, they must be "capable of accumulation."

In comparing these two definitions, it should be recognized at the outset that Aristotle's term "genuine" does not mean "truly economic," as it might in Mill, but rather "legitimate wealth" as distinguished from that gained from false finance (χρηματιστική);[3] also that his "necessary to life" and "limited in extent" are not used in the economic but in the moral sense, as opposed to luxury and extreme interest in money-making. Mill's "all useful and agreeable things" presents a marked contrast to this in spirit. Aristotle's "useful" means "what subserves the final good" (πρὸς ἀγαθὴν ζωήν), while Mill's means "things that give sensations of comfort or pleasure." Thus Aristotle's wealth is necessarily limited, while Mill's is unlimited, since, as Barker observes, "only an infinity of wealth can satisfy an infinity of need."[4] It will be seen from the following discussion, however, that Aristotle includes more than "necessary things" in his category of economic wealth. He does not specify "material things," as does Mill, but it seems probable that this is his meaning.[5] In all the passages where he enumerates the different kinds of wealth, only material things are

---

[1] i. 8. 1256b28–32. The term ἄπειρος, as applied to wealth, is used by Plato and Aristotle of undue love of money (*Rep.* 373D, 591D; *Laws* 870A); for Aristotle, cf. passage above and *infra*. There is a sense, even from the economic standpoint, in which wealth is not unlimited.

[2] *Prin. of Pol. Econ.*, preliminary remarks, and Book I, chap. iii, 3.

[3] On this term in Plato and Aristotle, cf. *infra* under exchange.

[4] *Op. cit.*, p. 374; cf. *infra* on the moral attitude of Aristotle to wealth.

[5] His unfair criticism of Plato seems to argue otherwise (*Rep.* 369C ff.; *Pol.* 1291a12–19), but cf. *infra*.

included, except slaves, who are counted as mere tools.[1]　One of these passages specifically excludes intellectual wealth by defining property as a "separable instrument."[2]　The use of the term for value (ἀξία) probably implies the same limitation.[3]　Though Aristotle does not mention exchange value specifically, it is clearly implied in his definition.　"Things useful for the association of a state" and things "capable of accumulation" must have exchange value, thus excluding illimitable utilities such as air and light.[4] His use of κτῆμα, "possession," and his recognition of cost of production and economic demand as the main factors in determining value,[5] are further evidence of this.　Moreover, as seen above, in the *Ethics*, he clearly makes exchange value an attribute of all wealth.[6]

From our comparison of the two definitions, then, it is evident that, though Aristotle is antithetical to Mill in putting the ethical interest first, and though his definition is not so scientifically specific, yet the two agree in recognizing the qualities of materiality, exchange value, and possibility of accumulation as necessary attributes of wealth.　We shall see below, also, that the Greek philosopher was the forerunner of the orthodox English economists in criticizing the common confusion of money with wealth.[7]

But, despite his grasp of the leading principles in the economics of wealth, he takes the same negative moral attitude toward wealth as does Plato, though his hostility is also directed primarily against the spirit that commercializes life and makes unlimited wealth the *summum bonum*.　To his mind, this idea that wealth is the sum of

[1] ii. 7. 1267b10 ff.; 1254a16 f.; *Rhet.* i. 5. 1361a12 ff.

[2] *Pol.* 1254a16ff.: κτῆμα δὲ ὄργανον πρακτικὸν καὶ χωριστόν, similar to Walker's term "transferability" (*Pol. Econ.*, 3d ed., p 5); cf. Mill, *op. cit.*, preliminary remarks on the term.

[3] *N. Eth.* iv. 1. 1119b26 f., cited on p. 84, n. 7.

[4] Cf. the discussion above on value; cf. Mill, *op. cit.*, Book I, chap. iii, 3, on the quality of "storableness" as an attribute of wealth.　Newman (*Pol. of Ar.*, II, note to 1256b26 ff.) asks if θησαυρισμός can be applied to slaves and cattle, and if the definition can include land.　These are all included; cf. n. 1, above.

[5] *Pol.* i. 9. 1257a6 and 14 f., and the discussion above of *N. Eth.* 1133a5 ff.

[6] Cf. n. 3.

[7] Cf. Smith, *op. cit.*, IV, for criticism of this basal confusion of the mercantile theory.

all goods is almost the necessary accompaniment of the possession
of superfluous wealth, but it is especially characteristic of the new-
rich (νεωστὶ κεκτημένοις).[1] Yet Aristotle is too practical to be
ascetic. He realizes that leisure (σχολή) is necessary for moral
development and for good citizenship, and that this cannot be
enjoyed except on a basis of sufficient wealth. A fair competency
is therefore desirable for the best life,[2] for men should live not only
temperately, but liberally.[3] Poverty produces civic strife and
crime.[4] Wealth in the absolute sense (ἁπλῶς) is always good,
though it may not always be fitted to a certain individual, or be
properly used by him.[5] Each, therefore, should choose what is
good for himself, and use it accordingly.[6] All this sounds saner
than the subjective notion of wealth taught by Plato. But right
here is the secret of the difficulty as Aristotle sees it. Just because
all external wealth is good in the absolute sense, the popular error
has arisen that it is the final cause (αἰτία) of all happiness,[7] whereas
the actual relation of wealth to happiness is the same as that of the
lyre to the tune. There can be no music without the intervention
of the musician.[8] External goods are therefore not of primary
importance to life. The goods of the soul should be placed first,[9]
for the virtues of life are not gained and preserved by material
wealth, but vice versa,[10] and the men of high character and

[1] *Rhet.* B. 16. 1390-91.

[2] *Pol.* i. 8. 1256b31 f.; *N. Eth.* i. 8. 1099a31-33, especially ἀδύνατον γὰρ ἢ οὐ
ῥάδιον τὰ καλὰ πράττειν ἀχορήγητον ὄντα; 1101a14 f., in the definition of the εὐδαίμων
man.

[3] *Pol.* iii. 6. 1265a32 f.: ἐλευθέρως; *N. Eth.* iii., chaps. 13-14 on σωφροσύνη, and
iv, chaps. 1, 2, on ἐλευθεριότης and ἀσωτία; but display of wealth is vulgar (iv. 2.
1123a19-22). Ruskin (*Stones of Venice*, VIII, 69 [Vol. X, 389]) refers to Aristotle on
liberality.

[4] ἡ δὲ πενία στάσιν ἐμποιεῖ καὶ κακουργίαν.

[5] v. 1. 1129b3; so *Mag. mor.* B. 3. 1199b6-9, 14-35; cf. *N. Eth.* i. 8. 1098b31 ff.
for a similar distinction between habit (ἕξις) and practice (χρῆσις) of virtue.

[6] v. 1. 1129b4-6; cf. *Pol.* i. 10. 1258a23-27 on the duty of the weaver or statesman; iv (vii). 15. 1334a36 f.; 13. 1332a22 f.

[7] *Pol.* 1332a25 f. [8] *Pol.* iv (vii). 13. 1332a26 f.

[9] *N. Eth.* i. 8. 1098b12-15; cf. *Pol.* 1323a25 f.; *Rhet.* i. 5. 1360b25 ff.; also *Mag.
mor.* A. 3. 1184b1-5 and *Eud. Eth.* ii. 1. 1218b32.

[10] *Pol.* 1323a40 f.; cf. Jesus' sentence, "Seek ye first," etc.; cf. also 1323b19 f.;
also pp. 24 ff., Plato.

intelligence are most happy, even though their wealth is moderate.[1]
The common attitude of the money-maker that wealth is unlimited
is contrary to nature.[2] Genuine wealth cannot be unlimited,[3] since
external goods are strictly defined by their utility for a certain
thing. Excessive wealth thus either harms the owner, or is, at
least, useless to him.[4] Neither can wealth be rightly made the
summum bonum, for it is really not an end at all, but only a collec-
tion of means to an end (ὀργάνων πλῆθος).[5] The inevitable result
of making it the end and measure of all is moral degeneration.[6] If
the highest interests of life are to be preserved, it must always be
kept subservient. First things must be placed first, both by the
individual[7] and by the state.[8]

PRODUCTION

It is often asserted that Aristotle denied the very existence of
a problem of production.[9] This statement has been based primarily on certain passages in the *Politics*.[10] These passages, however, are not a denial of the importance of production. Their
purport is merely to show that the chief aim of life is not to produce
or to provide wealth, but to use it for the advancement of life's
highest interest. From this standpoint, both acquisition (κτητική)
and production (ποιητική) are subordinate arts.[11] So far is Aris-

[1] *Pol.* 1323b, 1–6.

[2] *N. Eth.* i. 5. 1096a5 f.: ὁ δὲ χρηματιστὴς βίαιος τίς ἐστιν. Cf. also *Pol.* 1256b28–
32, discussed above, and i, chaps. 8 and 9, discussed under exchange.

[3] Cf. n. 2.   [4] *Pol.* 1323b7–11, and discussion above.

[5] 1256b36; *N. Eth.* i. 5. 1906a6 f.; χρήσιμον γὰρ καὶ ἄλλου χάριν; 7. 1097a27:
δῆλον ὡς οὐκ ἐστι πάντα τέλεια.

[6] *Pol.* i. 9. 1258a2 ff.; cf. also *Mag. mor.* B. 3. 1200a-b.

[7] 1258a10–14, similar to Plato *Rep.* i on the arts and their function; cf. a similar
passage from *Isocrates* (*Paneg.* 76) on the virtues of the Persian War heroes.

[8] *Pol.* iii. 9. 1280a25–32; the chief ambition of a state is not τῶν κτημάτων χάριν,
but εὖ ζῆν. Cf. above on the similar preachments of Plato, for their relation to
modern economic ideas and conditions. Cf. Plato *Crito* 48B: οὐ τὸ ζῆν περὶ πλείστου
ποιητέον, ἀλλὰ τὸ εὖ ζῆν.

[9] Cf. Souchon, *op. cit.*, p. 69; for Greek terms for production, cf. p. 66 and notes.

[10] i. 10. 1258a19–38; 4. 1254a7: ὁ δὲ βίος πρᾶξις, οὐ ποίησίς ἐστιν.

[11] 10. 1258a33 ff., τῆς ὑπερετικῆς, impossible for the economist, but true, for the
moralist; cf. p. 69 for his distinction (1254a1 ff.) between ὄργανα ποιητικά and κτῆμα
πρακτικόν.

totle from giving no place to production, that a later chapter
of the *Politics* is devoted to the consideration of the scheme of
supply, including production.[1] To be sure, he does not lay much
emphasis on genuine production in his enumeration. Industry is
barely mentioned, while agriculture is discussed in detail. His
"free-holder" is a consumer of the gifts of nature, rather than a real
producer.[2] He classifies the truly productive employments that
work for themselves (αὐτόφυτον) as those of the nomad, the farmer,
the brigand, the fisherman, and the hunter, and makes those that
live by barter (ἀλλαγῆς) or trade (καπηλείας) parasitic.[3]

In another passage, finance, strictly defined (οἰκειατάτη), is
limited to all forms of agriculture, and even the hired labor (μισθαρνία) of industry is included in unnatural finance.[4] Aristotle
has thus often been compared to the physiocrats, who distinguished
between creative and parasitic classes of workers, upheld the
"natural" order as the ideal, and eulogized agriculture and the
"extractive" industries as the only productive ones. As Souchon[5]
has observed, however, the resemblance is only superficial. Yet
the fact that he fails to see that exchange is productive of a time
and place value, and the fact that he includes hired labor, skilled
and unskilled, among the unnatural activities, are sufficient evidence that he had only a superficial grasp of the principles of production.[6] But the frequent assertion that he includes brigandage

---

[1] i. 2.; on both the above, cf. Newman, *op. cit.*, *in loc.*

[2] Cf. especially 1258a34 ff.: μάλιστα δὲ, καθάπερ εἴρεται πρότερον, δεῖ φύσει τοῦτο
ὑπάρχειν. Cf. Susemihl and Hicks, *Pol. of Ar.*, I (1894), Intro., p. 30.

[3] 1256a40 ff., αὐτόφυτος, "self-existent," with ἐργασία, as here, equals αὐτουργία,
"agriculture."

[4] 1258b9–27.

[5] *Op. cit.*, pp. 96, 98 f., n. 1; cf. Haney, *op. cit.*, p. 47; Kautz, *op. cit.*, p.138;
Ingram, *op. cit.*, p. 18. The physiocrats thought that commerce and industry increased
the value of raw materials only enough to pay for labor and capital expended. Commerce was an expensive necessity, a tax on agriculture. For a good summary, cf.
Haney, pp. 138 ff. Quesnay (*Tableau Econ.* [1776]) followed Xenophon (*Econ.* v. 17)
as his motto. But the motive of the physiocrats was economic, not moral and political,
as was that of Aristotle.

[6] *Pol.* 1258b21 ff.; probably implied also in 1256a40 ff.; but cf. vi (iv). 4. 1291a-
1 ff., where the mechanic and hired laborer are counted among the necessary parts of
the state.

and war among the productive arts is unwarranted, for he classifies them only among the acquisitive means.[1]

Aristotle almost outdoes Plato in his subordination of all production to ethics, though he keeps their respective aims more distinct. According to him, the productive arts are not ends in themselves. They are means to the supreme end of the moral life, whose first interest is not in production, but in right action.[2] As seen in our discussion of Plato, such a doctrine is not fruitful, economically. If interpreted too rigidly, it stifles commerce and industry. Yet, at bottom, it holds a great truth which modern economists are emphasizing—the fact that wealth and production alike must be subordinated to the general individual and social good. Moreover, the philosopher should not be interpreted in too hard-and-fast a manner. Barker is extreme in his statement that the economic theory of Aristotle is a mere treatise on "the ethics of family life" and that "the fundamental characteristic of his idea of production is a reactionary archaism, which abolishes all the machinery of civilization in favor of the self-supporting farm and a modicum of barter."[3] Bonar's assertion is also unwarranted, that "Aristotle thinks it beneath the dignity" of his discourse to give the practical details of agriculture and industry "more than a cursory notice."[4] Such details were not germane to the plan of his work, and would certainly be considered out of place in a modern general text on economics. Aristotle's economic doctrine, as a whole, is certainly far broader in scope than the family, and, while based upon ethics, is something more than an ethical treatise. As seen above, he recognizes the necessity of a moderate acquisition of wealth, both for the prosperous state and for the virtuous man, and demands only that the human interest be put first.[5]

---

[1] 1256*40 ff.; 1256*b*23 f. To him, production is a branch of acquisition. Cf. p. 28, on Plato's use of the terms.

[2] 1258*a*19–38; 1254*a*7, cited on p. 88, n. 10.   [3] *Op. cit.*, pp. 358, 375 f.

[4] *Op. cit.*, p. 39, on the basis of *Pol.* 1258*b*34 f.: τὸ δὲ κατὰ μέρος ἀκριβολογεῖσθαι χρήσιμον μὲν πρὸς τὰς ἐργασίας, φορτικὸν δὲ τὸ ἐνδιατρίβειν. φορτικόν may mean merely "tiresome," not "vulgar."

[5] Cf. Zmavc, *Archiv.*, etc., p. 431; cf. passages cited *infra*, on the attitude of Aristotle to labor; cf. vi (iv). 4. 1291*a*1 ff., especially ἔστι δὲ τοῦτο τὸ περὶ τὰς τέχνας ὧν ἄνευ πόλιν ἀδύνατον οἰκεῖσθαι.

Agriculture.—Of the factors that enter into production, Aristotle is, like the other Socratics, most interested in natural resources. He emphasizes especially the agricultural life. To his mind, it is the only true foundation of "natural finance," since the financial means should be provided in nature herself.[1] Natural finance (οἰκειατάτη) is made to include only a proper knowledge of the care of land, cattle, bees, fowl, and other natural resources.[2] It is natural, since it does not earn at the expense of others, as do retail trade and other methods of false finance. Aristotle also reveals his interest in agriculture by giving a bibliography of the subject. He names Charetides of Paros, Apollodorus of Lemnos, "and others on other branches"—a hint that many such works on practical economics may be lost to us.[3] However, his interest, even in this primary industry, is not of a practical nature, like that of Xenophon. He relegates it to the non-citizen classes, along with commerce and the mechanical arts.[4]

Capital.—Aristotle is the only Greek thinker who has given a clear definition of capital. After defining the slave as an instrument (ὄργανον), in order to distinguish still more sharply, he differentiates between the two kinds of wealth—that which is used for consumption, and that which is employed for further production.[5] As an example of the former, he uses the bed and the dress, and of the latter the weaver's comb (κερκίς).[6] He points out that all wealth is produced for consumption, but that part of it is consumed indirectly in manufacture. Here is an approach to Adam Smith's[7] definition of capital, as "that part of a man's stock which he expects to afford him revenue." Unfortunately, however, the Greek fails to pursue his distinction farther. The theme of his thought is, after all, not capital or production either, but the status of the slave, though, from his standpoint, the slave is capital. He proceeds with the very uneconomic assertion that life consists in action

---

[1] *Pol.* 1258a34–38, cited on p. 89, n. 2.   [2] 1258b9–21.

[3] *Ibid.* 40 ff.; cf. Newman, *op. cit.*, II, 204, on the statements of Varro *De re rustica* i. 1. 8 and *Columella* i. 1. 7 that Aristotle and Theophrastus wrote on agriculture. Cf. also (Plato) *Axiochus* 368C.

[4] *Pol.* iv (vii). 9. 1329a1 f.   [6] 1254a2–4.

[5] 1254a1 ff.; cf. pp. 68 and 88 for Greek terms.   [7] *Op. cit.*, ii, chap. i.

($\pi\rho\hat{a}\xi\iota s$), not in production ($\pi o\acute{\iota}\eta\sigma\iota s$),[1] and concludes with the real goal of his argument, that the slave is an assistant ($\acute{\upsilon}\pi\epsilon\rho\acute{\epsilon}\tau\eta s$), or an animate instrument in the realm of action, not of production.[2] The slave is therefore an instrument to increase the life or action of his master, who himself is not represented as a producer, but as a consumer of the present stock. Thus what bids fair to be a fruitful distinction ends in a denial of the primary importance of production. The purpose of Aristotle is here similar to that in some passages of Ruskin[3] and Adam Smith,[4] to emphasize consumption rather than production.

In another passage, he repeats his definition of capital in different terms. Goods are classified as for "purposes of production" or for "mere enjoyment,"[5] but here again no theory of capital is developed. Yet these two definitions are sufficient evidence that he advanced beyond his predecessors in his apprehension of the meaning of the term.[6] His division of production and finance, however, into the natural or limited, which deals only with natural resources,[7] and the unnatural, which is unlimited, and includes commerce, usury, and even industry,[8] reveals a mind neither greatly interested in capital, nor clear as to its true economic importance. His assertion in the Ethics[9] that the prodigal ($\check{a}\sigma\omega\tau os$) benefits many by his reckless expenditures, and that parsimoniousness ($\grave{a}\nu\epsilon\lambda\epsilon\upsilon$-$\theta\epsilon\rho\acute{\iota}a$) is a worse evil than prodigality also shows that he did not sufficiently emphasize the importance to society of economy, the

---

[1] Pol. 1254a7; cf. p. 88, n. 10.

[2] Pol. 1254a8 ff. He thinks chiefly of the domestic slave.

[3] Unto This Last, p. 61, an unjust criticism of Mill; ibid., IV, 78: "Production is primarily for the mouth, not for the granary."

[4] Op. cit., IV, chap. viii: "Consumption is the sole end and purpose of all production; . . . . and the interest of the producer ought to be attended to only so far as it may be necessary for promoting that of the consumer."

[5] For reference and Greek terms, cf. p. 68.

[6] For his term $\grave{a}\phi o\rho\mu\acute{\eta}$, cf. p. 68, n. 8, and infra. It probably was a mere business word to him. DuBois (op. cit., p. 38) thinks that he had a very clear idea of its significance.

[7] Pol. 1258b12–21; cf. 1258a37 f.

[8] Ibid. 21–27, and entire chaps., 8–11. For terms, cf. infra.

[9] iv. 1121a29; 1122a14 f.; cf. the stress on $\delta\acute{o}\sigma\iota s$ and $\chi\rho\hat{\eta}\sigma\iota s$ rather than on $\kappa\tau\hat{\eta}\sigma\iota s$ and $\lambda\hat{\eta}\psi\iota s$, 1120a8–13; b14–16, and Stewart's notes, I, 323.

mother of stored capital. On this point, Plato has the saner view,[1] and the extreme attitude of Aristotle is certainly not characteristic of the Greeks in general.[2] His failure to grasp the true theory of interest is a further evidence of his superficial apprehension of the function of money capital. He does not see, with Adam Smith, that money represents so much stored capital, potentially productive, and that "since something can everywhere be made by the use of money, something ought everywhere to be paid for the use of it."[3] In justice to him, however, it should be observed that, though he failed to see the importance of unlimited economic progress through constant increase in the capitalistic stock, there is after all a sense in which he was right. There is a natural limit to just acquisition, and it is especially with the individual in relation to wealth that he is dealing. He is thus, with Plato, a forerunner of the present tendency in economics, which is inclined to set a limit to the amount that one can justly earn in a lifetime by his own work.[4]

Labor and industry.—Aristotle's attitude to labor, the third factor in production, is similar to that of Plato, though he lays greater emphasis on the evil physical and moral effect of the "banausic" arts. They are defined as those that "render men unfit for the practice of virtue."[5] They not only cause the body to degenerate,[6] but, being "mercenary" employments, they also

[1] *Rep.* 552B, discussed above.

[2] Souchon (*op. cit.*, p. 121) seems to think it was.

[3] *Pol.* 1258b8, but cf. p. 39 and *infra* on this word τόκος. Cf. also Ar. *Clouds* 20; 1285 ff.; A. Smith, *op. cit.*, II, chap. iv.

[4] Souchon (*op. cit.*, p. 97) is hardly fair to Aristotle on this point, but cf. also p. 96, n. 1; cf. Ruskin, *Time and Tide*, XV, 81 (Vol. XVII, 388); *Mun. Pul.*, Pref., 21 (Vol. XVII, 144); *ibid.*, VI, 139 (p. 264); *ibid.*, 153 and note (p. 277), which cites *Laws* 743C, on the doctrine that the just are neither rich nor poor.

[5] *Pol.* v (viii). 2. 1337b8–11. The terms for mechanical labor are τέχνη, of ability through practice; δημιουργός, of one who works for the people, rather than for himself or one other; βάναυσος, originally of work by the fire, but later the common term for mechanical labor, usually with a derogatory sense in the philosophers; cf. βαναυσία, "vulgarity," *N. Eth.* iv. 4. 1122a31; βάναυσος, "vulgar man," *ibid.* 1123a19; *Etymol. mag;* Schol. to Plato *Rep.* 495E; Pollux i. 64. 50; Hesychius, *s.v.* The Greeks did not clearly distinguish the finer from the mechanical arts; cf. Büchsenschütz, *op. cit.*, p. 266; *Pol.* vi (iv). 4. 1291a1 ff., where all are included under βάναυσον. Cf. Cope-Sandys, *Ar. Rhet.*, 2d ed., I, 9, 27, note. Cf. above, p. 33, n. 7, for Ruskin's attitude.

[6] *Pol.* 1337b12; 1258b37.

vulgarize the soul.[1] The occupations that require the most physical labor are the most "slavish."[2] The life of artisans and laborers is mean (φαῦλος) and has no business with virtue.[3] The citizen youth should be taught none of the illiberal pursuits of the tradesmen.[4] No citizen should enter into industrial labor or retail trade, since they are ignoble (ἀγεννής) and hostile to virtue.[5] Even all the agricultural work must be performed by slaves, that the citizens may have leisure for personal development and for service to the state.[6] In addition to his other objections to retail trade and the arts, Aristotle considers them to be naturally unjust, since they take something from him with whom they deal.[7] Indeed, the productive classes have but slight recognition in his ideal state. They seem to be tolerated only as a necessary evil, and are in a state of limited slavery ἀφωρισμένην τινὰ δουλείαν. Virtue is even less possible for them than for slaves, and they lead a less tolerable life.[8] All hired labor belongs to the category of "false finance" which degrades individual and state alike.[9] The state that produces a multitude of mechanics and but few hoplites can never be great.[10]

Here we have the very antithesis of the modern commercial standpoint. However, the truth is not all with the moderns, for a highly developed commerce and industry and the general prosperity of the mass of the people are not always necessarily coincident. Moreover, it is hardly fair to interpret Aristotle too rigidly. He understood well the necessity of craftsmen and all other industrial workers to the state.[11] The burden of his attack was directed against retail trade. Like Plato's his prejudice had a moral and political root,[12] and was arrayed against the extreme application

[1] 1337b13 f.

[2] 1258b38 f.

[3] vii (vi). 4. 1319a26–28.

[4] v (viii). 2. 1337b5–7.

[5] iv (vii). 9. 1328b37–41; cf. iii. 5. 1277b33 ff.

[6] 1329a1; 1330a25–31.

[7] 1330a25–31; cf. also the pseudo-*Econ.* i. 2. 1343a26 ff.

[8] i. 3. 1260a40 ff.; cf. *infra* for discussion of this idea.

[9] 1258b25–27; *Rhet.* i. 9. 27, 1367a; ἐλευθέρου γὰρ τὸ μὴ πρὸς ἄλλον ζῆν. His entire argument for the slave as a mere "instrument" (cf. *infra*) shows the same attitude. Stewart (*op. cit.*, II, 316) says that he failed to see that labor is "an essential function of the social organism, something καλόν and not merely ἀναγκαῖον."

[10] *Pol.* iv (vii). 4. 1326a22–24.

[11] 1328b19–23; vi (iv). 1291a1–3.

[12] 1329a1; i. 11. 1258b38 f.

to labor, and against its false purpose, rather than against labor itself. He insisted that even intellectual work, when carried to an extreme, and pursued with the wrong aim, might become equally demoralizing.[1]

Here is a doctrine which our modern age, that would place even education on a bread-and-butter basis, and that tends to kill initiative and vision by extreme specialization, might well consider. Even Latin literature, when taught as it too often is, merely as a syntactical grind to prepare teachers to pursue the same folly is no more one of the humanities than is industrial chemistry.[2] Furthermore, Aristotle and Plato are doubtless right in their belief that a necessary extreme application to physical labor to earn the daily bread inevitably prevents mental and moral development and the proper performance of the duties of citizenship. And our modern democracies with their boasts of universal suffrage are still something of a farce, as long as economic conditions are such that the mass of the population has left no time to think of anything, except how to provide the bare physical necessities. Aristotle's insistence upon leisure for the life of the citizen is no demand for aristocratic indolence.[3] Neither is it Jowett's "condition of a gentleman," or merely the idealized notion of an "internal state" in which "the intellect, free from the cares of practical life, energizes or reposes in the consciousness of truth." It is rather a demand for release from material cares, so as to insure the highest degree of activity in self-development and political service.[4]

It may well be observed too, that Aristotle, the special champion of slavery, and reputed scorner of physical labor for freemen, exhibits a real interest in industry, in unguarded moments. One

---

[1] v (viii). 2. 1337b15–22, especially 17 f.: ἔχει δὲ πολλὴν διαφορὰν καὶ τὸ τίνος ἕνεκεν πράττει τις ἢ μανθάνει.

[2] The difference in employments and studies is largely one of method and aim. The most humanizing pursuit becomes ἀνελεύθερον and βάναυσον, if followed to an extreme or with a sordid purpose, merely. Cf. Plato Laws 918B–919C, and the criticism of the superficial method and merely vocational motive in mathematical study (Rep. 525C ff.). Cf. above, p. 33, n. 7, for Ruskin's idea on this point.

[3] Aristotle also has the aristocratic idea of labor as robbing a freeman of his independence, Pol. v (viii). 1337b15–22; Rhet. 1367a, cited on p. 94, n. 9.

[4] Pol. iv (vii). 9. 1328b39 ff.; N. Eth. x. 7. 1177b4; cf. Jowett, Ar. Pol., I, 144, cited by Stewart, op. cit., II, 446.

of his arguments against communism is that it would take from the
citizen the desire to work.[1] He repudiates the life of indolence,
and finds happiness in action.[2] He considers a practical knowledge
of agriculture as essential to the successful economist,[3] and defines
the just as those who live upon their own resources or labor, instead
of making profit from others, especially the farmers, who live from
the land which they cultivate.[4] We have seen above also that he
makes labor one of the prime factors that determine value, and
thus the most important element in production.[5] Moreover, he
shows that he has a practical grasp of the importance of productive
employment for the citizens of a democracy. He advises the rich
to furnish plots of land (γήδια) to the poor, from the public revenues,
or else that they give the poor a start (ἀφορμή) in other business,
and thus turn them to industry.[6]

On the division of labor, Aristotle adds little to Plato's and
Xenophon's theory. He agrees with Xenophon against Plato that
it implies a necessary distinction between the work of men and
women.[7] He also applies the principle more extensively, so as to
include all nature, whereas Plato seems to limit its application to
man. Nature (ἡ φύσις) he observes, does not produce things like
the Delphian knife, in a poverty-stricken manner (πενιχρῶς) to
serve many purposes, but each for a single purpose (ἓν πρὸς ἕν).[8]
Like Plato, he makes the principle of reciprocity (τὸ ἴσον ἀντιπεπονθός), out of which the division of labor arises, the saving element
in the state.[9] He is also fully as emphatic in his application of the
law to politics and citizenship.[10]

---

[1] *Pol.* ii. 3. 1261b33–38.   [2] 1325a31–33.   [3] 1258b12–20.

[4] *Rhet.* ii. 4. 9. 1381a, where the word αὐτουργοί is used; cf. above on Euripides.

[5] Cf. above on value, and *N. Eth.* v. 8–9. 1133a5–18.

[6] *Pol.* vii (vi). 6. 1320a38 ff.; cf. p. 92, n. 6.   [7] i. 12. 1259b1 ff.

[8] 1252b1 ff.; cf. Adam's note to *Rep.* 370B; Susemihl and Hicks's note to *Pol.*
1252b3, for an exception to the rule (*De part. Anim.* iv. 6. 11. 683a22). ἀλλ' ὅπου μὴ
ἐνδέχεται καταχρῆται τῷ αὐτῷ ἐπὶ πλείω ἔργα.

[9] *Pol.* ii. 1261a30 f.; *N. Eth.* v, 5.

[10] *Pol.* 1261a37–39; 1328b ff. Fontpertuis (*op. cit.*, p. 359) accounts for the comparative superficiality of the Greek theory of labor by the fact that their political
constitution diminished its importance, but cf. our introduction. Capitalistic employment of free labor was probably not extensive.

SLAVERY

We have seen that the references to slavery in Xenophon and Plato are incidental, and reveal a certain unconscious naïveté as to the actual social problem involved. By Aristotle's day, however, the criticisms of the Sophists had shaken the foundations of all traditional institutions, and their thesis that slavery is contrary to nature had become through the Cynics a prominent social theory.[1] The thought on the subject had crystallized into two leading doctrines—one including benevolence in justice, and hence denying the right of slavery; and the other identifying justice with the rule of the stronger, and hence upholding slavery as based on mere force.[2] The practical Aristotle, an upholder of slavery, not from tradition, but through conscious belief in its economic necessity, thus takes his stand midway between the two opposing theories. He champions the old view of natural slavery, but rejects the basis of mere force for that of morality and benevolence.[3] His thesis is that slavery is a natural and necessary relation in human society, not accidental or conventional. The slave, being property, which is a multitude of instruments ($\dot{o}\rho\gamma\acute{a}\nu\omega\nu$ $\pi\lambda\hat{\eta}\theta o s$), is an animate instrument ($\ddot{o}\rho\gamma\alpha\nu o\nu$ $\ddot{\epsilon}\mu\psi\nu\chi o\nu$) conducive to life ($\pi\rho\dot{o}s$ $\zeta\omega\acute{\eta}\nu$).[4] He is just as necessary to the best life of the citizen as are inanimate instruments, and will be, until all tools work automatically, like the mythical figures of Daedalus or the tripods of Hephaestus.[5] The slave is a servant in the realm of action ($\pi\rho\hat{a}\xi\iota s$), not of production ($\pi o\acute{\iota}\eta\sigma\iota s$). He is not a producer of commodities

---

[1] Cf. above, p. 16, n. 6; p. 17, n. 1.

[2] On the theory of the Sophists, cf. above, pp. 16 f. On the Cynics, cf. *infra;* also Zeller, *op. cit.*, II, 2, 376; Ar. *Pol.* 1253*b*20–23. Barker (*op. cit.*, p. 359), who has a very clear and discriminating criticism of Aristotle's theory of slavery, also states that slavery had been attacked by the "logic of events"—e.g., the enslavement of Athenians in Sicily, and the freeing of Messenian Helots, during the Theban supremacy, by which Greek freemen had become slaves and Greek slaves had become free. Cf. *Pol.* 1255*a* ff., especially 17 f. and 21–23, for the two theories.

[3] The *locus classicus* for his theory is *Pol.* i. 4–7. 1253*b*14 ff.; 13. 1259*b*21 ff. For good criticisms, cf. Wallon, *Histoire de l'esclavage dans l'antiquité*, 2d ed., pp. 372 ff.; and Barker, *op. cit.*, i. Cf. also Newman, *op. cit.*, I, 143 ff.

[4] *Pol.* i. 8. 1256*b*36; 1253*b*32.

[5] *Ibid.* 33–39. Aristotle would have been satisfied with electricity.

(ποιητικός), but of services (πρακτικός),[1] and just as property is merely a part or member (μόριον) belonging wholly to something else, so the slave, as property, belongs entirely to his master, and has no true existence apart from him.[2] From these facts, the whole nature and power of the slave are evident. One who, though a human being, is merely property is a natural slave, since he is naturally not his own master, but belongs to another, in whom he finds his true being.[3] As Barker has observed, this conclusion of the first part of Aristotle's argument is inevitable if we admit his premises of the identity of "instruments" and property, but this is an unreal identity.[4] "Natural" (φύσει) is the saving word in his argument, but "human" (ἄνθρωπος) refutes it, as the philosopher practically admits later.

He now proceeds to ask the question whether this "natural" slave of his hypothesis actually exists, for whom such a relation is just, or whether all slavery is contrary to nature, as some allege. He answers in the affirmative. The principle of rule and subjection he declares to be a foundation law of all life.[5] Men are constituted for either condition from birth, and their development follows this natural bent.[6] This law may be observed in inanimate things,[7] in the natural subordinate relation of the body to the soul, of domestic animals to man, of female to male, of child to parent, and of subjects to rulers.[8] Thus all who are capable only of physical service hold the same relation to higher natures as the body holds to the soul, and are slaves by nature.[9] This is the only relation for which the slave is naturally fitted, since he can apprehend reason without himself possessing it, being midway between animals and truly rational men.[10] Usually also nature differen-

---

[1] 1254a8, cited on p. 88, n. 10. This relieves the severity of the doctrine, since it shows that he thinks chiefly of domestic slavery. But in his proposed state, all industry is manned by slaves. Cf. iv (vii). 1330a25-31.

[2] *Pol.* 1254a9-13; cf. *Eud. Eth.* 1241b17-24.

[3] 1254a13-17.   [4] *Op. cit.*, p. 362.

[5] 1254a28-31; 1254b15. As Wallon (*op. cit.*, p. 391) points out, his radical error is a constant confusion of hypothesis with reality.

[6] 1254a23-24.   [7] *Ibid.* 33 f.

[8] *Ibid.* 30-40; 1254b10-13; 1253b7; 18 f., cf. *Eud. Eth.* 1241b17 ff.

[9] 1254b16-19.   [10] *Ibid.* 20-26.

tiates both the bodies and the souls of freemen and slaves, suiting them to their respective spheres and functions.[1]

This relation of slavery, Aristotle argues, is not only natural and necessary, but also beneficial for those who are so constituted.[2] Just as the body is benefited by the rule of the soul, and domestic animals by the rule of man, so it is distinctly to the advantage of the "natural slave" to be ruled by a rational master. This is universally true, wherever one class of persons is as inferior to another as is the body to the soul.[3]

The philosopher's frank admissions, in which he opposes the doctrine that slavery is founded on mere force, are fatal to his first argument on the natural slave. He admits that nature does not always consummate her purpose; that the souls of freemen are sometimes found in the bodies of slaves, and vice versa;[4] that it is difficult to distinguish the quality of the soul, in any event;[5] that the claim that slavery is neither natural nor beneficial has in it a modicum of truth, as there are sometimes merely legal slaves, or slaves by convention;[6] that slavery based on mere might without virtue is unjust;[7] that captives of war may be wrongly enslaved;[8] that only those who actually deserve it, should meet this fate;[9] that the accidents of life may bring even the noblest of mankind into slavery;[10] and that only non-Greeks are ignoble and worthy of it.[11] He even insists that the terms "slave-master," "freeman," "slave," when rightly used, imply a certain virtue or the lack of it, and therefore that to be justly a master, one must be morally

---

[1] *Ibid.* 26 ff.   [2] 1254a21 f.

[3] 1254b6–10; 11 f.; 16–20; 1255b6–15; a doctrine emphasized by Plato, *Rep.* 590D; *Laws* 645B, 714A, 818A, 684C, as also by Carlyle and Ruskin; cf. Shorey, *Class. Phil.*, IX (1914), 355 ff. Though Ruskin believed that natural slavery was the inevitable lot of many men, he did not uphold negro slavery, *Mun. Pul.*, v, 133 (Vol. XVII, 256 f.); Time and Tide, p. 149 (Vol. XVII, 438). But he pointed to the white economic slavery as equally bad, *Stones of Venice*, II (Vol. X, 193); Time and Tide, p. 105 (Vol. XVII, 403); *Crown of Wild Olive*, 119; *Cestus Aglaia*, p. 55.

[4] 1254b32–34; 1255b5 ff.

[5] 1254b38 f.   [7] *Ibid.* 19–21 and next note.

[6] 1255a3–7.   [8] *Ibid.* 24 f.

[9] *Ibid.* 25 f.: καὶ τὸν ἀνάξιον δουλεύειν οὐδαμῶς ἂν φαίη τις δοῦλον εἶναι.

[10] *Ibid.* 26–28.   [11] *Ibid.* 33 ff.

superior.[1] The question of the possession of the higher virtues
by slaves is recognized by him to be a difficult problem, for an
affirmative answer breaks down his distinction of "natural"
slave, yet it seems paradoxical to deny these virtues to him as a
human being.[2] Nor can the difficulty be avoided by positing for
the slave a mere difference in degree of virtue, for the distinction
between ruler and subject must be one of kind.[3] In any event,
temperance and justice are necessary even for good slave service.[4]
Aristotle therefore evades the difficulty, and begs the question by
concluding that both master and slave must share in virtue, but
differently, in accord with their respective stations.[5]

With this admission, he places slaves on a higher plane than
free artisans, in that he denies virtue to such classes, since it cannot
be produced in them, except as they are brought into contact with
a master.[6] He thus makes slavery a humanitarian institution,
and the slave a real member of the family.[7] But the admission
most fatal to his theory is in agreeing that the slave *qua* man may
be a subject of friendship,[8] and in advocating his manumission
as a reward for good behavior. With this, the attempted distinction between him, *qua* slave and *qua* man, utterly breaks down,
and the existence of natural slaves is virtually denied.[9] Thus the
great champion of slavery in the ancient world, by his very defense
of it, repudiates its right as a natural institution. His actual
conception of the relation is, indeed, not far from the ideal of Plato,
a union for the best mutual service of rulers and ruled, in which

---

[1] 1255*b*20–22. Barker (*op. cit.*, p. 369, n. 1) well observes that this is a challenge
of the right of slavery, not an argument for it, and that it may have impressed his
contemporaries so. Cf. Ruskin: "So there is only one way to have good servants;
that is to be worthy of being well served" (*Letters on Servants and Houses*, Vol.
XVII, 5–18, App. V); cf. also pp. 520 ff.

[2] 1259*b*26–28.   [3] *Ibid.* 36–38.   [4] *Ibid.* 39–41.

[5] 1260*a*2–4; 14–16; cf. 33 ff., which sets a limit on the slave's virtue.

[6] 1260*a*39–42; 1260*b*2 f. Cf. Ruskin, *Fors Clav.*, III, Letter 28, 14, on the virtue
of the "menial" condition.

[7] Cf. Barker, *op. cit.*, p. 370.

[8] *N. Eth.* 1161*b*1–10, especially 5: ᾗ μὲν οὖν δοῦλος, οὐκ ἐστι φιλία πρὸς αὐτόν, ᾗ δ'
ἄνθρωπος.

[9] Cf. his reference to Cleisthenes' gift of Athenian citizenship to many slaves;
also his own emancipation, by will, of five of his own slaves (Diog. L. V. 1. 9).

the slave receives from his master a moral exchange value for his physical service.[1]

There is a certain economic and moral truth, also, in the attitude of Aristotle toward slavery, that, as Ruskin has observed,[2] higher civilization and culture must have a foundation of menial labor, and that the only justification of such a situation is in the assumption that some are naturally fitted for the higher, and some for the lower, sphere.[3] Such modern laborers are not technically slaves, but Aristotle would insist that they are in a still worse condition, since they are deprived of the humanizing and moralizing influences of a rational master. The plausibility of such a contention would be well illustrated by the wretched condition of multitudes of negroes after the Civil War, as also by the hopeless life of a large portion of the modern industrial army. Moreover, the economic slavery of many of the common toilers today is less justifiable than the domestic slavery advocated by Aristotle, for it too often means a life of indolence and self-indulgence for the masters, instead of that Greek leisure which gave opportunity for higher activity.[4]

MONEY

To the theory of money Aristotle makes a substantial contribution. He agrees with Plato that money found its origin in the growth of necessary exchange, which in turn resulted from an increased division of labor. Unlike Plato, however, he gives a detailed history of the development of money.[5] Before its invention, all exchange was by barter.[6] But with the growth of commerce, barter became difficult, and a common medium of

[1] Cf. Barker, *op. cit.*, p. 370.

[2] *Sesame and Lilies*, end of lecture on "Kings' Treasuries"; cf. *Fors Clav.*, VII, 9 (Vol. XXIX, 230); *Mun. Pul.*, 130, note; cf. *Fors Clav.*, III (Vol. XXVII, 515 f.). Lett. 28, 13 ff., on the workman as a serf.

[3] Barker, *op. cit.*, 368.

[4] On the servile condition of the modern laborer, cf. Ruskin as above; a common idea also of Carlyle and of many modern economic writings.

[5] *Pol.* 1257a31 ff., praised for its exactness and insight. Cf. Poehlmann, *op. cit.*, I, 585; Dühring (*op. cit.*, p.23) belittles it. Newman (*op. cit.*, II, 184) points to ξενικωτέρας as implying that the increased distance between buyers and sellers also caused the origin of money.

[6] *N. Eth.* v. 5.1133b26–28.

exchange was agreed upon.[1] Something was chosen that was a commodity, having intrinsic value (ὁτῶν χρησίμων αὐτὸ ὄν) and that was easy to handle (εὐμεταχείριστον) in the business of life such as iron, silver, or other metal.[2] It was first uncoined, defined merely by size and weight.[3] Finally, to avoid the inconvenience, it was given a stamp (χαρακτήρ) representative of the quantity (σημεῖον τοῦ πόσου).[4] Thus arose the use of money as a convenience in necessary exchange, but once having arisen, it became the foundation of false finance and retail trade, which are pursued as a science of gain.[5] All this accords well with the facts as now accepted, yet how utterly different is Aristotle's standpoint from that of the modern historian of economic institutions is revealed by his last statement, and indeed by the setting of the entire passage. His history of money is merely incidental to his purpose of showing that money is the parent and the very life of the false finance which he decries.

He is also more explicit than the other Greek theorists on the function of money. He clearly recognizes the two functions noted by Plato,[6] but he deals with them in a much more detailed manner. His discussion grows out of his theory of distributive justice presented in the Ethics.[7] Money was introduced as the exchangeable representative of demand (ὑπάλλαγμα τῆς χρείας),[8] since diverse products must be reduced to some common denominator.[9] It is thus a medium of exchange, acting as a measure of all inferior and superior values, by making them all commensurable (συμβλητά).[10]

---

[1] Pol. 1257a31-36; ξενικωτέρας γὰρ γενομένης τῆς βοηθείας τῷ εἰσάγεσθαι ὧν ἐνδεεῖς καὶ ἐκπέμπειν ὧν ἐπλεόναζον, ἐξ ἀνάγκης ἡ τοῦ νομίσματος ἐπορίσθη χρῆσις, etc.

[2] Ibid. 36-38; εὐμεταχείριστον could mean "malleability," but probably not, since he considers coinage to be an afterthought.

[3] Ibid. 38 f.   [4] Ibid. 39-41.   [5] 1257b1-5.

[6] As a symbol of exchange (ξύμβολον τῆς ἀλλαγῆς) it is a medium of exchange and a measure of value (Rep. 371B; Laws 742A-B, 918B).

[7] v. 8. 1133a18-1133b28.   [8] 1133a29.   [9] Ibid. 5-19; 25; 27 f.; 1133b10, etc.

[10] 1133a19-22, 25 f.; 1133b16; 22; ix. 1164a1 f.; Pol. 1258b1-5, μεταβολῆς χάριν; 1257a30 ff. Stewart (op. cit., I, 416 ff.) thinks that the author meant to apply the corrective (διορθωτικόν) function of justice also to money, in that it makes exchange more fair and uniform. As evidence, he points to N. Eth. 1131a18 ff. and 1133a19-22, where the functions of justice and money are defined in similar terms. Cf. also his interesting remarks on the dianemetic function, which prompts exchange and distribution.

The other important function of money recognized is as a guaranty (ἐγγυητής) of future exchange. It represents the abiding, rather than the temporary, need, and is thus a standard of deferred payments.[1] The importance of money in the fulfilment of these functions is great, in the opinion of Aristotle. The possibility of fair exchange, or indeed the very existence of organized society depends upon it.[2]

He is also clearer than Plato and Xenophon in his definition of the relation between money and wealth. He severely criticizes the current mercantilistic theory of his day, which identified wealth with a quantity of current coin (νομίσματος πλῆθος).[3] He immediately follows this, however, with a more extended presentation of the opposite error of the Cynics, that money is mere trash (λῆρος), depending for its value entirely upon convention (νόμῳ). This theory, he points out, is based on the fact that, if money ceased to be recognized as legal tender, it would be useless; that it satisfies no direct necessity; and that one might starve like Midas, though possessed of it in superabundance.[4]

Aristotle is here somewhat ambiguous as to his own attitude toward this doctrine. He fails to object that money does not necessarily become valueless when it ceases to be legal tender, and that a similar argument might be used to prove that clothing is not wealth. Instead, he uses the idea as a means of refuting the opposite error, which is more obnoxious to him, and on the basis of it he plunges into his discussion of the true and false finance.[5] This, together with a passage in the *Ethics*, might point to the conclusion that he agreed with the doctrine of the Cynics on money. He states that it was introduced by agreement (κατὰ συνθήκην); that, owing to this, it is called νόμισμα, because its value is not natural but legal; and that it may, at any time, be changed or made

---

[1] 1133*b*10–13.

[2] *Ibid.* 15–18: οὔτε γὰρ ἂν μὴ οὔσης ἀλλαγῆς κοινωνία ἦν, etc.

[3] *Pol.* 1257*b*8 f.

[4] 1257*b*10–18; for the theory of the Cynics, cf. *infra*, especially on *Eryxias*. Cf. Newman, *op. cit.*, II, 188, note, and his reference to Macaulay's note on the margin of his edition of the *Politics*.

[5] 1257*b*19 ff.; cf. the transitional sentence, 18, a slight hint that he accepts the theory.

useless.[1]   In the light of other evidence, however, it seems probable
that he here meant to emphasize merely the fact that the general
agreement of a community is necessary before anything can be
used as a symbol of demand.   In stating that it may be made
useless, he probably referred to money itself, rather than the
material of it, which is, of course, true.   His determined opposition to the mercantile theory of money, as the basis of false
finance, caused him to appear to subscribe to the opposite error.
That, in actual fact, he did recognize the necessity of intrinsic
value as an attribute of money is clearly evidenced by another
passage, where he specifies it.   He says that the material chosen
as money was a commodity and easy to handle.[2]   This can mean
only that it is subject to demand and supply, like any other object
of exchange.   This inference is substantiated by another passage,
which declares that the value of money fluctuates, like that of other
things, only not in the same degree.[3]   Moreover, in his enumeration
of the diverse kinds of wealth, money is regularly included.[4]   It
seems evident, therefore, that he did not fall a victim of either
error, but recognized that, though money is only representative
wealth, yet it is itself a commodity, whose value changes with
supply and demand, like other goods.[5]   Since he understood the
use of money as a standard of deferred payments, he also saw
clearly the necessity of a stable monetary standard.[6]

Though Aristotle defines money as representative wealth, like
Plato, he fails to apprehend its meaning as representative, and
therefore productive capital.[7]   In his eyes, such a use of money is

[1] N. Eth. v. 5. 1133a29–31; cf. 1133b20 f., ἐξ ὑποθέσεως; cf. infra, where the
pseudo-Economica takes it for granted.

[2] Pol. 1257a36 f., cited on p. 102.

[3] N. Eth. v. 5. 1133b13 f.: οὐ γὰρ ἀεὶ ἴσον δύναται · ὅμως δὲ βούλεται μένειν μᾶλλον.

[4] Cf. p. 86, n. 1, for passages.

[5] Blanqui (op. cit., pp. 36, 88), Ingram (op. cit., p. 18), DuBois (op. cit., p. 51 and
n. 1), Zmavc (Zeitschr. f. d. ges. Staatswiss. [1902], pp. 76 f.), Palgrave's Dictionary
(art. "Aristotle," p. 54), all admit this conclusion.   Barker (op. cit., p. 380) says that
the idea is hinted at.   Souchon (op. cit., pp. 110 f.) accepts the other view, stating that
this was his purpose, to show the folly of making merely imaginary goods the goal of
all life.

[6] Cf. N. Eth. v. 5. 1133b13 f.

[7] Pol. 1257b5–8, and the whole of 1257b; 1258b1–5.

unjust and contrary to nature. He counts usury (τοκισμός) to be a large part of that false finance, which turns money from its true function to be made an object of traffic.[1] Those who lend small sums at a high rate of interest are contemptible.[2] and petty usury (ἡ ὀβολοστατική) is the most unnatural and violent form of chrematistik, since it makes money reproduce money.[3] It is to be observed, however, that his criticism is directed chiefly against petty interest, and that he does not appear to be thinking of "heavy loans on the security of a whole cargo, but of petty lendings to the necessitous poor, at heavy interest."[4] Though his entire account of false finance exhibits an animus against the precious metals, as its basal cause, and as the source of individual and national degeneration,[5] yet he clearly appreciates their necessary function in the state, and his hostility is actually directed against the spirit of commercialism. Money, the means, has usurped the place of the end, until domestic and public economy alike have come to mean only the vulgar art of acquisition.[6]

The usual explanation of the fact that the Greek theorists failed to grasp the fact of the productive power of money is that loans were almost entirely for consumption, and hence seemed like an oppression of the poor.[7] This explanation, however, does not accord with the facts of Athenian life, at least for Aristotle's day. It is clear from the *Private Orations* of Demosthenes that there did exist an extensive banking and credit system for productive

[1] 1258b25.

[2] *N. Eth.* 1121b34: καὶ τοκισταὶ κατὰ μικρὰ καὶ ἐπὶ πολλῷ. Cf. Zell's translation.

[3] *Pol.* 1258b1–8; but cf. p. 39 on this point. The etymology should not be taken seriously. Ruskin cites Aristotle on this point. Cf. above, p. 39, n. 10.

[4] Cf. Barker, *op. cit.*, p. 385 and n. 2, where he criticizes Poehlmann for his idea that Aristotle "is attacking a great credit system," and "is enunciating a gospel of socialism." But cf. *infra*.

[5] *Pol.* 1257b5 ff.

[6] *Ibid.* 33 ff.; for further discussion of chrematistik, cf. *infra*.

[7] Cf. Haney, *op. cit.*, p. 49: "In Athens, the circulation of capital was inconsiderable, and money was not lent for productive purposes as often as for the purpose of relieving distress"; Souchon, *op. cit.*, p. 93, though (pp. 106 f.) he recognizes the other side.

purposes in the Athens of his time.[1] Moreover, the hostility to
interest and credit was not the rule, but the exception, for Demosthenes and not the philosophers should be accepted as voicing
public opinion on this point. He considered credit to be of as
much importance as money itself in the business world,[2] and
declared one who ignored this elementary fact to be a mere know-
nothing.[3] Indeed, the money-lenders were, to him, the very
foundation of the prosperity of the state.[4] The prejudice of Plato
and Aristotle represent merely the exceptional attitude of the
pure moralist, who because of the questionable tactics of money-
lenders, and the injustice and greed in some phases of contemporary
business life, became critics of all money-making operations.[5]

EXCHANGE

Aristotle, in both the *Politics* and the *Ethics*, deals at considerable length with the subject of exchange.[6] He states that it
arose out of the natural situation (κατὰ φύσιν) and defines this
as "the fact that men had more of some commodities and less of
others than they needed."[7] At first, all exchange was by barter
(ἀλλαγή) and there was no trading except for specific need.[8] The
development of an international commerce of import and export
was made possible by the invention of money. It is this significant
fact that furnishes the line of division between the old natural

---

[1] Cf. Paley and Sandys ed., especially *Or.* xxxvi; Isoc. *Trapeziticus;* Boeckh,
op. cit., I, 160 ff.; V. Brants, "Les operations de banque dans la Grèce antique,"
Le Muséon, I, 2, 196–203; Koutorga, *Le trapézites,* (Paris, 1859); cf. also E. Meyer,
Kleine Schriften.

[2] *Or.* xx. 25.

[3] *Or.* xxxvi, 44: εἰ δὲ τοῦτ' ἀγνοεῖς, ὅτι πίστις ἀφορμὴ τῶν πασῶν ἐστὶ μεγίστη πρὸς
χρηματισμόν, πᾶν ἂν ἀγνοήσειας.

[4] *Ibid.* 57 ff.

[5] Cf. p. 105, n. 7, on Souchon; E. Boehm von Bawerk (*Capital und Capitalzins,*
[1900] I, 17 f. says: "Die Geschäftsleute und Praktiker standen sicher auf der zins-
freundlichen Seite." He accounts for the fact that almost the only passages against
interest are in the philosophers by the inference that to uphold interest was superfluous, and to oppose it was useless. Poehlmann exaggerates both the degree of
credit operations, and the prejudice of Aristotle.

[6] For the Greek terms, cf. p. 40.

[7] *Pol.* 1257a15–17   [8] *Ibid.* 22–28; *N. Eth.* v. 5. 1133b26–28.

economy and the era of commerce and finance, when exchange and money have become the tools for unlimited individual enrichment.[1]

His theory of exchange and just price grows out of his application to exchange of his definition of corrective justice, as a mean between two extremes of injustice.[2] Trade is just when each party to it has the exact equivalent (ἴσον) in value with which he began. Exchange is a mean between profit and loss, which themselves have no proper relation to its true purpose.[3] This does not mean that the traders must receive the same in return (τὸ ἀντιπεπονθὸς κατ' ἰσότητα), but an equivalent, or proportional requital (τὸ ἀντιπεπονθὸς κατ' ἀναλογίαν).[4] It is this fact of proportional requital that makes exchange, and indeed human society, possible.[5] The meaning is illustrated by a proportion in which the producers bear the same relation to each other as their products.[6] By joining means and extremes, the exchangers are brought to a basis of proportional equality (τὸ κατὰ τὴν ἀναλογίαν ἴσον).[7] Thus is determined how many shoes, the shoemaker's product, must be given for a house, the builder's product, and the prices of the two commodities are justly settled, with relation to each other.[8] It is very necessary for just exchange, that such proportional equality be effected before the requital or actual transfer takes place. Otherwise one will gain both superiorities (ἀμφοτέρας τὰς ὑπεροχάς), and

---

[1] *Pol.* 1257a30 ff. These two periods of οἰκονομική and χρηματιστικὴ correspond well to the German terms *Naturalwirtschaft* and *Geldwirtschaft*. Kautz (*op. cit.*, p. 137, n. 4) says that this antithesis was about as clear to Aristotle as it is to moderns. For the terms, cf. *infra*.

[2] *N. Eth.* v. 4. 1132b11–1133b28; cf. also under value and money, above; cf. *Mag. mor.* i. 33. 1193b19 ff.

[3] 1132b11–20; cf. *Rep.* 369B–C; 370B, for a similar idea of Plato.

[4] 1132b33.

[5] *Ibid.* 32–34, especially τῷ ἀντιποιεῖν ἀνάλογον συμμένει ἡ πόλις; 1133b6; 17 f.; Stewart, *op. cit.*, I, 449.

[6] 1133a5–10, cited on p. 83, nn. 2–7; cf. *Eud. Eth.* vii. 10. 1243b28–38.

[7] 1133a10 f.

[8] Cf. p. 83, n. 7. The less valuable product must make up in quantity what it lacks in quality. The proportion thus becomes, γεωργός : σκυτοτόμος : : : *x* pairs of shoes : a quantity of grain of equal value (1133a32 f.). Cf. other methods of statement, 1133b4 f., 22 f.; Stewart, *op. cit.*, I, 453 f.

equality becomes impossible,[1] since the cost of production of things is very diverse.[2] Indeed, the arts themselves could not exist, unless the advantage to the consumer were similar in quantity and quality to the cost to the producer.[3]

The common element in diverse products that makes them commensurable is need, or demand (ἡ χρεία), for reciprocal services.[4] But on the basis of the need of the moment, or under the régime of barter, just exchange would be practically impossible, since the concrete needs of A and B, at any given moment, are not likely to correspond. In such a case, exchange would be a gross disregard of the cost of production. This has been avoided by the introduction of money as a substitute for demand,[5] a symbol of general, rather than specific need. Thus just exchange becomes possible, for money, as the representative of general need, is always equally in demand by all, and, as the common denominator of value, it alone renders it possible for proportional amounts of each product to be exchanged.[6]

Aristotle's basal premise in this theory of fair exchange, that unless an equal quantum of value is received by each party, one must lose what the other gains, has been severely criticized by Menger.[7] He objects that the determining consideration in exchange is not the equal value of exchanged goods. On the con-

---

[1] 1133b1–4.

[2] 1133a11 f.; 16–18: ἑτέρων καὶ οὐκ ἴσων. Cf. Rep. 369C, 370B; Ar. Pol. 1261a22 for a similar idea. Stewart (op. cit., I, 464 f.), following Jackson, interprets, on the basis of 1132a33, the buyer's two advantages to be, if he buys too cheaply, the part of the article still unpaid for, and the money he should have paid for it. Cf. ibid. pp. 455–67 for other interpretations.

[3] 1133a15 f.: ἀνῃροῦντο γὰρ ἄν, εἰ μὴ <ὃ> ἐποίει τὸ ποιοῦν καὶ ὅσον καὶ οἷον, καὶ τὸ πάσχειν ἔπασχε τοῦτο καὶ τοσοῦτον καὶ τοιοῦτον. I follow Jackson, note, pp. 97 f.; Rassow, Forsch., p. 18 (Peters' trans., p. 154, n. 2), in accepting this difficult passage as an integral part of its context, and in interpreting it as above, though aside from the context, it would hardly bear this meaning. Stewart (op. cit., I, 455 ff.) thinks it is an interpolation or note, referring merely to the mechanical fact in the arts that material is receptive to the impression.

[4] 1133a18 f.; 25–28; 1133b6–8; 19 f.; cf. Rep. 369C.

[5] 1133a19–29; cf. Stewart's excellent comments, op. cit., I, 459 ff.

[6] 1133b14–16; 20–22: τοῦτο γὰρ πάντα ποιεῖ σύμμετρα; e.g., if a house is equal to five minae and a bed is worth one, five beds equal one house (23–26).

[7] Handwörterbuch der Staatswwissenschaft, art. "Geld," 2d ed., Bd. IV, 82 f.

trary, men trade only when they expect to better their economic condition. "Um ihres economischen Vortheils willen, nicht um gleiches gegen gleiches hinzugeben; sondern um ihre Bedürfnisse so vollständig als unter den gegebenen Verhältnissen dies zulässig ist zu befriedigen." Each gives the other only so much of his own goods as is necessary to secure this end, and it is this competition in open market that fixes prices. Barker[1] also criticizes Aristotle on the ground that he takes no account of demand in his theory of just price. He states that if the cost of production were the only element to be considered, the doctrine might be correct, but with the entrance of demand, one may buy at a low price and sell at an advance without injustice.

Of course, the bald theory that, in exchange, one necessarily loses what the other gains, is untenable. Yet there is still something to be said for Aristotle. He recognized, as well as Menger, that exchange, as pursued by the retailers, did not square with his idea of just price. This is the very reason why he objects to retail trade. He is presenting exchange, not as it is, but as he believes it should be pursued. His doctrine, in a nutshell, is that the primary purpose of exchange is profit, *defined as economic satisfaction of mutual needs*, not profit in dollars and cents. The equality that he seeks, too, is not so much an equality of value in obols and drachmas, but that each shall receive an equal quantum of economic satisfaction. This is the true standpoint at bottom, and when, as is common, the mere purpose of money-making dominates in the pursuit of exchange, the profit is too often at the expense of the other party. Such exchange certainly does not mean economic advance or general prosperity. It merely makes possible an increase in the inequalities of wealth and poverty. There is much of fallacy in the prevalent idea that business necessarily increases the wealth of a state. Ruskin, though like Aristotle extreme and one-sided in his view, struck at the root of this error. He also declared that the result of exchange should be advantage, not profit, and repudiated the idea that the mere fact that goods change hands necessarily means general enrichment.[2]

[1] *Op. cit.*, p. 384.

[2] Cf. citations above, p. 42, n. 7, and p. 44, n. 2. Cf. DuBois, *op. cit.*, p. 46.

The central truth in their protest needed to be spoken, though both erred in not sufficiently recognizing that the labor involved in exchange creates an added time and place value, and therefore has a right to be called productive. They also failed to observe the fact of the necessary risk involved in the business of exchange, which should be repaid with a fair additional profit. For the cornering of markets and the manipulation of prices, for the sake of individual enrichment, modern economists and statesmen, with Aristotle and Ruskin, are fast coming to have only words of protest.

Moreover, contrary to Barker's assertion, demand, as an element of price, is prominent throughout this discussion of Aristotle. He objects, however, to allowing the effect of demand to overcome unduly the cost of production, thus causing inequality and injustice. According to his idea, each receives the equivalent in value of what he gives, in the sense that it is a resultant of the proportionate influence of both cost and need.[1] We may, nevertheless, observe an excellent example of inconsistency in the fact that, despite his insistence upon just exchange, he appears to treat monopoly as a legitimate principle of finance for both men and states,[2] though his intention in the passage may have been to discuss actual conditions, rather than to idealize.

Naturally, the philosopher shows no concern for a tax on imports as a means of building up the industry and commerce of his state, since he is especially desirous of limiting both. However, he is not blind to the advantages of export and import trade for a nation,[3] but would regulate them with an ethical, rather than an economic purpose.[4] His doctrine of exchange as a form of production has been discussed above,[5] and will be touched upon further in the following pages. His general criticism of what he terms "false finance" or "chrematistik" ($\chi\rho\eta\mu\alpha\tau\iota\sigma\tau\iota\kappa\acute\eta$) remains for more extended treatment.

We have seen that he recognizes the necessity of a limited form of exchange, free from the purpose of gain, and considers such

[1] Cf. Haney, *op. cit.*, p. 48.   [2] *Pol.* 1259a2 f.; 33–35.   [3] iv (vii). 6. 1327a25–30.

[4] *Rhet.* i. 4. 7: $\pi\epsilon\rho\grave\iota\ \tau\hat\omega\nu\ \epsilon\grave\iota\sigma\alpha\gamma\omicron\mu\acute\epsilon\nu\omega\nu\ \kappa\alpha\grave\iota\ \grave\epsilon\xi\alpha\gamma\omicron\mu\acute\epsilon\nu\omega\nu$, as among the subjects for a statesman's consideration; cf. also 11.

[5] Pp. 89 and notes.

trading to be natural and in accord with that interdependence
which nature demands.¹ He calls it the very bond of the social
organization,² and even considers international commerce to be
necessary for the prosperity of a state.³ We have also seen that
he goes so far as to advise the rich in a democracy to give the poor
a start in business,⁴ but that exchange, in its prevalent form, is
to him a method of cheatery, in which one gains what the other
loses.⁵

On the basis of this prejudice, he builds his argument for
domestic economy (οἰκονομική) as opposed to false finance.⁶ We
will therefore consider his entire theory of this relation at this
point, for the term "chrematistik," though more inclusive than
exchange (μεταβλητική), has trade in either goods or money (καπηλική) as its predominating element, and the two terms are often
used by him as synonyms. He employs the word χρηματιστική
in several significations—usually of unnatural finance, or the art
of money-making by exchange of goods or money; sometimes as
synonymous with κτητική, the general term for the entire business
of acquisition, including both natural and unnatural finance;⁷
again, of the natural finance, which is a part of domestic economy.
His confusion results partly from his futile attempt to separate
landed property from general industry and commerce.

His main contention is that there is a vital distinction between
domestic economy, whether of householder (οἰκονόμος) or statesman, and the art of acquisition or finance, as usually pursued.

¹ *Pol.* 1257a28–30; vi (iv). 4. 1291a4–6; 1291b19 f.; vii (vi).7. 1321a6, all seem
to take retail and wholesale trade in the state for granted. But it is not named in the
list of necessary callings in the ideal state, 1328b24 ff.; 5 ff.; cf. also 1329a40 ff. Of
course the citizens are not to engage in it (1328b37 ff.).

² *N. Eth.* v. 8. 1132b4 f.; 1133a27; all of chap. 8; cf. above, on just exchange.

³ *Pol.* iv (vii). 6. 1327a25–28.

⁴ vii (vi). 5. 1320a39: ἀφορμὴν ἐμπορίας. Cf. p. 96.

⁵ Cf. discussion above of just exchange.

⁶ *Pol.* i. chaps. 8–11. Ruskin does not seem to have used the term "chrematistik,"
and he has no reference to this passage, though, as seen above, he has much to say in
the same general spirit.

⁷ *Pol.* 1256a11 f.; cf. p. 40 on Plato's terms for trade. For the word χρηματιστική,
cf. *Rep.* 415E, contrasted to soldiers; *Gorg.* 477E, the art that frees from poverty;
452C; *Euthyd.* 304C, of the Sophists; Xen. *Econ.* ii. 18, where no prejudice is implied.

The primary function of the art of finance is to provide, while that of domestic economy is to use what is provided.[1] There are, however, many methods of acquisition (κτητική; χρηματιστική), some of which truly belong to the sphere of domestic economy.[2] The provision of all that is furnished by nature herself, as necessary to human existence, then, if not already at hand (ὑπάρχειν), belongs properly to domestic economy.[3] It both uses and provides genuine wealth, such as is limited in amount (οὐκ ἄπειρος) yet sufficient for independence (αὐτάρκεια) and the good life.[4] But the use of such wealth is its chief business.[5] The other kind of acquisition, which is unlimited, or chrematistik, is contrary to nature, and is not in the province of domestic economy.[6] This unnatural finance, since it deals chiefly in the exchange of money and other commodities, may be termed retail trade (καπηλική).[7] Though itself false, it is a logical outgrowth (κατὰ λόγον) of the true form of exchange that is limited to actual needs[8] as a result of the invention of money.[9] But the real reason for its pursuit is to satisfy an evil and unlimited desire for material things.[10] It produces money merely through the exchange of money (διὰ χρημάτων μεταβολῆς,[11] and its beginning and end is unlimited currency.[12]

---

[1] *Pol.* i. 8. 1256a10–12; but cf. *N. Eth.* i. 1. 1094a9: τέλος οἰκονομικῆς δὲ πλοῦτος; and *Pol.* iii. 4. 1277b24 f.: ἐπεὶ καὶ οἰκονομία ἑτέρα ἀνδρὸς καὶ γυναικός· τοῦ μὲν γὰρ κτᾶσθαι τῆς δὲ φυλάττειν ἔργον ἐστίν. An American economist would hardly make the latter distinction. Newman (*op. cit.*, II, 166) thinks that in these two passages he states the actual condition, but cf. *infra*, where Aristotle admits a degree of acquisition in domestic economy.

[2] 1256a15 ff.   [3] 1256b26–39.

[4] *Ibid.* 30–37; cf. above on the definition of wealth.

[5] 1258a19 ff. He would combat the common idea that the first business of economics is to provide unlimited revenue (1259a35; 1254a1 f.)

[6] 1256b40–42; 1257a4 f.; 17 f.; cf. *Eud. Eth.* iii. 4. 1232a6–9.

[7] 1257b1 f.; 9 f.   [8] 1257a18 f., 28–30; 1257b19 f.; 31 ff.

[9] 1257a31 ff. Poehlmann (*op. cit.*, I, 599) cites Schaeffle, *Bau und Leben des sozialen Körpers*, I, 256, that this analysis of the change from natural to capitalistic economy holds "im Kern die ganze moderne Kritik des Kapitals," but the standpoint of the two is essentially different.

[10] 1258a1–14. Extreme desire demands superfluity (ὑπερβολή).

[11] 1257b20 f.   [12] *Ibid.* 23 ff.

This false form of acquisition is often confused with necessary exchange, because both deal with money.[1] Their aims, however, are quite diverse. The latter treats the accumulation of money (αὔξησις) as a means, while the former treats it as the supreme end of life.[2] In fine, then, Aristotle teaches that necessary chrematistik has to do with the supply and use of life's necessities, is natural (κατὰ φύσιν or οἰκειοτάτη) and limited,[3] its prime function being the proper disposal of products.[4] It is an honorable pursuit,[5] dependent chiefly upon fruits and animals,[6] and involves a practical knowledge of stock (κτηνή), farming, bee-culture, trees, fish, and fowl.[7] The false finance, on the other hand, is unnatural, dishonorable, and enriches at the expense of another.[8] Its chief business is commerce (ἐμπορία), including sea-trade (ναυκληρία), inland trade (φορτηγία), and shop-trade, (παράστασις).[9] It also comprises usury (τοκισμός) and hired labor, both skilled and unskilled (μισθαρνία ἡ μὲν τῶν βαναύσων τέχνων ἡ δὲ ἀτεχνῶν).[10]

Aristotle also distinguishes a third type of finance (χρηματιστική) which shares in the nature of both those above described. It deals with natural resources and their products, but with things

[1] *Ibid.* 35 f. The two uses overlap (ἐπαλλάττει).

[2] *Ibid.* 36–39. [3] 1258a16–18.

[4] *Ibid.* 19 ff. The other function is secondary (ὑπερετική).

[5] *Ibid.* 39 f. [6] *Ibid.* 37 f. [7] 1258b12–21.

[8] *Ibid.* 1 f.; cf. 1256a40 ff., where καπηλεία is opposed to αὐτόφυτον ἔχουσι τὴν ἐργασίαν.

[9] 1258b20–23.

[10] *Ibid.* 25–27. This contrasted yet overlapping relation between the two kinds of finance is well represented by Haney, *op. cit.*, 46, by two circles, as follows:

Cf. also Ashley, *op. cit.*, p. 340, for a synopsis of the divisions of κτητική.

which, though useful, are not fruits (ἀκάρπιμα), such as wood-cutting (ὑλοτομία) and mining in all its branches (μεταλλευτική).[1] The meaning may be best apprehended if, with Ashley,[2] we observe that οἰκονομική is characterized, not only by direct acquisition of nature's products, but also by a personal use of the same, while the unnatural finance has neither of these qualities. The medium kind, then, is like the former, in that it involves direct acquisition of natural resources, but like the latter, in that it does not acquire for directly personal use, but for exchange. It consists, therefore, not so much in the arts themselves, as in the exchange that is based on them.

In the discussion of the so-called false finance, Aristotle thus reveals a markedly hostile attitude to any extensive development of exchange. The middleman is considered to be a parasite and necessarily degenerate by the very fact of his business.[3] As seen above, his criticism was doubtless directed chiefly against the mean and dishonest spirit in the actual retail trade and money-loaning of his day.[4] Yet here also, just as in the *Ethics* passage above discussed, his prejudice blinds him to the fact that exchangers may be real producers, and that, after all, even the alleged false finance is not unlimited, but that it is distinctly bounded by economic demand.[5] Still worse, he includes hired labor of every kind under unlimited acquisition, merely because it has·some of the other qualities of that type of economy, though it certainly does not tend to unlimited enrichment even as much as agriculture.[6] However, he should be given credit of being a forerunner of the modern

---

[1] 1258b27-33.

[2] *Op. cit.*, pp. 333 ff., more satisfactory than Jowett's idea that the intermediate-ness consists either in exchange for money of the direct products of the earth, or else that wood-cutting and mining are themselves the intermediate form; or than New-man's (*op. cit.*, II, 202 f.) theory that it consists in the fact that in this type wealth is sought, not from fruits or animals, but from things, just as exchange seeks wealth from other men or from money, as Ashley shows. However, two questions still remain unanswered: why Aristotle has three forms in chap. 11 and only two elsewhere; and why the terms, ἀκάρπων, wood-cutting, and mining are so prominent, if their relation to the thought is only incidental.

[3] *Pol.* iv (vii). 1328b39 ff.; 1327a29-31.

[4] This was a common Greek feeling (Dem. xxv. 46).

[5] But he seems to recognize it elsewhere (*N. Eth.* v. 8).

[6] Cf. DuBois, *op. cit.*, p. 48.

humanitarian economy, which insists that the final goal of all
economics should be proper consumption, and that acquisition
must be relegated to its true place as a means, the supreme end
being human welfare.[1]

POPULATION

Aristotle exhibits an interest in the problem of population in
relation to subsistence in his criticism of Plato for limiting the
amount of property and making it indivisible, while failing to
provide against a too high birth-rate.[2] He states the principle
that, if property is to be limited, there must be a corresponding
limitation on the increase of population,[3] and that the let-alone
policy must be followed by increased poverty.[4] He therefore
criticizes the Spartan law, for encouraging the largest possible
families.[5] It is evident, however, that, as in the case of Plato, his
interest in the problem is prompted chiefly by a moral and political
motive. It arises merely from his desire to limit individual
acquisition, in a small state, artificially constructed, and is to him
in no sense a question of world food-supply.[6]

DISTRIBUTION

In the *Ethics* passage discussed above,[7] Aristotle approaches
a scientific theory of distribution. He observes that just distribution will be a mean between two extremes of unfairness.[8] Unlike
some moderns, however, he realizes that this will not mean
equal shares for all. There must be the same ratio between the
persons, or services, and the things.[9] In the "mutual exchange of

[1] Cf. the entire criticism of chrematistik, and especially 1257b40–42, the contrast between ζῆν and εὖ ζῆν. On this point, cf. above, pp. 109 f. and 87 ff. Zmavc (*Zeitschrift*, etc., p. 52), rightly states that even Adam Smith made his economic theory a subordinate part of his practical philosophy.

[2] An unfair criticism, as seen above.   [4] 1265b6–12.

[3] *Pol.* 1266b8–14; iv (vii). 1335b22 ff.   [5] 1270a40 ff.

[6] Cf. iv (vii). 4. 1326a25–30, especially, τῶν γοῦν δοκουσῶν πολιτεύεσθαι καλῶς οὐδεμίαν ὁρῶμεν οὖσαν ἀνειμένην πρὸς τὸ πλῆθος. Cf. entire chapter.

[7] 1130b ff.; cf. under value, money, and exchange. The terms are διανομή or ἡ τῶν κοινῶν διανομή.

[8] 1131a11.

[9] *Ibid.* 21: καὶ ἡ αὐτὴ ἔσται ἰσότης, οἷς καὶ ἐν οἷς. Cf. above, pp. 55 f. and 60 f., on Plato's idea of equality; cf. *infra* for further comments on Aristotle.

services," the law must be proportional requital.¹ In other words, each should receive an equivalent to what he contributes.² Distribution must thus proceed according to a certain standard of worth or desert (κατ' ἀξίαν τινά).³ If the individuals are unequal, their shares cannot be equal, and it is a prolific source of dispute, whenever equals receive unequal shares, or unequals receive equal.⁴ On the other hand, Aristotle recognizes that it is a difficult matter to determine this standard, by which just distribution is to proceed.⁵ At this point, again, he shows clearly that his paramount interest in the problem is not economic. He names four possible standards—freedom, wealth, noble birth, and general excellence—all of which are distinctly political in their reference.⁶

Though he insists on a fair distribution of wealth to the citizens, he can hardly be said to exhibit as much interest in the welfare of the common people as does Plato. He had not a very ideal conception of human nature in general. He would have thought it not only impracticable, but undesirable to give his doctrine of leisure any extensive application. As seen above, he includes all hired labor under false finance, and relegates all industry, including agriculture, to the slaves and strangers. The life of mechanic and commercial alike is to him ignoble.⁷ He advises that measures be taken to hold the workers in submission and obedience.⁸ His unfair criticism of Plato's *Republic*, however, on the ground that it fails to emphasize sufficiently the welfare of the parts of the state, and that it does not distinguish clearly enough the status of the commons, reveals a spirit that does not entirely disregard the masses.⁹ His demand that no citizen shall lack subsistence,¹⁰ his

---

¹ 1132b32 f.; cf. pp. 107 ff. and notes for a more detailed discussion, and for Greek expressions.

² 1131b27–32: ἡ διανομὴ ἔσται κατὰ τὸν λόγον τὸν αὐτὸν ὅνπερ ἔχουσι πρὸς ἄλληλα τὰ εἰσενεχθέντα. Cf. *Mag. mor.* i. 33. 1193b36 ff. Stewart (*op. cit.,* I, 432) says that the expression ἡ τῶν κοινῶν διανομή, must mean more than distribution by some central authority, for the most important form of it is the distribution of wealth, operating under economic laws that regulate wages and profits.

³ 1131a24–26.

⁶ *Ibid.; Pol.* iii. 1280a7 ff.; 1282b23 ff.

⁴ *Ibid.* 22–24. For Plato, cf. pp. 55 f.

⁷ Cf. above, pp. 113, and 93 ff. on labor.

⁵ *Ibid.* 26–29.

⁸ *Pol.* ii. 4. 1262b2 f.

⁹ 1264a11–17; 36–38; 1264b11–13, all discussed above under Plato.

¹⁰ iv (vii). 1329b41 ff.

provision of the *sussitia* for all,[1] his insistence that, in the market, mere economic self-interest shall not rule,[2] and his emphasis on the importance of a strong middle class in the state,[3] all show that, in the interest of the perpetuity of the state at least, he had some regard for the economic well-being of all classes. It would be wrong to infer from his suggestions for the aid of the masses in a democracy, that he would offer similar advice for the ideal state. Moreover, his chief emphasis in the passage is upon the idea of Mill, that mere hand-to-mouth help of the poor is wasteful, and that what is needed is to aid them to become economically independent.[4] Nevertheless his suggestion does show that he saw clearly the relation that exists in a democracy between the economic condition of the masses and the stability of the state.[5] He says that the genuine friend of the people (ἀληθινῶς δημοτικός) will see that the masses are not very poor, for the best assurance of the abiding welfare of the state is the solid prosperity of the great majority of the population. He therefore advises the rich to contribute money for furnishing plots of land or capital for small business enterprises to the needy poor.[6] However, while the advice seems, on the surface, to favor the commons, it is really a prudent suggestion to the upper classes, appealing to their selfish interest to avoid by this method the danger of a discontented proletariat.[7] Nevertheless, the general economic attitude of Aristotle would warrant including him, with the other Greek thinkers, in the statement of Roscher: "Die hellenische Volkswirtschaftslehre hat niemals den grossen Fehler begangen, über dem Reichtume die Menschen zu vergessen, und über der Vermehrung der Menschenzahl, der Wohlstand der einzelnen gering zu achten."[8]

[1] 1271*a*29–37; 1272*a*12–21.

[2] *N. Eth.* v. chaps. 4–5, discussed above.   [3] *Pol.* vi (iv). 1295*b*35 ff.

[4] v (vi). 1320*a*33 ff.; cf. pp. 95 f.; cf. especially 35: τεχναστέον οὖν ὅπως ἂν εὐπορία γένοιτο χρόνιος, and 1267*b*3 ff. on the insatiety of the masses. He believed hat the state doles for mere consumption aggravated the evil—a very sane doctrinet which our city charity organizations are prone to overlook.

[5] Cf. Poehlmann, *op. cit.*, II, 339 f., on this passage.

[6] Cf. above, n. 4 above, and pp. 95 f.

[7] 1320*a*36: ἐπεὶ δὲ συμφέρει τοῦτο καὶ τοῖς εὐπόροις, and 34, τοῦτο γὰρ αἴτιον τοῦ μοχθηρὰν εἶναι τὴν δημοκρατίαν; viz., undue poverty of the masses.

[8] *Op. cit.*, p. 7; cf. Poehlmann, *op. cit.*, I, 600, on this point.

Aristotle makes clear his attitude toward the institution of private property and other related questions, both in his criticism of other thinkers, and in his own positive suggestions for the ideal state. Through his objections to the systems of Phaleas and Plato, he has acquired the reputation of being the great defender of private property in Greece. We shall see the extent to which this interpretation of him is correct. Our consideration of his theory may be summarized under certain topics which are fundamental to the problem of distribution.

He admits that the doctrine of economic equality may have some wisdom in it.[1] The attempt to equalize possessions may tend slightly to prevent civic discord.[2] Yet it is liable to arouse sedition on the part of the exploited classes,[3] and such relief measures will satisfy the masses only for a time, for they are notoriously insatiate.[4] In his opinion, therefore, the saner remedy is equalization of desires rather than of property,[5] which must be realized by proper education and a right constitution, whereby the upper classes shall not oppress, and the masses shall be held in check. We have here still a valid argument against the more radical type of socialism. It is suggestive of the modern doctrine of private property as a public trust,[6] and presents clearly the antithesis between the attitude of Greek thinkers and that of the modern social democracy.[7]

Aristotle argues further that equalization of property would be powerless to prevent anything more than the merely petty crimes, for the grossest ones are the result of inordinate desire, rather than of inability to provide life's necessities.[8] Moreover, there are many other natural inequalities of life what would remain to arouse discontent.[9] This is a sensible observation that has often been

---

[1] *Pol.* ii. 7. 1266*b*14–25, as advocated by Phaleas; cf. above. Cf. *infra* for Aristotle's advocacy of equality in landed property.

[2] 1267*a*37–39.   [3] *Ibid.* 39–41.

[4] 1267*b*1–4; vii (vi). 1320*a*31; cf. p. 117 on this idea. He does not consider the rise in the cost of living.

[5] 1266*b*28–30.   [6] Cf. Bonar, *op. cit.*, p. 45.

[7] Aristotle, like Plato, strongly emphasizes education as a great cure for the ills of the state (1310*a*15 ff.). It should be common to all citizens, and be publicly supervised (1336*a*22 ff.).

[8] 1267*a*13–17.   [9] 1266*b*38–1267*a*2.

overlooked by modern radical socialists, though its author might have objected further that such personal diversities would also render an abiding equality of property impossible. His previous argument, however, that immorality and crimes are the result of inordinate desire, rather than of economic need, might be answered today by the results of investigations upon the relation of wages to morality.

The doctrine of communistic equality, as preached by some theorists in fifth- and fourth-century Greece, and as satirized by Aristophanes,[1] had no appeal for Aristotle. It was, to him, merely a thinly veiled individualism. He saw through the selfish partisanship of both oligarchs and democrats, and recognized that all men are poor judges in matters that concern themselves.[2] The excessive individualism of the radical democrat of his day, which permitted the majority to confiscate the property of the minority in the name of a false equality, was as hateful to him as it was to Plato.[3] As seen above, he insisted that economic or political equality should not be demanded, except on the basis of equality of service.[4] Exploitation by the radical democracy was, in his eyes, as bad as the rule of a tyrant,[5] and the ruthless individualism of the classes was no better.[6] Like Plato, he would oppose to both of these the common interest, and would unite both masses and classes in the aim to realize the highest moral life for the individual through the state.[7] He refuted the Sophist's theory of social contract and of justice as a mere convention.[8] As Stewart has observed he realized that "more powerful causes than the mere perception

---

[1] *Ecclesiazusae.* Poehlmann (*op. cit.*, I, 403) argues that such ideas were widespread in Greece.

[2] *Pol.* iii. 9. 1280a14–21: σχεδὸν δ' οἱ πλεῖστοι φαῦλοι κριταὶ περὶ τῶν οἰκείων. Cf. 7–31, his discriminating remarks on equality in general.

[3] vii (vi). 5; iii. 10; cf. Haney *op. cit.*, p. 45.

[4] Cf. above on fair exchange; also p. 116 and notes.   [5] vi (iv). 4. 1292a4–38.

[6] vii (vi). 3. 1318b1–5, especially οἱ δὲ κρατοῦντες οὐδὲν φροντίζουσιν; cf. iii. 9. 1280a, especially 22–30, on the false idea of equality on both sides.

[7] i. 1: ζῷον πολιτικόν; 1280a31 ff.; 1252b30 f.; cf. all of chap. 9 to 1281a10.

[8] 1280b10–12, against Lycophron; cf., above, p. 16; καὶ ὁ νόμος συνθήκη καὶ . . . . ἐγγυητὴς ἀλλήλοις τῶν δικαίων, ἀλλ' οὐχ οἷος ποιεῖν ἀγαθοὺς καὶ δικαίους τοὺς πολίτας.

of material advantage brought men into social union and keep them in it."¹ Each citizen, he held, is not his own master, but all belong to the state. Each is a member (μόριον) of the social body, and the concern of each is naturally relative to the good of the whole.²

Aristotle's further criticisms, of minor significance, on the suggestions of Phaleas and Plato for equality of possessions are as follows: They have taken no precautions to regulate population accordingly.³ They set no proper limit between luxury and penury for individual possessions.⁴ Plato's system is not thoroughgoing, since it allows inequalities in personal property, a criticism also valid against his own proposals.⁵ Phaleas failed to include personal property in his system of equality.⁶ Such strictures seem to proceed from his pedantic desire to criticize inconsistency. However, he may have apprehended more clearly than did Plato the danger of the press of poverty that must eventually result from a system like that of the *Laws*.⁷

Our author is also strong in his denial of either the wisdom or feasibility of the communism in the *Republic*.⁸ He argues that Plato's proposed family communism is based upon the false principle that a state must be composed of like elements,⁹ and shows that it must fail to accomplish its end of harmony, for Plato's "all" must mean all collectively.¹⁰ But this must result, if realized, in a decrease of devotion,¹¹ and thus in a lack of the very harmony sought,¹² since one of the chief sources of attachment in the world is exclusive ownership.¹³ He would deem such a measure,

---

¹ *Op. cit.*, II, 304.

² *Pol.* v (viii). 1. 1337a27–30, a remarkable passage, suggestive of Plato and of St. Paul's analogy of the body. Aristotle paints vividly the antithesis between political and economic equality, whereby there grows up a state within a state (1295b-13 ff.), for he believes with the author of *Eud. Eth.* vii. 10. 1242a, that man is not only a πολιτικόν, but also an οἰκονομικόν ζῷον. Cf. Poehlmann, *op. cit.*, I, 276 ff.

³ 1266b8–14; 1265a38–42; unfair to Plato, as seen above.

⁴ 1266b24–28; 1265a28–38.   ⁵ 1265b22 ff.   ⁶ 1267b9–13.

⁷ Cf. his criticism of the Spartan system, 1270a40 ff.

⁸ On its wisdom, cf. *infra;* on its feasibility, cf. 1263b29: πάμπαν ἀδύνατος.

⁹ 1261a16–1261b15.   ¹¹ 32–35.

¹⁰ 1261b30–32; 24–28.   ¹² 1262b4–24.   ¹³ 22–24.

therefore, more fitting for the third class, since a weakening of their ties of affection might result in greater submission to the rulers,[1] another striking evidence of the gulf that separates the ideal of Greek political thought from the spirit of modern democracy.

Moreover, he considers Plato's assumption that a state, to be a unity, must be devoid of all private interests, to be gratuitous,[2] and argues that the common possession of anything is more likely to cause strife than harmony.[3] In his opinion, the present system of private property, if accompanied by a right moral tone and proper laws, combines the advantages of both common and individual ownership.[4] The tenure of property should therefore be private, but there should be a certain friendly community in its actual use.[5] Thus will be avoided the double evil of strife and neglect, which must result from dissatisfaction and lack of personal interest under communism.[6] He offers as a substitute for the Platonic doctrine, then, his own ideal of reciprocal equality (τὸ ἴσον τὸ ἀντιπεπονθός) as the real cement of society.[7] In any event, he asserts, the present evils do not result from private property, but from the depravity of human nature (μοχθηρίαν),[8] and the aim should be to improve this by moral and intellectual culture, rather than to attempt amelioration by the establishment of an entirely new system.[9] The latter method would result, even if successful, not only in escape from some of the present evils, but also in the loss of the present advantages of private tenure.[10]

The foregoing arguments all show remarkable practical insight, and have been common in the modern criticism of socialism. The objection that individual effort and industry would be paralyzed if bereft of the stimulus of personal interest and ownership, while a general fact of human nature, need not be valid against a system where each has opportunity to develop up to his capacity. There

[1] 1262a40–1262b3.   [3] 1263a11–16.
[2] 1263b30 ff., and preceding note.   [4] 22–26; 39 f.
[5] 26–30, citing the proverb κοινὰ τὰ φίλων. Cf. 1329b14 ff. N. Eth. viii. 8 f. on φιλία; Pol. 1252b29; 1280a25; cf. Xen. Laced. Pol. vi. 3–4.
[6] Cf. preceding note, and 1261b32 ff.   [8] 1263b22 f.
[7] 1261a30 f. N. Eth. v. 5.   [9] 37–42. But Plato used both methods.
[10] 1263b27–29; e.g., besides the personal satisfaction (1263a40 f.), the opportunity for liberality (1263b11–13).

is certainly little to impel the great mass of people to industry under an individualistic system, except the proverbial wolf at the door. But Aristotle is not thinking of the masses. The objection that the evils result from human nature, not from the economic system, may well be pondered by modern socialists and doctrinaire reformers, yet this very fact is an additional reason why the system should be reformed so as to curb such wrong tendencies. The emphasis upon education as a cure for the existing ills is wise, and it might well be more fully recognized by modern socialists, though both Aristotle and later critics of proposed social reforms are wrong in implying that the two methods are mutually exclusive. The warning that, by giving up the régime of private property, we should not only be rid of its evils, but also lose its advantages, should be pondered by agitators against the existing economic system. Modern socialists might also learn much from Aristotle and the other Greek thinkers in regard to the true social ideal, as not primarily materialistic and selfish, but moral and social. On the whole, it may be observed that Aristotle's criticism of Plato's alleged communism in the *Republic* would be far more applicable against modern socialism.

As to the *sussitia*, Aristotle proposes a system similar to that of Plato's *Laws*.[1] He harshly criticizes the Spartan method, which required every citizen, rich and poor alike, to contribute to the common meals on pain of loss of citizenship.[2] He praises, on the other hand, the Cretan system, which permitted the entire citizenship, including women and children, to be nourished at the common table, at public expense.[3]

We have seen that Plato, in the *Laws*, while apparently granting private property in land, really denies this, since he makes the product of the land practically public property.[4] Aristotle, despite his strictures against communism, advocates a system of land tenure quite similar. His limitation of the freedom of donation or testament, purchase or sale; his demands that the lot shall

---

[1] iv (vii). 10. 1330a5 ff. He would make part of the land public. In the *Laws*, the expense is met by making the product public.

[2] 1271a29–37.

[3] *Ibid*. 28 f.; 1272a12–21.   [4] Cf. above on socialism in the *Laws*.

never leave the family, that it shall always be handed down by legitimate succession, and that no citizen shall ever be allowed to hold more than one allotment, are all Platonic, and make him unquestionably an advocate of family, rather than of private ownership of land.¹ His collectivism is more direct than that of the *Laws*, since he makes part of the land entirely public, to defray the expense of worship and the common meals.² The assignment of lots to the citizens is on the same terms as in the *Laws*, with the exception that the owners are masters of the product of their lots.³ Despite his criticism of Plato's division of homesteads, he has the same plan.⁴ As in the *Laws*, only citizens are landowners, and this includes only the governing and military classes,⁵ while all husbandmen are to be public or private slaves.⁶ Unlike Plato, however, Aristotle does not attempt to avoid undue inequalities in personal property.⁷ He sets no maximum above which limit goods must be confiscated, nor does he, as Plato, establish a rigorous system of laws to hamper trade and to make money-making operations practically impossible. He recognizes that such regulations are not feasible, and his legislation is therefore more considerate of human nature, despite the fact that his hostility to the ideal of commercialism is even more pronounced than is that of Plato.⁸

It is evident from the preceding outline of Aristotle's negative and positive doctrine on the matter of private property that his system is in substantial agreement with that of Plato's second state.⁹ Besides the points of similarity noted above, he agrees with his predecessor in emphasizing strongly the power of the state over the life of the citizens. Both insist that the citizen belongs, not

---

¹ *Pol.* ii. 1270*a*21 f.; viii (v). 1309*a*23–25, though rather a measure for an oligarchy; vii (vi). 1319*a*8–13, for a democracy, also against mortgage on land; cf. Guiraud, *La Prop. fonc.*, p. 591. Like Plato, he opposes free disposal of dowries (1270*a*23–25).

² Cf. p. 122, n. 1.   ³ 1330*a*9–23.   ⁴ 1265*b*24–26.   ⁵ iv (vii). 1329*a*18–21.

⁶ 1330*a*25–31; 1328*b*40; 1329*a*2; cf. Souchon, *op. cit.*, pp. 169 f., on his system as compared with that of the *Laws*.

⁷ Cf. p. 120, n. 5; but cf. viii (v). 1308*b*16–19 for a recognition of the desirability of such a regulation.

⁸ Cf. above, his criticism of chrematistik, *Pol. i.* chaps. 8–10.

⁹ So Souchon, *op. cit.*, p. 167; cf. above for differences in detail.

to himself, but to the state, and can realize his best life only through the state.[1] Thus Aristotle is far from being a defender of private property in the absolute sense. On the other hand, his emphasis upon the social obligation of individual possession is, if not social-istic, at least very modern. He is certainly a much better socialist than the alleged communist of the *Republic*, whom he criticizes so severely. Like the Plato of the *Laws*, he is a semi-collectivist. As Barker has observed,[2] Aristotle thought in terms of land, while modern socialism thinks in terms of capital and labor. Both standpoints involve social ownership and the limitation of the indi-vidual, and in this respect the Greek thinker was socialistic in tendency. But despite their social spirit and their trend toward nationalism, which is so strong in all progressive countries today, neither he nor Plato was a socialist, in the modern sense, in spirit or in aim.[3] Any attempts at direct comparison with modern social-ism, therefore, are likely to be fanciful and confusing. Whatever analogy there is between them is of a very general nature and should not be pressed.[4]

[1] Cf. pp. 119 f.; 1280b35 ff. He does not overlook the complement of this prin-ciple, that the prosperity of the whole involves that of the parts (iv [vii].1328b37 ff.; 1329a18–21), his unjust criticism of Plato on this point. Zmavc (*Zeitschrift*, etc., p. 56, n. 3) rightly observes that there is more truth in this Greek doctrine of the relation of the individual to the state than moderns are prone to recognize.

[2] *Op. cit.*, p. 391.

[3] Francotte (*L'Industrie*, II, 250) strongly emphasizes their extreme limitation of the individual. Souchon (*op. cit.*, p. 170) refers to them as precursors of Marx, though he recognizes the difference in their aim.

[4] Poehlmann is an example of such exaggerated analogy. Cf. I, 599, where he makes Aristotle's theory of interest the source of the Marxian theory of value, and unduly presses the analogy between his chapter on chrematistik and modern criti-cisms of capital. For further Greek communistic theories after Aristotle, cf. *infra*.

CHAPTER VII

MINOR PHILOSOPHERS, CONTEMPORARIES OR SUCCESSORS OF PLATO AND ARISTOTLE

The minor philosophers, contemporaries or successors of the Socratics, present in their extant fragments some ideas on wealth and other economic problems that are worthy of note. For purposes of convenience, we shall group them all here, though some of them would chronologically precede one or both of the greater philosophers. The successors of Plato in the Academy, Speusippus, Xenocrates, and Crantor,[1] carried forward the teaching of the Socratics on wealth, as opposed to the more extreme doctrine of the Cynics and Stoics.[2] There was, however, probably less emphasis on matters economic in their writings, since their prime interest was in practical individual ethics rather than in the political morality of Plato and Aristotle, though Xenocrates is known to have written an *Economicus*.[3]

Theophrastus,[4] the first and greatest successor of Aristotle in the Peripatetic school, was the author of a treatise on wealth, of which we know only the name.[5] He also probably dealt somewhat with economic subjects in his *Ethics* and *Politics*, but only slight fragments of either work are extant. He reveals slightly greater regard for the importance of external goods than Aristotle, perhaps because of his special love for the quiet and leisure of the scholar's life.[6] There is, however, no evidence that he went so far as to

---

[1] Third century B.C.; cf. Zeller, *op. cit.*, II, 1, 986 ff.

[2] Cic. *De fin.*, iv. 18. 49; Plut. *Adv. Stoicos*, p. 1065: οἱ τοῦ Ξενοκράτους καὶ Σπευσίππου κατηγοροῦντες ἐπὶ τῷ μὴ τὴν ὑγείαν ἀδιάφοραν ἡγεῖσθαι μηδὲ τὸν πλοῦτον ἀνωφελές. On Crantor, cf. *Ap. Sext. Emp.* (Bekker, p. 538, ll. 4 ff.); on the above, cf. Heidel, *Pseudo-Platonica* (dissertation, Chicago, 1896), p. 60, n. 5; cf. also *Def.* 140, of Speusippus (Mullach, *op. cit.*, III, 80): πλοῦτος κτῆσις σύμμετρος πρὸς εὐδαιμονίαν.

[3] For discussion of all the *Economica*, cf. *infra*.

[4] Born *ca.* 370 B.C. (Zeller, *op. cit.*, II, 2, 807, n. 1), a voluminous writer, from whom a substantial amount is extant, notably his *Characters*.

[5] περὶ πλούτου (*Aspas. in Eth.* 451; and Cic. *De officiis* ii. 16. 56).

[6] Cf. Zeller, *op. cit.*, II, 2, 856.

ascribe a positive value to wealth as such. On the contrary, he advises that one render himself independent of it by living a simple life,[1] and urges against vulgar display.[2] Like Aristotle, he prefers moderate wealth,[3] and finds its chief value in the fact that it enables one to have the distinction of giving splendid gifts to the people.[4] He approaches the cosmopolitan spirit of the Stoics in his emphasis upon the natural relationship of all men,[5] a result of the broadening vision due to the unification of Greece under the Macedonian Empire. There is nothing of interest from other members of the Peripatetic school, except the *Eudemian Ethics* and *Magna moralia*, which were included in our discussion of Aristotle, and the pseudo-Aristotelian *Economica*, which will be discussed in the following pages.

THE ECONOMICA

Economica were one of the characteristic types of Greek literature, after the *Economicus* of Xenophon.[6] They discussed wealth from the ethical standpoint, dealt largely with domestic, rather than public, economy, and considered questions of human relations, such as slavery and the married life. They are, in general, imitations of Xenophon and of Aristotle's *Politics*, and add very little of interest to the economic theory of the Socratics. Aside from the work, falsely ascribed to Aristotle, to be discussed below, *Economica* were written by Antisthenes,[7] Xenocrates,[8] Philodemus,[9]

---

[1] Stob. *Flor.* iv. 283, No. 202, ed. Mein.: ὁ αὐτὸς (Theophrastus) ἔλεγεν ὀφείλομεν ἑαυτοὺς ἐθίζειν ἀπὸ ὀλίγων ζῆν, etc.

[2] *Theophrasti Opera*, ed. Wimmer, iii. 231. fr. 86 f.; Plut. *Lycurg.* 10.

[3] Theoph. *Op.* iii. 182. fr. 78: οὐδὲν πλέον ἔχουσιν οἱ πλούσιοι τῶν μέτρια κεκτημένων, etc. (Plut. *Cupid. Divit.* 527).

[4] Cic. *De officiis* ii. 16. 56.

[5] Porph. *De abstin.* iii. 25.

[6] Cf. above on Xenophon.

[7] Cf. *infra* on Cynics; Diog. L. vi. 1. 16; not extant.

[8] Diog. L. iv. 12; not extant.

[9] περὶ οἰκονομίας; for fragments, cf. ed. Jensen (Teubner). He was an Epicurean; cf. M. Hoderman, "Quaestionum Oeconomicarum Specimen," *Berliner Studien f. Class. Phil.*, XVI, 4 (1896), 38 f., for a summary statement of his teaching.

Metrodorus of Lampsacus,[1] Hierocles,[2] Dio Chrysostom,[3] Plutarch,[4] and the New-Pythagoreans,[5] Bryson,[6] Callicratidas,[7] Periktione,[8] and Phintys.[9]

The pseudo-Aristotelian *Economica*[10] require no extended discussion, since most of the material that is of interest in them is an imitation of Aristotle's *Politics* and Xenophon's *Economics*. Book i

[1] Diog. L. x. 11. 24: περὶ πλούτου; probably opposed to the Cynic ideas on wealth. Cf. Hoderman, *op. cit.*, 37 and note.

[2] For the few fragments, cf. Stob. lxxxv. 21 (Vol. III, p. 150, ed. Mein.), of Stoic tendency. Cf. F. Wilhelm, "Die Oeconomica der Neupythagoreer," *Rhein. Mus.*, XVII, 2 (1915), 162.

[3] For frag., cf. Stob. *Flor.* xlii. 12 (Vol. II, p. 78, ed. Mein.); 46 (Vol. II, p. 366); lxxiv. 59 (Vol. III, p. 362); lxxxv. 12 (Vol. III, p. 138); of Stoic tendency, though the fragments may not be from him. Cf. Wilhelm, *op. cit.*, p. 162; Hoderman, *op. cit.*, pp. 40 f.

[4] Cf. his *Conjugalia moralia*, which, though it does not bear the name *Economica*, is similar in content to them. Cf. Hoderman, *op. cit.*, p. 43; cf. also his essay, Περὶ Φιλοπλουτίας, which moralizes on the folly of inordinate desire for wealth, in the Stoic vein, e.g., ed. Bern., Vol. III, 524D, p. 357: πενία γὰρ οὐκ ἔστιν ἀλλ' ἀπληστία τὸ πάθος αὐτοῦ καὶ φιλοπλουτία.

[5] Jamblichus (*Vit. Pyth.* 72. 89. 169 f.) says that among the follcwers of Pythagoras were those who were called οἰκονομικοί. They date from about the middle to the end of the second century B.C. Cf. Wilhelm, *op. cit.*, pp. 161–224.

[6] Cf. Stob. v. 28. 15 (p. 680, 7 ff., ed. Wachs.; called οἰκονομικός. Wilhelm (*op. cit.*, p. 164, n. 3) thinks that the entire essay may be extant in a Hebrew translation. Bryson was Peripatetic in tendency. He makes a third division of slaves, in addition to κατὰ φύσιν and κατὰ νόμον; viz., κατὰ τρόπον τᾶς ψυχᾶς. He also gives a catalogue of vocations, similar to that of Xen. *Econ.* i. 1–4, and raises the question as to the function of economics.

[7] Cf. Stob. v. 28. 16 (p. 681, 15 ff.); iv. 22. 101 (p. 534, 10 ff.); v. 28. 17 (p. 684, 16 ff.); v. 28. 18 (p. 686, 16 ff., ed. Wachs.): περὶ τᾶς τῶν οἰκήιων εὐδαιμονίας; composed largely of negative utterances on the rich, and of observations on the relations of the sexes; Platonic and Stoic in tendency. Cf. Wilhelm, *op. cit.*, pp. 177, 222.

[8] Cf. Stob. iv. 25. 50; v. 28. 19 (ed. Wachs.): περὶ γυναικὸς ἁρμονίας and περὶ γυναικὸς σωφροσύνας; similar to Stoics.

[9] Cf. Stob. iv. 23. 61 f. (p. 588, 17 ff., ed. Wachs.); Stoic-Peripatetic in tendency. The two latter deal chiefly with the marriage relation. On the general subject of *Economica*, cf. Hoderman and Wilhelm, as above.

[10] Book iii, in Latin, is of later origin, and is of no economic interest. Book i is perhaps from Eudemus of Rhodes, a pupil of Aristotle and Theophrastus (Zeller, II, 2, 869 ff.), but Philodemus (*De vita* ix) assigns it to Theophrastus (Zeller, II, 2, 944); cf. Susemihl, introduction to his edition of the *Economica*, 1887. Book ii is later, but from the Peripatetic school (Zeller, II, 2, 945).

is largely a repetition of some of Aristotle's theories of domestic economy, the marriage relation, and slavery, with a few unimportant additions and slight differences.[1]   Book ii is almost entirely composed of practical examples of how necessary funds have been provided by states and rulers.

The most distinctive point about the doctrine of the first book is its separation of οἰκονομική from πολιτική as a special science.[2] The author agrees with Aristotle, however, that it is the function of economics both to acquire and to use, though without his specific limitations upon acquisition.[3]   He distinguishes four forms of economy—acquiring, guarding, using, and arranging in proper order.[4]   Elsewhere, he makes a different classification on another basis—imperial, provincial, public, and private.[5]   These are each further subdivided, the first including finance, export and import commerce, and expenditures.[6]

Agriculture is especially eulogized by the author, in the spirit of Xenophon and Aristotle.   It is the primary means of natural acquisition, the others being mining and allied arts whose source of wealth is the land.[7]   It is the most just acquisition, since it is not gained from men, either by trade, hired labor, or war,[8] and it contributes most to manly strength.[9]   Retail trade and the banausic arts, on the other hand, are both contrary to nature,[10] since they render the body weak and inefficient (ἀχρεῖα).[11]

The work agrees with Aristotle, against Plato, in his doctrine that men and women are essentially different in nature, and hence that their work should be distinct.[12]   No attempt is made to justify

---

[1] Cf. Susemihl, *op. cit.*, p. v, n. 1, for a list of parallel passages from Xenophon and Aristotle.

[2] 1343a1–4, especially ἡ μὲν πολιτικὴ ἐκ πολλῶν ἀρχόντων ἐστίν, ἡ οἰκονομικὴ δὲ μοναρχία. Cf. also 14 f.   Cf. Aristotle, above.   Zeller (II, 2, 181, n. 6) points out that *Eud. Eth.* makes a similar distinction, in that he places economics between ethics and politics.

[3] 1343a8 f., though 25 ff. implies the limitation, κτήσεως δὲ πρώτη ἐπιμέλεια ἡ κατὰ φύσιν.

[4] 1344b22 ff.   [6] *Ibid.* 20 ff.: νόμισμα, ἐξαγώγιμα, εἰσαγώγιμα, and ἀναλώματα.

[5] ii. 1345b13 ff.   [7] 1343a25–27.

[8] *Ibid.* 28–30.   Cf. Aristotle, who makes war a natural pursuit.

[9] 1343b2 f.   [10] Cf. preceding n. 8.   [11] 1343b3 f.   [12] *Ibid.* 26 ff.

slavery, though Aristotle is followed in his advice to grant emancipation, as a special reward for faithfulness.[1] The author of Book ii seems to have taken for granted the Cynic theory that money need have no intrinsic value, at least for local purposes. Coinage of iron,[2] tin,[3] bronze,[4] the arbitrary stamping of drachmas with a double value,[5] are all offered apparently as a proper means of escape from financial difficulty. Like Aristotle, he accepts monopoly as a shrewd and legitimate principle of finance.[6] Elsewhere, however, in striking contrast to such uneconomic suggestions, the author states the important economic principle that expenditures should not exceed income.[7] In accord with Greek usage, he is familiar with a tax on exports for revenue and as a means of guarding against depletion of supply.[8]

CYRENAICS

The Cyrenaics were the forerunners of the Epicureans in their more liberal attitude toward wealth. Aristippus,[9] the founder of the school, was a man of the world, who believed in enjoying life as it came.[10] He held that pleasure was always a good, and that all else was of value only as a means of realizing this end.[11] If consistent, therefore, he must have valued highly moderate wealth. His principle that one should aim to realize the highest degree of pleasure with the least economic expenditure is somewhat analogous to the modern economic doctrine of the smallest means.[12] Bion of Borysthenes became a Cyrenaic in his later life, but his satires are almost entirely lost.[13]

---

[1] 1344*b*15 f.; 1344*a*23–1344*b*11.   [3] 1349*a*33 ff.

[2] 1348*b*17 ff.   [4] 1350*a*23 ff.

[5] 1349*b*31 ff. Debasement of the currency was common in the time of the author.

[6] 1346*b*24 ff.; 1347*b*3 ff.; cf. Ar. *Pol.* 1259*a*6–35.

[7] 1346*a*14–16: τὸ τἀναλώματα μὴ μείζω τῶν προσόδων γίνεσθαι.

[8] 1352*a*16 ff.; cf. above on the Socratics, under exchange.

[9] Of Cyrene (435 B.C.), a pupil of Socrates. No genuine fragments of his writings are extant. Cf. Zeller, II, 1, 346 ff.

[10] Cf. Horace *Ep.* i. 17, 23.

[11] Cf. Zeller, II, 1, 346, n. 2, and Xen. *Mem.* ii. 1. 9.

[12] Zeller II, 1, 346, n. 2; cf. Oncken, *op. cit.*, p. 47, a basal principle of hedonism.

[13] Cf. Hor. *Ep.* ii. 2. 60.

EPICURUS AND HIS SCHOOL

Epicurus, though the apostle of hedonism, and heir of the Cyrenaics, taught a doctrine of wealth somewhat similar to that of the Stoics.[1] His "happiness" consisted in living a simple and prudent life. He taught that spiritual wealth is unlimited, and that the wise are contented with things easy to acquire ($εὐπόριστα$);[2] that external wealth, on the other hand, is limited,[3] and that it is not increase of possessions but limitation of desires that makes truly rich.[4] He believed the simplest food to be best,[5] both for pleasure and for health, that many wealthy find no escape from ills,[6] that he who is not satisfied with little will not be satisfied with all,[7] and that contented poverty is the greatest wealth.[8] In accord with his teaching, he seems to have lived very simply.[9] However, he did not go to the extreme of the Cynics and Stoics, but taught that the wise will have a care to gain property, and not live as beggars.[10] He exhibits no tendency toward communism, but rather toward the extreme individualism of the Sophists, and was in sympathy with their social contract theory.[11] Later Epicureanism degenerated by taking the hedonistic principle of its founder too literally. Like the Sophists, the school has influenced modern economic thought through its conception of justice, as a mere convention for mutual advantage.[12]

[1] 342–270 B.C. His theory was far different than the Cyrenaic doctrine of the pleasure of the moment.

[2] Diog. L. x. 130, 144, 146; Stob. *Flor.* xvii. 23.

[3] Usener, *Epicurea* (1887), pp. 300–304, ὥριϲται.

[4] *Ibid.*, p. 302, fr. 473; p. 303, fr. 476.

[5] Diog. L. x. 130 f.

[6] Usener, p. 304, fr. 479.

[7] *Ibid.*, p. 302, fr. 473 f.; cf. Stob. *Flor.* xvii. 30.

[8] Usener, p. 303, and fragments.

[9] Stob. xvii. 34; Seneca *Ep.* 25. 4 f.; Cic. *Tusc. disp.* v. 31.

[10] Diog. L. x. 119; Philod. *De vit.* ix. cols. 12 ff., 27, 40.

[11] Cf. Barker, *op. cit.*, p. 37; cf. above on Sophists; also Dunning, *Political Theories Ancient and Mediaeval* (1913), pp. 103 f.

[12] Cf. Hasbach, *Allgemeine philosophische Grundlagen der Pol. Econ.* (1890), pp. 76 and 36 f.; Dunning, as above.

CYNICS

The Cynics developed the negative attitude of the Socratics
toward wealth to its extreme in asceticism.   Their doctrine was subversive of all economic interest.   Antisthenes, the founder of the
school, was a contemporary of Plato, a Sophist in his youth, but
later associated with the Socratic circle.   He appears prominently
in the *Symposium* of Xenophon.[1]   He urged a return to nature
in the literal sense.[2]   His book on the nature of animals περὶ ζώων
φύσεως) probably presented examples from the animal world as
models for natural human living.   Like many writers of his time
and later, he idealized the life of primitive and barbarous peoples.[3]
In utter antithesis to Aristotle,[4] he declared city life and civilization to be the source of all injustice, luxury, and corruption.
In his opinion, Zeus punished Prometheus, not because he envied
men any good, but because the discovery of fire was the source
(ἀφορμή) of all effeminacy and luxury for men.[5]   Material wealth
was, to him, if not an absolute evil, something about which men
should be entirely indifferent, for in essence, good and evil could have
only a moral reference.[6]   The craving for wealth or power was a
vain illusion.   Nothing was good for a man except what was actually
his own,[7] and this was to be found only in the soul.[8]   Wealth without
virtue was not only worthless, but a fruitful source of evil,[9] and no
lover of money could be either virtuous or free.[10]   He thus advanced

[1] For his life, cf. Zeller, II, 1, 280 ff., and Diog. L. vi.   A few fragments of his
philosophical dialogues are extant.   Cf. above, p. 126, n. 7. for his *Economicus*.   He
and Diogenes are discussed at this point, since the Cynic movement as a whole is
logically post-Aristotelian.

[2] Diog. L. vi. 1. 15; cf. Gomperz, *op. cit.*, II, 117 and note, with citations from
Dio of Prusa; also Zeller, *op. cit.*, II, 1, 325 f. and note, who thinks Plato's ironical
"city of pigs" (*Rep.* ii) may well have been a reference to the ideas of Antisthenes.

[3] Cf. preceding note, and *infra*, on later ideal states.

[4] *Pol.* i. 1253a1–4: ἄνθρωπος φύσει πολιτικὸν ζῷον, etc.

[5] Dionis Prus. *Opera* (ed. Arnim, 1893, or vi. 25 f.), ascribed to Diogenes, but
it was also the idea of Antisthenes. Cf. Gomperz, *op. cit.*, II, 118; compare Rousseau.

[6] Diog. L. vi. 104.   [7] *Ibid.* vi. 12; cf. chap. 9, 105.

[8] Xen. *Symp.* iv. 34, 34–43, on the advantages and disadvantages of the two kinds
of wealth; iii. 8; *Econ.* i. 7 f.; ii. 2 f.

[9] Xen. *Symp.* iv. 35 f.

[10] Mullach, *op. cit.*, II, p. 289, fr. 86: φιλάργυρος.

beyond the Socratic doctrine of ability to use as the criterion of value.

However, though despising wealth, Antisthenes upheld the dignity of free labor. He believed it to be a good by which alone virtue is gained, the source of independence.[1] Like the rest of the Cynics, he was thus doubtless opposed to slavery. The Cynic principle that all diversities in men, except differences in moral character, were merely accidental was a direct argument against slavery.[2] It is also probable that he held the Cynic doctrine that intrinsic value in money is unnecessary.[3]

Diogenes of Sinope, "the philosopher of the proletariat, "became more famous than Antisthenes, owing to his eccentric personality.[4] He carried the Cynic doctrine of wealth to its *reductio ad absurdum* by applying it literally in his own life. His repudiation of wealth and civilization was even more emphatic than that of his predecessor. He taught that wealth without virtue is worse than poverty.[5] Lovers of wealth are like men afflicted with the dropsy, always athirst for more.[6] The desire for money is the very source and center (μητρόπολιν) of all ills.[7] Virtue cannot dwell either in a wealthy state or in a wealthy house.[8] Poverty better accords with it, and is no real cause of suffering.[9] Truly noble men despise wealth and are above being troubled by poverty and other so-called ills.[10]

---

[1] Diog. L. vi. 2, καὶ ὅτι ὁ πόνος ἀγαθὸν συνέστησε διὰ τοῦ μεγάλου Ἡρακλέους καὶ τοῦ κύρου. Heracles, the toiler, was their patron saint. Antisthenes is said to have written two dialogues called Heracles (Diog. L. vi. 2. 18), but Zeller, (*op. cit.*, II, 1, 307, n. 4) thinks only one was genuine.

[2] Cf. *infra* on Diogenes. Ar. *Pol.* 1253b20–22 probably refers to the Cynics, as holding it to be κατὰ φύσιν, οὐδὲ δίκαιον, and βίαιον. Cf. Newman, *op. cit.*, I, 140, n. 2, on this. He cites Strabo, p. 15; 110, on the opposition of the Cynic Onesicritus to slavery. Cf. above, pp. 97 ff.; Zeller, *op. cit.*, II, 1, 280 ff., 323 f.

[3] Cf. *infra* on Diogenes and *Eryxias;* Ar. *Pol.* 1257b10, probably Cynic.

[4] 412-323 B.C.; cf. Zeller, *op. cit.*, II, 1, 280 ff.

[5] Mullach, *F.Ph.G.*, II, 326, fr. 276; cf. Diog. L. vi. 47: τὸν πλούσιον ἀμαθῆ, πρόβατον εἶπε χρυσόμαλλον.

[6] Mullach, II, 302, fr. 27; 327, fr. 285; cf. *infra* on Teles, for like idea.

[7] Mullach, II, 316, fr. 168; Chrysost. *Homil.* lxiv in Matthew points to Paul's parallel, I Tim. 6:10: ῥίζα γὰρ πάντων τῶν κακῶν ἐστὶν ἡ φιλαργυρία.

[8] Mullach, II, 305, fr. 63.   [9] *Ibid.* fr. 66; 65.   [10] *Ibid.* fr. 61; p. 327, fr. 285.

Diogenes was doubtless opposed to slavery and taught that under proper conditions of the simple life there would be no reason for it.[1] In his opinion, the truly free were not slaves, even though they might be in a state of servitude, but the mean-spirited were slavish even though free.[2] He wrote a *Republic* in which he seems to have advocated fiat money to take the place of the hated gold and silver[3] and to prevent the extensive accumulation of movable wealth. He also advocated the community of wives and children,[4] and perhaps some system of land tenure other than private ownership.[5] Crates, the poet of the Cynics,[6] expresses similar sentiments of scorn for wealth, supreme regard for virtue,[7] and glorification of poverty,[8] Menippus and Monimus left little of economic interest.

"ERYXIAS"

The pseudo-Platonic dialogue, *Eryxias*, is of special interest for our study, since it is the only extant work in Greek literature which deals directly and exclusively with the problem of wealth.[9] The work presents nothing new, however, which had not already been observed by the Socratics. The statement of Heidel,[10] that it is "distinctly the most valuable contribution of antiquity to the science of political economy," is therefore an exaggeration.

[1] Gomperz, *op. cit.*, II, 133; Zeller (*op. cit.*, II, 1, 323 f.) is not sure that the Cynics taught a positive anti-slavery doctrine, but cf. p. 132, n. 2.

[2] Diog. L. vi. 66, 74 f.; cf. Epict. *Dissert*. iii. 24. 67.

[3] *Athen.* iv. 159c: Διογένης δ' ἐν τῇ πολιτείᾳ νόμισμα εἶναι νομοθετεῖ ἀστραγάλους.

[4] Diog. L. vi. 72: ἔλεγε δὲ καὶ κοινὰς εἶναι δεῖν τὰς γυναῖκας, etc. Aristotle (*Pol.* ii. 7. 1266a34) names Plato as its sole advocate, but cf. Zeller, *op. cit.*, II, 1, 321 f., n. 4, and Gomperz, *op. cit.*, II, 132, though they think that he did not hold it in the extreme form stated by Diogenes Laertius.

[5] There is no specific evidence, though it would accord well with his other teachings. Cf. Gomperz, *op. cit.*, II, 132.

[6] Called "Thebaios"; flor. *ca.* 328 B.C.; cf. Diog. L. vi. 87.

[7] Mullach, *F. Ph. G.*, II, 334, fr. 6; 338, frs. 38, 39; cf. also Diog. L. vi. 86.

[8] Cf. *The Beggar's Wallet*, an amusing parody of the *Odyssey* (von Arnim, *Leben und Werke des Dio von Prusa* [1898], 255 ff. Gomperz (*op. cit.*, II, n. 545 to p. 125) doubts its genuineness for Crates, but thinks it is from a Cynic source; cf. also *infra* on Teles.

[9] The pseudo-Aristotelian *Economics* is a possible exception. The *Economics* of Xenophon has a broader theme, and the *Revenues* is for practical purposes.

[10] *Pseudo-Platonica*, p. 59.

Nevertheless, the essay is worthy of more notice than it has usually received in histories of ancient economic thought.[1] Whatever consideration has been given to it has been largely devoted to the question of its origin. It reveals points of contact with Plato, the later Socratics, and especially with Antisthenes, the Cynic, with whom the author seems to have been most in sympathy.[2]

The two theses that form the goal of the *Eryxias* are that the wisest men are in reality the wealthiest, and that material wealth is an evil, since they who possess most of it are the most needy of all, and hence most depraved.[3] The keynote of the dialogue is the question of Socrates concerning the wealthy Sicilian, "What sort of a man was he reputed to be in Sicily?"[4] The double thesis is illustrated concretely by Socrates, the wisest, and the Sicilian, the richest but worst of men. The first idea is prominent in *Euthydemus*,[5] and elsewhere in Plato and Xenophon.[6] The second is a favorite doctrine of the Cynics and Stoics,[7] though the general thought may be traced back to Socrates.[8]

Some insight is exhibited by the author into the problem of value. Like Xenophon, he defines property ($\chi\rho\dot\eta\mu\alpha\tau\alpha$) as that which is useful, and thus recognizes this element in value.[9] He also distinguishes general from economic utility.[10] In answer to the question in respect to what particular use wealth possesses utility, he

---

[1] It is given mere passing mention in Boeckh, *op. cit.*, I, 693; Hoderman, *op. cit.*, p. 9; Francotte, *L'Industrie*, II, 310, n. 1; Cossa, *op. cit.*, p. 146; Oncken, *op. cit.*, p. 37; Bonar, *op. cit.*, p. 11, n. 1; Kautz, *op. cit.*, p. 121; Simey, *op. cit.*, p. 474; Hagen, *Observationum oec. pol. in Aesch. dialog.*, *qui Eryx. inscribitur* (dissertation, 1822). The latter has not been examined.

[2] On its origin, cf. Otto Schrohl, *De Eryx. qui fertur Platonis* (dissertation, 1901) which gives a full bibliography, pp. 5 ff.; Heidel (*Pseudo-Platonica*, p. 61), following Steinhart (Mueller, VII, 14), attributes it to a later Socratic, in sympathy with Antisthenes; p. 69, n. 3, he thinks it grew out of *Euthyd.* 288E ff.; for other points of contact, cf. Schrohl, 10 ff.

[3] On the first, cf. 393A–394E, 402E–403C; on the second, cf. 396E–397D, 405C–406B.

[4] Cf. preceding n. 3.   [5] 278E–282.   [6] Cf. above, *in loc.*   [7] For Stoics, cf. *infra*.

[8] Xen. *Mem.* i. 6, especially end: ἐγὼ δὲ νομίζω τὸ μὲν μηδενὸς δεῖσθαι θεῖον εἶναι, etc.; cf. Schrohl, *op. cit.*, pp. 26–28.

[9] 400E, 401A.

[10] 401A: ἀλλὰ ποῖα δὴ τῶν χρησίμων, ἐπειδή γε οὐ πάντα. Cf. also 400E.

states tentatively that it is with respect to bodily needs,[1] an idea
suggestive of the organon theory of Aristotle. By this, he doubtless
means food, clothing, and shelter, which have the quality of rarity.
This, however, is only a step in the argument, which has for its
goal the thesis that intellectual attainments constitute the most
important part of one's wealth, and possess a very real economic
value.[2] The author thus agrees with Plato, Xenophon, the Cynics,
and the Stoics, in his emphasis upon spiritual goods. The distinction between value in use and value in exchange and the necessary dependence of the latter upon the former are also suggested
in the statement that nothing can have economic value except as
there is a demand for it. The money that passes current in one
state may be valueless in another, as also would be the mansion of
the wealthy Polytion to Scythian nomads, since there would be
no demand for them.[3]

The *Eryxias* has no clear or satisfactory definition of wealth.
It is recognized that wealth must be defined before its character
as good or evil can be determined, but the final answer nowhere
appears.[4] In this vagueness of result, one is strongly reminded of
some of Plato's minor dialogues. There is also a certain ambiguity
throughout the work, similar to that observed in Plato,[5] between
wealth in its strict economic sense and excessive wealth. We may
gather from the course of the argument, however, that the author
would define wealth as consisting of things that possess utility, and
are subjects of economic demand, whether external, physical, or
intellectual goods.

The attitude of the *Eryxias* toward wealth is an extreme ver-
sion of that with which we have become familiar in the Socratics,
and is best characterized as Cynic. As seen above, the author
considers external wealth to be an absolute second to wisdom,[6]

[1] 401B, 401E.

[2] 402E, 393E–394E, and the general thesis that the wisest are richest.

[3] 400A-E, 394D, arguing that economic demand might make a man's wisdom
more valuable than another's house.

[4] 399E.

[5] Cf. 399E, where Eristratos defines $\pi\lambda o\hat{v}\tau os$ as $\tau\grave{a}\ \chi\rho\acute{\eta}\mu\alpha\tau\alpha\ \pi o\lambda\lambda\grave{a}\ \kappa\epsilon\kappa\tau\hat{\eta}\sigma\theta\alpha\iota$.

[6] 393A, 393D–394A; cf. above, pp. 24 ff. and notes for Plato and others.

since wisdom is not only itself a means of providing material needs,[1] but also and especially because through it alone does any material wealth become truly valuable.[2] When the latter is made the *summum bonum*, it becomes the greatest evil. Like Plato, Jesus, and Ruskin, he insists that the kingdom of wisdom be given the first place,[3] for things derive their good or evil quality from the character or knowledge of the user.[4] The ironical account of how the Greek fathers, even of the best classes (τῶν μεγίστων δοκούντων) urge their boys to seek wealth, since without this they are, of no account, is almost in the language of Pastor Wagner's condemnation of the extreme commercialism of this age.[5] Material goods, when unwisely used, are a fruitful source of ills,[6] and excessive wealth is always evil.[7] However, the political motive, which prompted the hostility of Plato and Aristotle to excessive wealth, is absent from the *Eryxias*.

Thus far the attitude of the author does not differ very essentially from that of the Socratics, but toward the end of the dialogue the doctrine is distinctly taught that wealth is an evil *per se*. He argues that one's needs are most numerous in a state of sickness, when he is in his worst condition.[8] One is at his best, on the other hand, when he has fewest and simplest needs.[9] But those who have most property are sure to need the largest provision for the service of the body.[10] Thus the richest, as being the most needy, are the most depraved (μοχθηρότατα διακείμενοι) and the most unhappy, and therefore external wealth is essentially evil.[11] Such a characteristically Cynic doctrine is essentially ascetic, and subversive of the very foundations of economics.

[1] 394D–E, 402E.

[2] 393E, 396E–397E, 403E, the insistence upon ability to use, so common in Plato, Xenophon, and Ruskin.

[3] 394D–E, which reads like a passage from the New Testament.   [4] 397E.

[5] 396C: ἂν μέν τι ἔχῃς, ἄξιός του, ἐὰν δὲ μή, οὐδενός. Cf. *The Simple Life:* "He who has nothing is nothing." Cf. Eurip. fr. 328, Danae (Nauck): κακὸς δ' ὁ μὴ ἔχων, οἱ δ' ἔχοντες ὄλβιοι.

[6] 396E–397E; cf. *infra*, the Stoic doctrine of "indifferents"; but they included health and wealth in the same class, while the *Eryxias* does not. Cf. Diog. L. vii. 103; cf. a similar passage in the *Euthydemus;* cf. Schrohl, *op. cit.*, p. 34.

[7] 396E–397E, as above; 393A.   [8] 405D.   [9] 405E.   [10] 406B.

[11] *Ibid.*, but cf. 134, n. 8, where Socrates approaches this asceticism.

The *Eryxias* hints at a definition of capital in the distinction between the direct consumption of wealth and its use for further production.[1] But it is far from the author's purpose to define capital, and he makes nothing of the distinction. The relation of money to wealth is also dealt with incidentally. Like Aristotle, he criticizes the definition of wealth as "the possession of much money,"[2] on the ground that the money of one country may not pass current in another, and hence cannot be true wealth.[3] This is suggestive of the Cynic theory of fiat money, since the examples used are those of the worthless currency of Carthage, Sparta, and Ethiopia.[4] But the argument proves too much, since it would be equally as effective against counting the house of Polytion as true wealth. There is, moreover, a peculiar shift in this part of the dialogue between money and property. The theory of the author is further upheld by the argument that a condition can be conceived in which our bodily needs might be supplied without silver or gold, in which case these metals would be worthless.[5] However, the necessity of intrinsic value for international currency is recognized,[6] and it seems hardly probable that the purpose of the dialogue was to contend that money is never wealth, since the very implication of the argument is that current money is wealth.[7]

TELES

The fragments of Teles exhibit the same extreme asceticism of the Cynics in relation to wealth.[8] His main thesis is that the possession of money does not free from want and need.[9] Many who

[1] 403E, distinguishing the materials of a house, the tools by which they are provided, and the tools for building. Cf. Plato and Aristotle, *in loc.*, for a like distinction.

[2] 399E.   [3] 400A-E.

[4] 400A-B. Heidel (*op. cit.*, p. 61) points to his "ostentatious display of learning" here.

[5] 402B-C, 404A-B.   [6] 400E.

[7] 400C-E, especially ὅσα μὲν ἄρα τυγχάνει χρήσιμα ὄντα ἡμῖν ταῦτα χρήματα, though at this point the term has been made to include all wealth; cf. also 402C: ἀλλὰ ταῦτ' ἂν εἴη (χρήματα) οἷς τὰ χρήσιμα οἷοί τ' ἐσμὲν ἐκπορίζεσθαι.

[8] Cf. *Teletis Reliquiae*, ed. Hense, Freiburg, 1889. The ancient source is Stobaeus. Teles, a Cynic of Megara, wrote about 240 B.C. Cf. Hense, *op. cit.*, XXI–XXXV; Gomperz, *op. cit.*, II, 129 ff. Fr. iv. A, pp. 24 ff., and iv. B, p. 34, are of special economic interest.

[9] Fr. IV, A, pp. 24 ff.

have great possessions do not use them, because of stinginess and sordidness.[1] But if wealth is not used, it is useless, and cannot free from need or want.[2] Here we meet a different application of the criterion of "use" from that with which we have become familiar in the Socratics, the *Eryxias*, and Ruskin. It is based on refusal, rather than inability to use, though the other idea is in the background. The author argues further that wealth does not free from need, because the wealthy life is always insatiate (ἄπληστος),[3] and wealth does not change the disposition,[4] by which change alone the life can be freed from need and slavery.[5] To try to accomplish this by wealth is like attempting to cure a patient of dropsy by stuffing him with water until he bursts.[6] Counsel is given, therefore, not to turn one's sons to the acquisition of wealth, but to study under Crates, who can set them free from the vice of insatiety.[7]

Poverty, on the other hand, does not change the disposition of the temperate man for the worse.[8] There is nothing distressing or painful about it,[9] for Crates and Diogenes were poor and yet passed their life in ease.[10] It is no harder to endure old age in poverty than in wealth, but all depends upon the disposition.[11] Poverty deprives the life of no positive good, but furnishes the opportunity of gaining good,[12] since it is conducive to the contemplative life of philosophy, while wealth is an obstacle to this.[13] It is the poor, rather than the wealthy, who have leisure.[14] They are also obliged to be strong (καρτερεῖν), while the wealthy become effeminate,

[1] Fr. IV, A, p. 24: δι' ἀνελευθερίαν καὶ ῥυπαρίαν.

[2] *Ibid.* 27; cf. the example of the Φορκίδες, who have an eye, but do not use it; cf. also the quotation from the "ancients" on the distinction between χρήματα, "used wealth," and κτήματα, "wealth merely possessed" (ll. 13 f.).

[3] P. 32, the unsated life will not be satisfied even with immortality, since it cannot become Zeus. L. 13 ff., kings are always in want, σπανίζουσιν. Cf. Xen. *Symp.* iv.36.

[4] P. 26, ll. 4 f., 6–12; p. 31.   [6] P. 29, ll. 6 ff.

[5] P. 28, ll. 13–29.   [7] P. 29; cf. pp. 30 f.; p. 26, ll. 11 f.   [8] P. 26.

[9] Fr.; Περὶ αὐταρκείας; p. 9: καὶ τί ἔχει δυσχερὲς ἢ ἐπίπονον ἡ πενία.

[10] *Ibid.*   [11] *Ibid.* Cephalus in *Rep.* i gives a more balanced judgment.

[12] *Ibid.*, pp. 6 f., citing Bion on the answer of poverty to her accusers. Cf. Aristoph. *Plutus* 558 f. on the power of poverty, cited by Ruskin, *Aratra Pentel.*, IV, 139 (Vol. XX, 296).

[13] Fr. iv. B, p. 34, he attacks the opposite thesis.

[14] *Ibid.*, ll. 5 f.; p. 35, good doctrine for a tramp; p. 34.

since they have no impetus to work.[1] Thus poverty, when accompanied with justice, should be more highly honored than wealth.[2] The author concludes that it is therefore best to despise wealth and turn to the life of philosophy, for this develops generosity instead of stinginess, and contentment instead of insatiety. Such a life uses what is on hand, and lives content with present blessings (τοῖς παροῦσι).[3] The marked contrast between this ascetic philosophy of poverty and the saner teaching of Plato, who was as much opposed to poverty as to excessive wealth, is patent.

STOICS

The Stoics were the natural descendants in thought of the Cynics, whom they resemble closely in their attitude toward external goods. According to their definition, a good must have an unconditioned value (absolutum, αὐτελές). Whatever exists merely for the sake of something else, or is of value only in comparison to something else, is not a good.[4] A similar doctrine was held concerning evil. Thus spiritual goods were counted to be the only true wealth,[5] and he who had the right attitude toward all,[6] and used all rightly, was thought to be the spiritual owner of all.[7]

Zeno, the founder of the school,[8] classified both wealth and poverty among the so-called "indifferents" (ἀδιάφορα),[9] as neither good nor evil per se. Like the Cynics, he eulogized poverty, though not to such an extreme degree.[10] He went with them only

---

[1] Ibid., ll. 13 ff.

[2] Ibid., pp. 36 f., a comparison of Aristides and Callias.

[3] Fr. iv. A, p. 28, purporting to be the answer of Crates as to what he would gain by being a philosopher.

[4] Cf. infra; also Cic. De fin. iii. 10. 33 f.; Zeller, op. cit., III, 1, 214.

[5] Cic. Paradox. 6, on the thesis that only the wise are rich.

[6] Seneca Benef. vii. 3. 2 f.; 6. 3; 8. 1.

[7] Diog. L. vii. 125. On both the citations above, cf. Zeller, III, 1, 251.

[8] Called Citieus, born 320 B.C., of Semitic descent.

[9] Stoic Vet. Fr., ed. Arnim, 1905, I, 47, fr. 190 (Stob. Ecl. ii. 7. 5, pp. 57 f., ed. Wachs.); Diog. L. vii. 101 f., 103–5.

[10] Von Arnim, op. cit., p. 53, fr. 220; Cic. De fin. v. 84: "At Zeno eum (mendicum) non beatum modo, sed etiam divitem dicere ausus est."

so far as to insist that wealth and poverty have no value, except in relation to the proper spiritual attitude.[1]

In his argument that temples are not especially holy places, since they are the work of artisans (βαναύσων), Zeno exhibits the common negative attitude of the philosophers toward manual labor.[2] His doctrine on money and exchange was also the negative teaching of the moralist, though his statements on these matters have special reference to an ideal future.[3] His attitude on the problem of distribution is not altogether clear, though he wrote a *Republic*,[4] in which he seems to have presented some communistic ideas. Like his followers, he looked to the time when the whole world should be one state, where artificial differences were no more, and all men were brothers.[5] His state is utopian and anarchistic, without temple, court, gymnasium, money, or exchange. All are to wear the same clothing, and there shall be no artificial modesty.[6] Community of wives, at least for the wise, was also probably among his utopian schemes,[7] though it is very unlikely that he held the doctrine in the crass form as reported.[8] His state is somewhat suggestive of the Christian ideal, as a unitary whole, a world-cosmos, united by love.[9]

There is a peculiar mixture of individualistic and social conceptions in the philosophy of the Stoics. In their pictures of an ideal future world-state, they advanced beyond Plato and other thinkers, who limited their communities to the small city-state. In calling their state a "cosmos" also, they gave a positive social

---

[1] Von Arnim (p. 52, fr. 216 [Stob. *Ecl.* ii. 7. 11g, pp. 99 f., ed. Wachs.]) cites Zeno as placing among the goods of the σπουδαῖος man the fact that he is οἰκονομικός and χρηματιστικός, while the φαῦλοι are opposite; cf. also p. 100.

[2] Von Arnim, p. 61, fr. 264 (Clem. Alex. *Strom.* v. 12. 76, p. 691*p*).

[3] Von Arnim, p. 62, fr. 268 (Diog. L. vii. 33): νόμισμα δ' οὔτ' ἀλλαγῆς ἕνεκεν οἴεσθαι δεῖν κατασκευάζειν οὔτ' ἀποδημίας ἕνεκεν. Oncken (*op. cit.*, p. 48) thinks that the Stoics were forerunners of the physiocrats.

[4] Plut. *De Alex. Fort.* i. 6: ἡ πολὺ θαυμαζομένη πολιτεία τοῦ . . . . Ζήνωνος. He says that it agreed in principle with the states of Plato and Lycurgus. Cf. Poehlmann, *op. cit.*, II, 341 ff., but cf. *infra*, p. 140 f. Cf. n. 2, above. Ar. *Pol.* ii. 4. 1266a: εἰσὶ δέ τινες πολιτεῖαι καὶ ἄλλαι, etc., shows that a series of ideal states had preceded his, though he says Plato's was the most radical.

[5] Plut. *De Alex. Fort.* i. 6.

[6] Diog. L. vii. 33, 131; cf. nn. 3 and 5 above.

[7] Diog. L. vii. 131; 33.

[8] Poehlmann, *op. cit.*, II, 342, n. 1.

[9] Cf. above, n. 5; *Athen.* xiii. 561c.

content to the narrow individualism of the Cynics.[1] Moreover, as seen above, their ideal undoubtedly contained some communistic elements. However, according to the fundamental tenet of Stoicism, as expressed by Zeno,[2] that only the wise can be free and citizens, we are still faced with the old duality and anti-socialistic ideal. The Stoics, like the Cynics, were after all essentially individualistic, and were probably believers in private ownership, though they dreamed of a future golden age of altruism, when private property would be no longer necessary.[3]

Chrysippus, the greatest of the Stoics,[4] continued and expanded the principle that virtue is the only absolute good, and that all other things are indifferents, depending for their worth upon right use.[5] But since the wise alone are capable of right use of externals, they alone are truly wealthy.[6] They are wealthy, even though beggars, and noble though slaves.[7] They are not eager for wealth[8] yet they are good economists, since they know the proper source,[9] time, method, and extent of money-making. The worthless, on the other hand, are most needy, even though wealthy.[10] Chrysippus seems to have advanced still farther, in teaching the negative doctrine that wealth is an evil, since it may come from an evil source,[11] an idea suggestive of the modern theory of "tainted money."Naturally, he with the other Stoics, was in sympathy with the Socratics, in objecting to the use of one's knowledge for purposes of money-making.[12]

---

[1] Cf. Poehlmann, *op. cit.*, I, 11, n. 8; also 346.   [2] Diog. L. vii. 33.

[3] On this double tendency in the Stoics, and reasons therefor, cf. Souchon (*op. cit.*, pp. 173 f.); Poehlmann (*op. cit.*, II, 342 f., and I, 111) and Wolf (*op. cit.*, pp. 116 ff.) exaggerate their socialistic tendency. For further discussion, cf. *infra*. Cf. L. Stein, *Soc. Frage*, pp. 171–80.

[4] 280–206 B.C. Aristo and Cleanthes, successors of Zeno, also emphasized similar doctrines in relation to wealth. Cf. von Arnim, I, p. 89, frs. 396, 397, 398, from Aristo; *ibid.*, p. 137, fr. 617, from Cleanthes.

[5] *Ibid.*, II, 79, fr. 240; III, 28, fr. 117; p. 29, frs. 122, 123; p. 32, fr. 135.

[6] *Ibid.*, III, 156, fr. 598; p. 159, fr. 618; p. 155, fr. 593.   [7] *Ibid.*, p. 155, fr. 597.

[8] *Ibid.*, p. 160, fr. 629, "Lucro autem numquam sapiens studet."

[9] *Ibid.*, p. 169, fr. 623: μόνον δὲ τὸν σπουδαῖον ἄνδρα χρηματιστικὸν εἶναι, γινώσκοντα ἀφ' ὧν, χρηματιστέον, καὶ πότε καὶ πῶς καὶ μέχρι πότε.

[10] Von Arnim, III, 168, fr. 674.

[11] *Ibid.*, p. 36, frs. 151, 152, "Bonum ex malo non fit: divitiae fiunt: fiunt autem ex avaritia divitiae ergo non sunt bonum" (Seneca *Ep.* 87. 22).

[12] Von Arnim, p. 172, fr. 686 (Stob. *Ecl.* ii. 7, p. 109, 10): . . . . λόγους καπηλεύειν, οὐ φαμένων δεῖν ἀπὸ παιδείας παρὰ τῶν ἐπιτυχόντων χρηματίζεσθαι.

The cosmopolitan attitude of the Stoics caused them to be opposed to the theory of slavery as a natural institution.[1] They taught that enforced service is no evidence of slavery,[2] but that the real slaves are the ignoble and foolish.[3]   The wise, on the other hand, alone are free, though they are slaves to countless masters.[4]

Chrysippus, like Zeno, probably had dreams of a future ideal state, where the highest eternal law would rule and individual strivings would be lost in the care for the common weal.[5]   If he taught family communism, it was doubtless in a Platonic form.[6]

Utopian social theories after the time of Aristotle were by no means limited to those of Zeno and Chrysippus. As Souchon has observed,[7] the period between the end of the fourth and the beginning of the second centuries was especially favorable to such speculation. The skeptical criticism of the Sophists had prepared the following generations to call in question the most elementary social principles. Ideal states, such as those of Phaleas and Plato, had opened the way for future imitations. The conquests of Alexander had broadened the vision of the Greek, so that he no longer thought in terms of Plato's circumscribed city, but rather in terms of a world-state. Moreover, the utter political confusion and unstable economic conditions of the time aroused the more serious-minded to dream of an ideal past or golden age; to idealize the simple, "natural" life of the so-called "pious" barbarian nomads,[8] or even of the animal world, as opposed to the "artificial" conditions of civilization; and to exaggerate the virtues and communistic

---

[1] Von Arnim, p. 86, fr. 352: ἄνθρωπος γὰρ ἐκ φύσεως δοῦλος οὐδείς; p. 87, fr. 358; cf. p. 141, n. 7, above.

[2] *Ibid.*, fr. 357.   [3] *Ibid.*, 89, fr. 365; p. 86, frs. 356, 354.

[4] *Ibid.*, p. 86, fr. 355; p. 88, fr. 362; p. 89, 364. Cf. Espinas, *Hist. des doctrines èconomiques*, 56 f., on the Stoics' attitude toward labor and slavery: "Ni les Cyniques ni les Stoiciens ne méprisaient le travail"; "La seule servitude déshonorante est celle des passions et du vice."

[5] Poehlmann (*op. cit.*, II, 342 f. and notes), citing von Arnim, III, 77, fr. 314, ὁ νόμος πάντων ἐστὶ βασιλεύς, etc., thinks Chrysippus' principle of the law of reason as king of all is anti-individualistic. He cites also Cic. *De fin.* iii. 19 (64), where the individual seems to be made to exist for the sake of the whole. But cf. above, p. 140 f. and notes.

[6] Cf. Diog. L. vii. 131, and above, p. 140, nn. 7 f.   [7] *Op. cit.*, p. 171.

[8] Cf. above, on Cynics and Stoics, and *infra;* cf. even in Plato, *Laws* 679A-B.

character of the old Spartan constitution.[1] The social theories
were largely Stoic in tendency, and thus present a strange com-
bination of individualistic and communistic ideas.[2]

Dichaearchus of Messana, a pupil of Aristotle, described an
original paradise, when men lived in accord with nature. In that
golden age, they did not depend upon animals for food, but sub-
sisted on fruits. Neither did they have any possessions to arouse
hate and strife, until the evil of private property developed, and
caused the degeneration of human society.[3]

Ephorus,[4] a disciple of Isocrates, represented the second tendency. He eulogized the life of the "milk-fed" (γαλακτόφαγοι),
barbarian nomads of the north as true to nature and righteous.[5]
Their piety and simple life precluded the social ills that arise from
individual ownership,[6] for their communism even extended to the
family, and all composed one brotherhood.[7]

The third tendency is evident in the writings of Isocrates,[8]
Ephorus,[9] Polybius,[10] Plutarch,[11] and was probably common to

[1] The Socratics were the pioneers in this regard also. On the unhistorical character of the alleged early communism in Sparta, cf. Poehlmann, op. cit., I, 75 ff. and
100 f.; on this triple tendency in the post-Aristotelian social thought, cf. ibid.,
pp. 99 ff., on "Der Sozialstaat der Legende und das sozialistische Naturrecht"; also
Souchon, p. 172.

[2] Cf. above, p. 140.

[3] Cf. Porphyry De abstin. iv. 1. 2; Mueller, F.H.G., II, 233. His Βίος Ἑλλάδος
was a history of the degeneration of Greek civilization from the primitive ideal. Cf.
Poehlmann, op. cit., I, 109 and n. 1, on his influence on Rousseau, who refers to him.
Cf. ibid., n. 2, for a similar idea of a golden age in Theoc. xii. 15.

[4] On his social ideas, cf. Poehlmann, I, 113 ff.

[5] Strabo vii, p. 463 (F.H.G., I, 256, fr. 76).

[6] Nic. Damasc. (F.H.G., III, fr. 123): διὰ τὴν τοῦ βίου κοινότητα καὶ δικαιοσύνην.
Cf. also ibid., I, 257, fr. 78, Ephorus.

[7] Ibid.; also fr. 76: πρός τε ἀλλήλους εὐνομοῦνται κοινὰ πάντα ἔχοντες τά τε ἄλλα
καὶ γυναῖκας καὶ τέκνα καὶ τὴν ὅλην συγγένειαν.

[8] Panathen. 178: ἀλλὰ παρὰ σφίσι μὲν αὐτοῖς ἰσονομίαν καταστῆσαι καὶ δημοκρατίαν
τοιαύτην, οἵαν περ χρὴ τοὺς μέλλοντας ἅπαντα τὸν χρόνον ὁμονοήσειν; also 153; for an
idealized picture of early Athenian life, cf. Paneg. 79; Areop. 31; 32, 35, 44, 83;
cited by Poehlmann, op. cit., I, 136 f.

[9] Cf. Polybius vi. 45, and Poehlmann's note (I, 122).

[10] Book vi. 10; 48; etc.; cf. Poehlmann, as above.

[11] Cf. his Lycurgus, especially 8, 9, 10, 3, 25, 30, 31.

many other thinkers whose works are no longer extant.[1] They idealized the ancient Spartan society, as a model of complete communism, which provided full equality and freedom for the citizens. It was free from the evils of luxury, excessive wealth, poverty, civic strife, commerce, and money-greed, a condition where all the citizens were wise, and where the Stoic ideal of independence (αὐτάρκεια) was fully realized.[2]

It was but a step from this to the projection of these bizarre idealizations of the past and of primitive life into the present and future. They took the form of ideal utopias such as that of Zeno,[3] or of romantic descriptions, purporting to portray ideal conditions as actually existing, such as found their model in Plato's *Atlantis*.[4] For a full discussion of this type of literature, the reader may consult Poehlmann's work.[5] We need give it only cursory notice here.

Theopompus, a pupil of Socrates, described a "Meropian" land.[6] His aim, however, was probably the entertainment of the reader, rather than social reform, as is evidenced by the fantastic nature of his stories. They picture not only ideal communistic conditions, but also a state of the wicked (πονηρόπολις), and crassly emphasize the alleged free-love of the Etruscans.[7]

The Cimmerian state of Hecataeus, an idealization of the kingdom of the Pharaohs, had a more serious social purpose.[8] It describes a state in which all conquered lands are equally divided among the citizens, and where landed property cannot be sold. The people are free from greed of gain, civic strife, and all the ills that follow it. The ideal is not the greatest increase of wealth, but the development of the citizens to the highest social ideal.[9]

Euhemerus wrote a "Sacred Chronicle" (ἱερὰ ἀναγραφή)[10] of an ideal society on an island near India, ruled by a priestly aris-

---

[1] Cf. Poehlmann, I, 122 and n. 3.   [3] Cf. above, p. 140.

[2] Cf. above, notes p. 143, nn. 4–6. especially 6.   [4] Cf. above, p. 62, n. 6.

[5] *Op. cit.*, II, 359 ff., though he has been too ready to see in them a direct analogy to modern socialism.

[6] Book viii of his *Philipp. Histories* (*Athen.* xii. 517*d* ff.).

[7] Cf. Poehlmann, I, 362 ff.

[8] Mueller, *F.H.G.*, II, 392, fr. 13; cf. 386 ff.

[9] Diod. i. 6. 93; 4, a platonic ideal.   [10] *Ibid.* v. 45. 3 ff.

tocracy. Here, labor was held in high regard. The artisans were in the priestly class, the farmers were second, and the herdsmen were on an equality with the soldiers.[1] All land and other means of production were common, except the house and garden (κῆπου).[2] The land was not worked collectively, but farmers and herdsmen alike brought their products to a common storehouse for common consumption.[3] Thus neither money nor commercial class was necessary.

Jambulus, in his "Sun State,"[4] outdoes even Euhemerus in his communistic ideas. He describes a sort of paradise of sun-worshipers at the equator. Here the trees never fail of ripe fruit, and the citizens never lose their strength and beauty. The whole social and economic life is under communistic régime. There is collective ownership of all the means of production, and each must take his turn at each kind of work.[5] The communism extends also to the family.[6] Thus Greek economic and social speculation, which always contained socialistic elements, ends in a communism for the whole citizenship, so thorough as to include both products and means of production, and to demand a leveling even of the natural inequalities that result from the different kinds of work.

[1] *Ibid.* 45. 3.

[2] Diod. v. 45. 5; 46. 1 shows that the artisans were included in the communism.

[3] *Ibid.* 45. 4: τοὺς κάρπους ἀναφέρουσιν εἰς τὸ κοινόν, etc.; though prizes were given for excellence in farming.

[4] *Ibid.* ii. 55-60.

[5] *Ibid.* 59.6: ἐναλλὰξ δὲ αὐτοὺς τοὺς μὲν ἀλλήλοις διακονεῖν, τοὺς δὲ ἀλιεύειν, τοὺς δὲ περὶ τὰς τέχνας εἶναι, ἄλλους δὲ περὶ ἄλλα τῶν χρησίμων ἀσχολεῖσθαι, τοὺς δ' ἐκ περιόδου κυκλικῆς λειτουργεῖν, πλὴν τῶν ἤδη γεγηρακότων. Cf. p. 34, n. 1, above, on Ruskin's idea that all should do some head and some hand work. Poehlmann (II, 391, n. 2) compares it to the socialism of Bebel. The implication that Plato's state is distinguished from this, as a society of citizens who do not work (402 f.), is hardly fair The proper distinction is rather that Plato insists that each citizen do the particular kind of work for which he is best fitted. It is needless to ask which had the saner view, from the economic or any other standpoint. Jambulus' repudiation of the division of labor in the interest of equality is certainly one of the most radical measures ever suggested in the history of communism.

[6] Diod. v. 58.1.

CHAPTER VIII

GENERAL CONCLUSIONS ON THE IMPORTANCE AND INFLUENCE OF GREEK ECONOMICS

Our conclusions as to the importance and influence of Greek economic thought have been fully presented in the previous discussion. A brief summary of the results, however, may be of advantage now, at the close of our survey. As seen above, despite the fact that Greek thought in this field was incidental to moral and political speculation, and despite a certain philosophic prejudice and limited economic vision, the contribution is by no means merely negative. We have seen that it included a recognition by one or more Greek thinkers of such important principles as the following: that society finds its origin in mutual need, and in the natural development of clan and family, not in the artificial social contract; that the state is a great business association, in which about the same economic laws apply as in private economy; that the final goal of economics is not property but human welfare; that the criteria of economic value are intrinsic utility, economic demand, and cost of production; that wealth must possess the quality of storableness; that true wealth consists only of commodities that minister to human welfare; that the three factors in production are land, labor and capital; that money originated in necessary exchange; that it serves as a medium of exchange, a standard of value, and a ticket of deferred payments; that it should possess intrinsic value, which is more stable than that of other commodities; that it should not be confused with wealth, but should be understood in its true function as representative wealth; that credit must play an exceedingly important part in business operations as representative capital; that agriculture is the basal industry, on which all others must depend; that the division of labor is the fundamental principle at the foundation of all exchange; that it results in certain important economic advantages, and that its extensive application depends upon large commercial development; that reciprocity is the fundamental principle in exchange, as also in the social structure; that exchange performs a legitimate social function in creating time and place values; that industrial expansion is limited by a law of diminishing returns; that the primary purpose of exchange should not be profit, but satisfaction of economic need; that commerce merely for its own sake does not necessarily increase the national store, but may produce only economic inequalities; that extremes of wealth and poverty cause industrial inefficiency, social strife, and crime; that excessive individual wealth is not usually compatible with just acquisition or just expenditure; that it also necessarily implies corresponding extremes of poverty; that the commercial spirit in nations is the chief cause of international differences; that the goal of economics is consumption rather than production, and that foolish consumption results in great economic waste; that all economic problems are moral problems; that private property is not a natural right, but a gift of society, and therefore that society may properly control its activities; that there is a certain unity in human nature, which is opposed to the doctrine of natural slavery; that the individual should have opportunity for personal development in accord with his capacities, aside from the mere struggle for physical existence; that true economic equality does not demand equal shares for all, but shares proportioned to capacities and services; and that gifts of charity merely for consumption are fruitful causes of poverty and indolence.

Besides the recognition of such principles, we have seen that many practical suggestions for the amelioration of economic and social conditions, which are being seriously presented today, were first proposed by Greek thinkers. Measures for the divorce of government from big business, state control of natural monopolies, conservation of natural resources, state supervision of trade and commerce, including regulation of prices and rates, publicity in business, pure food laws, and the socialization of industry and its products were all first proposed by Greeks. On the other hand, we have seen that practically all the modern stock arguments against socialism were long ago presented by Aristotle, and that the ideal of the Greek socialist was not primarily materialistic and selfish, as the modern, but moral and social.

Such a list of positive economic principles and practical suggestions should surely give the Greeks some claim to recognition
in the field of economic thought. But they should be judged
primarily, not by their positive contribution to economic theory
or by the practical nature of their suggestions for legislation, but
rather by the extent to which they realized the existence of the
great economic and social problems, which are still crying for a
solution. From this standpoint, we have seen that Plato and
Aristotle especially reveal remarkable economic insight. Moreover, there still remains the outstanding fact that the Greeks were
the forerunners of the moral, humanitarian, and social emphasis
in present-day economy. This alone should give to them a distinct
place in the evolution of economic thought, and should make it
impossible for Souchon to conclude: "Ces mépris [of G. B. Say]
sont pour nous apparaître plus justifiés que les admirations de
Roscher."[1]

The influence of Greek thought upon later economic theory,
however, seems not to have been very direct or extensive, probably
owing to the incidental nature of their speculation. To be sure,
mediaeval economic thought presents, in many respects, an
unbroken continuity with the Greek. In their emphasis on the
moral, in their doctrines on usury, just price, importance of agriculture, exchange for profit, and in their general conservative attitude toward money and commercial development, mediaeval
thinkers are very similar to the Socratics.[2] Doubtless much of
this similarity may be traced to the direct influence of Aristotle, as
is especially evident in the work of Thomas Aquinas and Nicholas
Oresme.[3] To a considerable extent, however, the economic ideas
of the Middle Ages were a direct outgrowth of the economic and
religious conditions under which the writers lived.[4] In the following

---

[1] *Op. cit.*, p. 195; Roscher is, of course, extreme in his appreciation.

[2] Cf. Brants, *Les théories écon. au XIIIᵉ et XIVᵉ siècle;* Espinas, *Histoire des doctrines économiques*, pp. 72 ff.; Haney, *op. cit.*, pp. 69 ff.

[3] In his *De origine, natura, jure, et mutationibus monetarum* (fourteenth century).
On their dependence upon Aristotle, cf. Zmavc, *Zeitschr. f. d. gesammt. Staatswiss.*,
1902, pp. 54 and 77 f.; and *Archiv f. d. Gesch. der Phil.*, 1899, 407 ff.

[4] Cf. Souchon, pp. 199 f., who observes that the Greek moral goal was perfection
of the individual through the state, while that of the Middle Ages was individual
salvation to another world.

8GENERAL CONCLUSIONS

centuries, some Greek influence may be traced in Adam Smith, in the physiocrats,[1] in utopian writers such as More, and in eighteenth-century thinkers like Rosseau.

It is usually asserted that the economic thought of the past century has been practically unaffected by Greek ideas. But our previous discussion has clearly shown that Plato and Xenophon, at least, dominated the economic thinking of Ruskin. If further evidence is needed, it is necessary only to turn to the names of Greek thinkers in the index to the monumental new edition of his works, which we have frequently cited above. He frankly and enthusiastically presents himself as an apostle of a "Greek theory of economics."[2] But despite some of his utopian and extravagant ideas, he is being ever more recognized by authorities in economics as having been one of the chief factors in the development of political economy to its present moral and humanitarian emphasis.[3] His repudiation of the abstract "economic man," his insistence upon human, moral, and social ideals in economics, his attempt to broaden the definition of economic value and wealth by emphasizing true utility, his constant stress upon proper consumption rather than upon production, his demand that all have opportunity up to their capacity, his opposition to the *laissez-faire* policy in economics

[1] Cf. Oncken, *op. cit.*, p. 38.

[2] He calls Plato the "master of economy" (*Fors Clav.* [Vol. XXVIII, 717]); cf. also Vol. XXXVIII, 112 on his Platonic discipleship. He says (*Arrows of the Chace*, Vol. XXXIV, 547): "The economy I teach is Xenophon's"; cf. also Vol. XXXVII, 550, Letter to Professor Blackie, II: "My own political economy is literally only the expansion and explanation of Xenophon's." Cf. Vol. XXXI, Intro., pp. xv ff.; Vol. XVII, pp. xlix and 18; cf. his preface to his translation of the *Economicus;* cf. also E. Barker, *Pol. Thought in England from Herbert Spencer to the Present Day* ("Home University Library"), pp. 191–96, who emphasizes this Greek influence. Cf. above, p. 23, n. 5; 64, n. 3.

[3] Barker, cited above, in n. 2, also emphasizes this fact. Cf. the edition of Ruskin above cited, Introduction to Vol. XVII, an excellent discussion of Ruskin's economic ideas and their influence, for a bibliography (p. cxii) and citations from many modern economists on the subject; e.g., the notable address in 1885, in recognition of his work, signed by a number of leading English economists; the striking citations from Ingram; from Stimson (*Quarterly Journal of Economics*, II [1888], 445), that the future political economy will make its bricks for building "from Ruskin's earth rather than from Ricardo's straw"; from the late regius professor of modern history at Oxford, "The political economy of today is the political economy of John Ruskin, and not that of John Bright or even of John Stewart Mill."

and politics, his emphasis upon right education, all have borne rich and abiding fruit in the last few decades, and these are all distinctively Greek ideas, as we have seen above. Thus indirectly, through Ruskin, Greek economic thought has exerted a potent influence upon the evolution of nineteenth-century economics, and thus there is much truth in the words of Wagner, as quoted by Oncken,[1] not merely for German, but for all modern economy: "Es ist im Grunde uralter wahrhaft classischer Boden, auf den jetzt die deutsche ökonomische und soziale Theorie und Praxis sich bewusst wieder stellen." Souchon's characterization of Greek economy as "morale étatisme"[2] could well be applied to much in the economic thought of today.

[1] P. 46, n. 3 (Wagner, *Die Akad. Nat.-oek. und der Socialismus*, 1895).

[2] *Op. cit.*, p. 201.

BIBLIOGRAPHY

The following bibliography includes: (a) histories of economic thought; almost all of these have only a cursory chapter on Greek theory, and several of them deal largely with economic conditions; (b) histories of socialism and social theory, to which the foregoing statement applies to a large extent; (c) chapters in works on different phases of Greek economic history; (d) other works of a more general type, which deal more or less extensively with Greek economic or social ideas; (e) articles and dissertations; (f) editions of Greek authors that are of special interest for our subject. It is manifestly impossible to name many of these latter, and we shall content ourselves with the mention of a few that have proved especially helpful. The works are listed in alphabetical order, for greater convenience in reference, and those of chief interest are starred.

Adam, James (The Republic of Plato, 1902).

Adler, G. *Geschichte des Socialismus und Kommunismus von Plato bis zur Gegenwart* (1899), pp. 6–52. On Greek.

Alesio. "Alcune reflessione intorno ai concetti del valore nell' antichita classica," *Archivio Giuridico*, 1889.

Ashley, W. J. "Aristotle's Doctrine of Barter," *Quarterly Journal of Economy*, 1895. An interpretation of Ar. *Pol.* i. 1258b27 ff.

Barker, E. *Political Thought of Plato and Aristotle* (1906), pp. 357–404.*

Blanqui, M. *Histoire de l'économie politique en Europe* (1842; 4th ed., 1860), I, 33–92. Somewhat indiscriminate in appreciation of Greek thinkers.

Bonar. *Philosophy and Political Economy* (1893).*

Brants, V. *Xenophon Economiste*, reprint from *Revue Catholique de Louvain*, 1881.*

Bussy, M. *Histoire et Réfutation du Socialisme depuis l'antiquité, jusqu' à nos jours* (1859). Superficial and prejudiced.

Cossa, L. *Histoire des doctrines économiques* (1899) (trans. from the Italian of 1876), pp. 144–50.*

———. "Di alcuni studii storici sulle teorie economiche dei Greci," *Saggi di Economia Politica*, 1878, pp. 3–14.

De Sam-Cognazzi. *Analisi dell economia publica e privata degli antichi* (1830).

Du Mesnill-Marigny. *Histoire de l'économie politique des anciens peuples* (1878, 3 vols.). Superficial.

De Villeneuve-Bargemont. *Histoire de l'économie politique* (Paris, 1841, 2d ed.), I. Chiefly on the facts.

Dietzel. "Beiträge zur Geschichte des Socialismus und des Kommunismus," *Zeitschrift für Literatur und Geschichte der Staatswissenschaften*, I (1893), 373 ff.*

Döring, A. *Die Lehre des Socrates als soziales Reform-System* (1895).

DuBois, A. *Précis de l'histoire des doctrines économiques dans leurs rapports avec les faits et avec les institutions* (1903), pp. 23–53. A good partial bibliography.*

Dühring, E. *Kritische Geschichte der Nationalökonomie und des Socialismus* (3d ed., 1879), pp. 19–25.

Dunning, W. A. *Political Theories Ancient and Mediaeval* (New York, 1913). Economic material only incidental.

Eisenhart, H. *Geschichte der Nationalökonomie* (2d ed., 1891). Mostly on economic history.

Espinas. *Histoire des doctrines économiques* (1891), chap. i.*

———. "L'art économique dans Platon," *Revue des Etudes Grecques*, XXVI (1914), 105–29, 236–65.*

Ferrara, J. "L'economica politica degli antichi," *Journal de Statis. de Palerme*, 1836.

Fontpertuis, F. de. "Filiation des ideés économiques, dans l'antiquité," *Journal des écon.*, September, 1871 ff.*

Francotte, H. *L'Industrie dans la Grèce ancienne* (Brussels, 1900). Sections on Greek theories of labor and socialism.*

Glaser. "De Aristotelis doctrina de divitiis" (dissertation, 1850), *Jahrb. für Gesellschafts- und Staatswissenschaft*, 1865.

Göttling. *De Notione servitutis apud Aristotelem* (dissertation, Jena, 1821).

Grote, G. *Plato* (4 vols.).

———. *Aristotle* (2 vols.).

Guiraud, P. *La main-d'œuvre industrielle dans l'ancienne Grèce* (1900), pp. 36–50. On theory.*

———. *La propriété foncière en Grèce jusqu'à la conquête Romaine* (1893), pp. 573–612. On socialistic ideas.*

———. *Etudes économiques sur l'antiquité* (1905), chap. i. On the importance of economic questions in Greece.*

Hagen. *Observationum oeconomico politicarum in Aeschinis dialogum qui Eryxias inscribitur* (dissertation, 1822).

Haney, L. W. *History of Economic Thought* (1911), pp. 39–52.*

Heidel, W. A. *Pseudo-Platonica* (dissertation, Chicago, 1896), pp. 59–61. On Eryxias.

Herzog, C. "Communismus und Socialismus in Alterthum," *Beilage zur allgemeine Zeitung*, 1894, No. 166. Conservative on the influence of socialism in the ancient world.

Hildebrand, B. *Xenophontis et Aristot. de oeconomia publica doctrinae illustrantur* (dissertation, Marburg, 1845). Part on Aristotle not published.

Hoderman, M. "Quaestionum oeconomicarum specimen," (dissertation, Berlin, 1896), *Berlin Studien für class. Philol. und Arch.*, XVI, No. 4. On the so-called *Economica*.

Ingram, J. K. *History of Political Economy* (1907), pp. 7–26.*

Jowett and Campbell. *Republic of Plato* (3 vols., 1894).

Kaulla, R. *Die geschichtliche Entwickelung der modernen Werttheorien* (1906), pp. 3 f. On Aristotle.

Kautsky, K. *Die Geschichte des Socialismus in Einzeldarstellungen* (1897), I, 1.

Kautz. *Theorie und Geschichte der national Oekonomie* (Wien, 2d ed., 1860), pp. 102–43).*

Knies, Karl. *Die politische Economie vom geschichtlichen Standpunkt* (1883). Of but slight interest for ancient theory.

Loos, I. A. "Studies in the *Politics* of Aristotle and the *Republic* of Plato," *Bull. of the University of Iowa*, 1899.

Mabille. "Le communisme et le féminisme à Athènes." *Mémoires de l'académie de Dijon*, 4 série, t. 7, pp. 317 ff. (Paris, 1900).

Martiis, S. de. *Cognetti* (Socialismo antico, Turin, 1899).*

Menger, Karl. Art. "Geld," *Handwörterbuch der Staatswissenschaft* (2d ed.), IV, 82 ff.

Newman. *The Politics of Aristotle* (Oxford, 1877, 4 vols.).*

Oncken, A. *Geschichte der Nationalökonomie* (1902), I, 27–49.

Palgrave's *Dictionary*. Art. "Aristotle." This and the above-named article on "Geld" will serve as sufficient notice of the several Dictionaries of Political Economy, to which other references might be made.

Platon, G. "Le socialisme en Grèce," *Devenir Social.*, January, 1897 ff.

Poehlmann, R. *Geschichte des antiken Socialismus und Kommunismus* (München, 1893–1901, 2 vols.; 2d ed., 1912, *Geschichte der sozialen Frage und des Socialismus in der antiken Welt*). A thorough treatment of Greek socialistic tendencies both in theory and in practice, though it exaggerates the development of capitalism in Greece, and draws analogies too freely between ancient and modern socialism. Our citations are from the second edition.*

———. "Die Anfänge des Sozialismus in Europa," *Sybel's Hist. Zeitschrift*, Bd. 79, H. 3, pp. 385–451.

Rambaud, J. *Histoire des Doctrines économiques* (Paris, 1902).

Regnier, M. *L'économie politique et rurale des Grecs.*

Robin, L. "Platon et la science sociale," *Revue de metaphysique et de morale*, March, 1913 (reprint by Armand Colin, Paris).*

Roscher. "Ueber das Verhältniss der national Oekonomik zum klassischen Alterthume," *Ansichten der Volkswirtschaft*, I (1878), 1–50.*

Roscher. *De doctrinae oeconomico politicae apud Graecos primordiis* (Leipzig, 1866).

Salvio, G. Salomo. *Il concetto della schiavitu secundo Aristotile* (Rome, 1881).

———. *Communismo nella Grecia antiqua* (Padua, 1883).

Schneider. *Die staatswirtschaftlichen Lehren des Aristotles* (dissertation, Neu Puppin, 1873).

Schrohl, O. *De Eryxias qui fertur Platonis* (dissertation, 1901). Chiefly on the authorship of the *Eryxias*.

Schulte, J. *Quomodo Plato in legibus publica Atheniensium instituta respexerit* (dissertation, 1907).

Sewall, H. "Theory of Value before Adam Smith," *Publication of American Economic Association*, II, Part 3. Four pages on Aristotle.

Shorey. Paul ("Plato's *Laws*," *Classical Philology*, October, 1914.

Simey, Miss E. "Economic Theory among the Greeks and Romans," *Economic Review*, October, 1900.

Souchon, A. *Les Théories économiques dans la Grèce antique* (1898; a 2d ed. in 1906, but slightly changed).*

Stein, Ludwig. *Das erste Auftauschen der sozialen Frage bei den Griechen* (dissertation, Bern, 1896).

———. *Die soziale Frage im Lichte der Philosophie* (Stuttgart, 1903, 2d ed.), pp. 150–82.

———. "Die staatswissenschaftliche Theorie der Griechen vor Arist. und Platon," *Zeitschrift für die gesammte Wissenschaft*, 1853, pp. 115–82 (Tübingen).

Stewart. *Notes to Ar., Nic. Ethics* (2 vols.).*

St. Hilaire, B. Preface to translation of the *Politics* of Arist.

Thill, J. *Die Eigenthumsfrage im klassischen Alterthum* (Luxembourg, 1892).

Thomissen. *Histoire du socialisme depuis l'antiquité jusqu'à la constitution française du 14 jan., 1852.*

Trinchera, F. *Storia critica dell' economia publia (epoca antica)* (Naples, 1873).

Vanderkindere, L. "Le Socialisme dans la Grèce antique," *Revue de l'Université de Brussels*, I, 4, pp. 241–46.

Vogel, G. *Die Oekonomik des Xenophon; eine Vorarbeit für die Geschichte der griechischen Oekonomik* (Erlangen, 1895).

Walcker, K. *Geschichte der Nationalökonomie und des Socialismus* (Leipzig, 1902).

Wallon. *Histoire de l'esclavage dans l'antiquité* (Paris, 1879, 2d ed.). One chapter on theories of slavery.

Wolf, H. *Geschichte des antiken Sozialismus und Individualismus* (1909). A merely popular treatment.

Wilhelm, F. "Die *Oeconomica* der Neupythagoreer," *Rhein. Mus.*, XVII, No. 2 (1915), 162 ff.

Zmavc, J. "Die Werttheorie bei Arist. und Thos. Aquino," *Archiv für die Geschichte der Philosophie* (Berlin, 1899), pp. 407 ff.*

Zmavc, J. "Die Geldtheorie und ihre Stellung innerhalb der Wirtschaft und staatswissenschaftliche Anschauungen des Arist., *Zeitschrift für die ges. Staatswissenschaft*, 1902, pp. 48–79.*

As stated, a large number of the foregoing list deal chiefly with actual conditions, rather than with theory. Besides these, many other works on phases of Greek economic history are cited in the course of our discussion, the names of which, with page-references, may be found in the index.   All other works that are incidentally cited are also listed there.   For an excellent presentation of the political economy of John Ruskin, and a selected bibliography on his work as a social and economic reformer, cf. the Library Edition of his works, from which we have often cited (George Allen, London, Introduction to Vol. XVII, 1905; bibliography, p. cxii).

INDEX OF SUBJECTS AND AUTHORS

INDEX OF GREEK TERMS

MWARCHTIN